Categorically Famous

Categorically Famous

Literary Celebrity and Sexual Liberation in 1960s America

Guy Davidson

Stanford University Press

Stanford, California

STANFORD UNIVERSITY PRESS
Stanford, California

Printed in the United States of America on acid-free, archival-quality paper

Library of Congress Cataloging-in-Publication Data
Names: Davidson, Guy, author.
Title: Categorically famous : literary celebrity and sexual liberation in 1960s America / Guy Davidson.
Description: Stanford, California : Stanford University Press, 2019. | Series: Post 45 | Includes bibliographical references and index.
Identifiers: LCCN 2018047095 (print) | LCCN 2018049525 (ebook) | ISBN 9781503602359 (cloth : alk. paper) | ISBN 9781503609198 (pbk. :alk. paper) | ISBN 9781503609204 (ebook)
Subjects: LCSH: Gay authors—United States—History—20th century. | Celebrities—Sexual behavior—United States—History. | Sexual minorities—United States—Identity—History. | Gay liberation movement—United States—History. | Fame—Social aspects—United States—History. | United States—Social conditions—1960-1980.
Classification: LCC PS153.G38 (ebook) | LCC PS153.G38 D39 2019 (print) | DDC 810.9/920664—dc23
LC record available at https://LCCN.loc.gov/2018047095

Cover design: Black Eye Design | Michel Vrana

Typeset by Kevin Barrett Kane in 10/15 Minion

Contents

List of Illustrations vii

Acknowledgments ix

Introduction 1

1 James Baldwin and Celebrity Shame 21

2 Baldwin and the Celebrity Novel 43

3 Susan Sontag's Impersonal Stardom 71

4 From Camp to Counterculture 99

5 The Moment of *Myra Breckinridge* 125

6 Gore Vidal's Sexuality in the Public Sphere 151

Afterword: Visibility, Revisited; or, Delete the Closet? 175

Notes 181

Index 221

Illustrations

1. Photo from "Homosexuality in America," 1964 66

2. Back dust-jacket portrait of Susan Sontag, *The Benefactor*, 1963 72

3. Cover of *Boston Area Mattachine Society Newsletter*, May 1959 92

4. Original print ad for Bantam edition of *Myra Breckinridge*, 1968 135

5. Cover of original hardback edition of *Myra Breckinridge*, 1968 137

6. Gore Vidal with publicist Jim Moran, *Myra Breckinridge* promotional tour, 1968 138

7. Back cover of original hardback edition of *Myra Breckinridge*, 1968 141

8. Cover of *The Myra Breckinridge Cookbook*, 1970 148

9. Screenshot of William F. Buckley Jr., Democratic Convention coverage, August 1968 152

10. Screenshot of Gore Vidal, Democratic Convention coverage, August 1968 159

Acknowledgments

The writing of this book was made possible by an Australia Research Council (ARC) Discovery Project grant (2015–17). I'm extremely appreciative of the financial support from the ARC, which gave me the time and means to travel to archives, research, and write. I'm also grateful for additional financial and logistical support provided by the Faculty of Law, Humanities and the Arts at the University of Wollongong (UOW). I'm very fortunate to have such estimable colleagues in the English and Writing discipline at UOW, and I thank them, as well as Sarah Miller, my head of school, and my former dean, Amanda Lawson, for their empathy and interest. Thanks also go to Anna Breckon for her fantastic research assistance.

I'm grateful to Loren Glass and Kate Marshall, the editors of the Post•45 series, and to Emily-Jane Cohen and Faith Wilson Stein at Stanford University Press for their enthusiastic and constructive support of this project. Post•45 was my dream venue for this book, and it's immensely gratifying to see this dream come true.

For various forms of intellectual support and provocation along the way, I thank Michael Bibler, Michael Cohen, Shady Cosgrove, Jonathan Goldberg, Melissa Hardie, Scott Herring, Craig Loftin, Christopher Looby, Kate Lilley, Heather Love, Michael Moon, John Plotz, Ashley Shelden, Vanessa Smith, Jeff Solomon, Clara Tuite, Lee Wallace, and Elizabeth Wilson. Henry Abelove has, as ever, been an invaluable adviser and delightful dining companion. For their careful reading of large parts of the manuscript as well as their general awesomeness, I owe major gratitude to Benjamin Kahan and Monique Rooney. Stephen Flanagan and Galina Laurie have been the best of friends. Nev Benazic has been the best of special friends.

Parts of Chapter 1 were published as "Sexuality and Shame in James Baldwin's Career," in *Literary Careers in the Modern Era*, ed. Guy Davidson and Nicola Evans (Houndmills, UK: Palgrave Macmillan, 2015); reproduced with permission of Palgrave Macmillan. Parts of Chapter 6 originally appeared in *Mosaic: An Interdisciplinary Critical Journal* 48, no. 1 (2015): 147–64.

Categorically Famous

Introduction

IN THE 1992 *SEINFELD* EPISODE "The Cheever Letters," a letter from John Cheever found in the burned ruin of George's girlfriend Susan Ross's family's cabin reveals that her father had a passionate affair with the writer.[1] Mr. Ross's decloseting—the letter is contained in a previously secreted box—parodically replays the revelations of Cheever's own same-sexuality in his daughter's memoir and in his own posthumously published journals and letters.[2] The *Seinfeld* version of this literary-historical event and subsequent narrative complications within the show constellate concerns central to this book. In his posthumous career, Cheever became paradoxically famous for being closeted, throwing into relief pre-Stonewall and post-Stonewall conceptions of homosexuality as they play out in relation to the public figure of the author. Exploiting Cheever's outing for humorous effect, *Seinfeld* indicates the tangled relations between sexuality, liberation, and mass-mediatized literary fame that are the focus of the following pages. An exemplar of popular media itself, *Seinfeld* draws on and further circulates the newly dominant image of Cheever that disrupted the notion of him as patrician husband and father that held sway during his lifetime. "The Cheever Letters" thus indicates how literary celebrity can be a flashpoint for understanding same-sexuality in both pre- and postliberation dispensations. But if the revelation of the Cheever-like Mr. Ross's homosexual past suggests a suppressed authentic identity that might have benefited from the liberationist emphasis on openness and pride, other aspects of the subsequent story line complicate this perspective. *Seinfeld* explicitly identifies Mr. Ross as "a homosexual" but juxtaposes this with representations of sexual "fluidity." Mr. Ross stays married, and his daughter Susan later goes through a lesbian phase that "doesn't take." Her girlfriend, meanwhile, who has "*never* been with a guy," instantaneously relinquishes her Kinsey 6 status when she comes within the orbit of Kramer's sexual charisma, prompting George's incredulous plaint, "I drive them to lesbianism, he brings 'em back."[3]

"The Cheever Letters" and subsequent episodes of *Seinfeld* suggest the complicated relations of individuals to sexual categorization. Representative recent critical understandings of Cheever's sexuality, however, divide into accounts that understand Cheever as either symptomatically repressed or as unclassifiable as gay, according to contemporary understanding. For Geoff Dyer, reviewing Cheever's *Journals* in 2009, Cheever's "slow discovery and eventual acceptance of his sexual identity conforms to the larger story of homosexuality in the 20th century." Quoting from the journals, Dyer presents Cheever as moving from efforts to suppress homosexual desire, supplemented by self-denying performances of homophobic censoriousness, to "gradual acceptance ('I am queer, and happy to say so'), celebration and realisation that real harm was caused not by one's sexual nature but by 'the force that was brought to crush these instincts and that exacerbated them beyond their natural importance.'"[4] By contrast, the historian Barry Reay, in *New York Hustlers: Masculinity and Sex in Modern America*, contends that Cheever's notoriously homophobic statements indicate resistance to homosexual categorization rather than self-loathing or denial. For Reay, Cheever illustrates his revisionist argument that the dominance of homosexual identity as the framework for understanding same-sexuality needs to be dated much later than is usually the case—effectively to the postliberation period. Because homosexual identity was widely understood to involve effeminacy, Reay argues, many normatively masculine men did not understand themselves as homosexual, "whatever their same-sex cravings."[5] If Dyer's account exemplifies the popular teleological narrative of gay emancipation that queer scholars have rightly challenged, Reay's argument is indicative of the inclination of queer studies to emphasize the deconstruction of the homosexual/heterosexual binary at the expense of appreciation of the social potency and political efficacy of sexual identity categories.[6] While his book usefully thickens our understanding of how many midcentury men lived their sexualities, Reay significantly underestimates the force of the homosexual/heterosexual binary by the midcentury period—thus necessarily ignoring Cheever's statements of self-acceptance, quoted by Dyer.[7] Reay also understates the flexibility with which the putatively monolithic category of "the homosexual" may be inhabited.

The *Seinfeld* story line I've briefly sketched indicates instead that sexual identity categories do not necessarily exclude epistemological ambiguity *and* the usefulness of postliberation gay and lesbian identities as political points of reference and as guides for everyday living. This double-edged claim is the founding assumption of *Categorically Famous*, which recognizes the contingency of sexual identity categories, but, through an examination of three celebrity writers—James Baldwin, Susan Sontag, and Gore Vidal—challenges the reflexive valorization of instability, indeterminacy, and opacity that has come to dominate queer studies: what we might, with apologies to Kant, dub "the anticategorical imperative." By contrast, *Categorically Famous* is animated by interest in what epistemological and political affordances might follow from treating sexual identities not as essences but as deeply meaningful for both individual and group experience.

My challenge to the anticategorical imperative concomitantly involves a revision of queer studies' antiliberation bias and its critique of gay visibility and audibility—a bias and a critique that I suggest involve a repression of queer theory's own indebtedness to liberation discourse. I argue that the importance of open assertions of gay and lesbian personhood is evidenced by an examination of the careers of Baldwin, Sontag, and Vidal. Despite their own objections to sexual identity categories, these three writers, through their widely publicized and widely read work and through their celebrity embodiments of queerness, contributed to the highly mediatized "sexual revolution" of the 1960s, particularly to the increasingly open discussion of homosexuality that helped construct a widespread, politically progressive understanding of gays and lesbians as an oppressed minority. This historical argument ramifies into two further central theoretical claims. First, I contend that an examination of the careers of Baldwin, Sontag, and Vidal enables a rethinking of the usual understanding within queer studies of gay and lesbian visibility as a form of social control. Second, I demonstrate that the example of postwar queer celebrity necessitates a reappraisal of the dominant view of the relations between privacy and publicity in celebrity studies. Celebrity is generally understood by scholars to involve a crossover or confusion between the public and the private. Graeme Turner, for instance, argues that public figures become celebrities at the point in which "media interest in their activities is transferred from reporting on their public role (such as their specific achievement in politics or sport) to investigating the details of their private lives."[8] But such general claims are complicated by the phenomenon of queer celebrities in the preliberation era, during which the media could not or did not usually directly comment on the homosexuality of public figures. The desire for knowledge and truth about the private life of the queer celebrity may certainly impel public and media interest during this period, but the homosexuality of that figure cannot be directly acknowledged—in the mass media at least. If sexuality in general is constituted in modern culture as the most private and therefore the most truthful aspect of the self, then homosexuality in particular—as the sexual orientation subject to the most intensive operations of secretion and disclosure—throws the operations of celebrity into fine-grained relief.

Baldwin, Sontag, and Vidal were all homosexual or bisexual in orientation, and for each their celebrity status was complexly related to their queerness. All three writers gained or consolidated their fame in the 1960s in part through their representation and embodiment of sexual daring. Yet Baldwin, Sontag, and Vidal each resisted open declarations of their sexuality. In refusing gay or lesbian identity, these writers could be seen as participating in the discursive regimes of the closet or the open secret, which queer studies has commonly understood as structuring homosexual identity in the preliberation period.[9] But *Categorically Famous* deemphasizes this reading, drawing attention to the ways in which the taboo-breaking careers of all three writers contributed to the increasing climate of openness about homosexuality during the 1960s that was an important precondition of liberation. Despite their various forms of resistance to gay identity, all three were persistently identified with it. If Cheever has become a byword for the dramatic move from the closet to visibility that liberation entails, these three writers, I suggest, manifest *proto-visibility* during the decade in which liberation emerged. While Cheever successfully avoided or kept at bay homosexual identification during his lifetime (despite the queer interests of much of his writing), Baldwin, Sontag, and Vidal in different ways modeled the possibilities of the open profession of homosexual orientation, however inadvertently.

The identification with homosexuality was differently elaborated for each writer and took place across different time frames. Commentary on Baldwin and Vidal was frequently shot through with gay innuendo, and this knowingness reached a kind of tipping point for both writers in 1968 with Eldridge Cleaver's homophobic attack on Baldwin in his best-selling *Soul on Ice* and the "outing" of Vidal on live TV by the right-wing pundit William F. Buckley Jr. Sontag's public association with queerness was more oblique. Her image had a sexually perverse cast that was importantly informed by her mediation of gay male sensibility, but this was offset by her public profile as an ostensibly heterosexual divorced mother, as well as by her conventionally feminine gender performance; it was not until the 1990s that Sontag's same-sexuality was widely discussed. Sontag thus cannot be understood as a proto-lesbian celebrity in quite the same way that (their protestations notwithstanding) Baldwin and Vidal can be understood as proto-gay ones; her career instead exemplifies how gay male culture, as the most widely publicized version of queerness, may enable other kinds of queer cross-identification.[10] Despite these different relations to gayness, I argue that all three writers proved unable to manage their association with homosexual identity. While I accord due respect to each writer's account of his or her own sexuality, and while I acknowledge the sometimes reductive and indeed derogatory effects of the associations of each writer with gay or lesbian identity, this book does not make a case for these writers' heroic resistance to sexual categorization. Departing from the emphasis within queer theory on sexual identity categories as coercive operations of power/knowledge, I draw on my analysis of Baldwin, Sontag, and Vidal to argue for the political and critical value of those categories.

Categorically Famous does not propose that same-sexuality is necessarily the most productive perspective through which to view all these authors' work. It does, however, argue for the crucial relations of career-defining moments for all three writers to the emergence of the discourse of gay and lesbian liberation. I elaborate my claims through close readings and thick descriptions of these moments, outlining each author's mobilization of homosexual meaning and his or her engagements with homosexual subcultures. At the same time I bring these authors' work into dialogue with queer theory to interrogate some of its foundational assumptions regarding identity, visibility, and liberation. While I concentrate on the decade leading up to the Stonewall Inn riots of 1969, conventionally understood as the beginning of the liberation period, I also occasionally move outside this time frame to chart the prehistories and aftermaths of each author's relation to queer identity and celebrity. My argument is sustained by the insights of celebrity studies that, as David Marshall puts it, "the celebrity . . . is an embodiment of a discursive battleground on the norms of individuality and personality within a culture"; and that, as Robert van Krieken puts it, the celebrity helps "co-ordinat[e] the ideas, choices and actions of large numbers of people," due to the exorbitant amount of attention she accrues.[11] I contend that the careers of Baldwin, Sontag, and Vidal involved discursive struggles over the norms of sexual identity and the permissibility of varieties of sexual expressions and attitudes that were played out in audience relations to their work and personas.

As is probably already apparent, my approach to these authors is in some ways quite sociological in spirit. Drawing on a wide range of work from the thriving field of celebrity studies—which concentrates on culture industries such as Hollywood cinema, TV, and popular music—I situate the fame of Baldwin, Sontag, and Vidal not only as the outgrowth of their particular achievements but also in relation to large forces of mediatization, commodification, and identity formation.[12] I balance this account with an awareness of the specificities of literary celebrity, an increasing focus of scholarship over the past few years, elaborated in studies that range from the beginnings of commodified literary fame in the eighteenth century to modern and contemporary contexts.[13] My promiscuous engagement with celebrity scholarship, taking up its diverse insights on a need-to-know basis as I move from one author to the next, is appropriate to the topic of celebrity itself. Opposing the tendency of many scholars to oversimplify celebrity by "labeling it either fully participatory or thoroughly manufactured, radically democratic or incipiently fascist, blasphemously secular or the newest expression of religious impulses, a rallying point for individualism or the imposition of mindless conformity," Sharon Marcus contends that celebrity is "always all these things: its omnivorousness is how and why it works."[14] With regard to mid-twentieth-century literary celebrity in particular, we can say that it is both a phenomenon of the impersonal machinery of mass media and publicity *and* directly connected to what Loren Glass calls "individual authorial consciousness."[15]

In *Authors, Inc: Literary Celebrity in the Modern United States*, a work dealing with the period directly relevant to *Categorically Famous*, Glass argues that the emphasis on individual authorial consciousness complicates "the easy dismissal of the celebrity's subjectivity" in celebrity studies scholarship that attends to the culture industries.[16] Glass suggests that modern literary celebrity is qualitatively different from culture industry celebrity, in that even though literary celebrities participate in media outlets such as TV and mass-circulation magazines, they also sustain "an ethos of individual creative production over and against the rise of these culture industries."[17] In tandem with or cued by Glass, other work on literary celebrity has elaborated the interpenetration of the ethos of authorial creativity and celebrity status, conceiving of "the structure of mass-mediated celebrity [as] a formal problematic" of works by celebrity authors, "not simply a condition of their reception."[18] Thus, various scholars have argued that the stylistic individualism of twentieth-century literary celebrities is simultaneously an inscription of subjectivity and a unique selling point in the marketplace of commodified personhood.[19] In *Categorically Famous* I synthesize these insights of literary celebrity scholars with Michel Foucault's contention about the centrality of sexuality to modern subjectivity. I argue that it is the expression of "individual authorial consciousness" that explains the preoccupation with same-sexuality in the work of Baldwin, Sontag, and Vidal. In this respect, I also draw on Edward Said's richly suggestive discussion of the modern authorial career. Said argues that from the late nineteenth century a cultural emphasis on individualism, as well as dramatic changes in the literary marketplace, displaces the "ritual progress" of the poetic vocation, forcing writers to produce "aboriginal," self-managed careers.[20] The resultant "tyrannical domination" of the literary career means that "even the writer's personal life . . . [becomes] matter for the writing project"; no clear distinction between authorial subjectivity and literary output remains.[21] I understand this principle to apply as much to Sontag's famously "impersonal" essays as to Baldwin's obviously autobiographical novel *Tell Me How Long the Train's Been Gone* (to make an indicative contrast), though the obviousness of the "confession" of sexual interest varies significantly depending on genre and mode.[22]

It is the tight reticulation of subjectivity, sexuality, and literature that in my view makes exemplars of literary fame especially germane to a discussion of the relations between celebrity and politicized gay consciousness before the 1970s. In *Categorically Famous*, I follow Henry Abelove and Jeff Solomon in arguing for the impact of literature on gay liberation, contending that, as Solomon argues of Truman Capote and Gertrude Stein, "the work and persons" of Baldwin, Sontag, and Vidal "served as essential influences on gay and proto-gay men and women before and after Stonewall, and were highly significant to the gay and lesbian rights movement as a whole."[23] Certainly there is no such connection evident in the case of culture industry celebrities, such as closeted Hollywood stars.[24] And famous literary authors had much more effect in this regard than, say, famous art-world figures such as Jasper Johns or even Andy Warhol, who may have worked with homosexual meaning but whose medium of expression allowed for more distance between that meaning and their public personas.[25] In any case, with the rule-proving exception of Warhol, the art world received much less media coverage in this period than literature. As many have observed, the postwar period up to around 1975 still accorded literature—and literary celebrity—significant authority, in ways that seem quaint in our current dispensation, in which literature has been absorbed into the leveling generality of "postmodern" cultural production.[26] Additionally, literature's exemplification and enablement of sexual frankness in the public sphere during the 1960s need to be connected to the legal challenges to obscenity that took place during the decade. These were not confined to cases of print media, but literature furnished many of the most prominent objects of contestation, with the decade seeing key legal decisions in favor of publishers of texts such as John Cleland's eighteenth-century pornographic novel *Memoirs of a Woman of Pleasure* and twentieth-century novels such as D. H. Lawrence's *Lady Chatterley's Lover*, William Burroughs's *Naked Lunch*, and Henry Miller's *Tropic of Cancer*.[27] Less "literary" print media works also played an important part in the censorship battles, with the Supreme Court decision in *Manual Enterprises v. Day* (1962) in favor of H. Lynn Womack, a publisher of gay pulp books and physique magazines, proving particularly enabling for explicitly homoerotic publications.[28] The net effect was an increase in the sexual license of print media (which already had greater license than media such as Hollywood film and TV). The essays and fiction of Baldwin, Sontag, and Vidal, which were both celebrated and excoriated for their sexual frankness, both benefited from and contributed to the increasingly sexualized public sphere that the censorship battles helped make possible.

If Baldwin, Sontag, and Vidal had ambivalent relations to sexual identity categories, their relations to celebrity were similarly vexed. All three authors were apprenticed in midcentury liberal intellectual culture, which adopted an oppositional stance toward the mass media that generates celebrity; in the case of each author, however, this stance was tempered by other investments and interests. Thus, Baldwin to some extent embraced his celebrity as a means of communicating his deeply felt views (about race, art, and sexuality) to a large audience and as a due reward for his struggle as an African American writer from unpromising beginnings; yet he was also often severely critical of celebrity culture, and *Tell Me How Long the Train's Been Gone* is an early entry in the subgenre of late twentieth-century novels engaging in fictionalized meditations on the Faustian bargain that celebrity supposedly constitutes for the literary author. Vidal's attitudes were less tortured and of a piece with his carefully cultivated "aristocratic" stance of aloofness toward bourgeois earnestness. One of his repeated quips was that he was a third-generation celebrity, and in many ways he reveled in his fame; yet, like Baldwin, he cast a jaundiced eye on the mass media and its putatively stupefying effects on the American populace. His masterpiece *Myra Breckinridge* (1968), the subject of Chapter 5, is a brilliant satire of celebrity culture, among other things, even as it is animated by Vidal's own fannish relation to 1940s Hollywood and its stars. Of the three authors I discuss,

Sontag was the most stringently critical of the mass media and its forms of fame. Notwithstanding her "with-it" celebration of popular and unsanctioned cultural forms—such as camp and science-fiction film—Sontag steadfastly eschewed any self-critical relation to her own iconic media image, disavowing any association with "pop celebrity."[29]

Categorically Famous argues, however, that just as all three authors were unable to manage their association with homosexuality, so they were unable to manage their celebrity.[30] This claim is not simply meant to point out a parallel. Rather, I contend that the figures of the homosexual and the celebrity are brought into strange intimacy in the immediate preliberation era of the 1960s. In these two figures, the always fraught relations between the nonetheless crucial cultural categories of public and private come into focus. If celebrity status is premised on the presumptive access of a mass audience to a public figure's private life, homosexuality for much of the postwar period was generally seen by both sympathetic and unsympathetic commentators as a personal or private matter, the public discussion of which should be minimal at best. During the 1960s, however, increasing media coverage of homosexuality, particularly of urban gay male subcultures, worked against this repressiveness. *Categorically Famous* places the work of Baldwin, Sontag, and Vidal in this context, arguing that what Joe Moran would call the "intertextual nature" of their celebrity—that is, the interlocking components of their works and their media images—contributed importantly to the making public of homosexuality that helped consolidate gay men and lesbians as a politicized minority.[31]

But why these three writers? There were other equally famous queer writers of this period who undoubtedly affected public conceptions of and attitudes toward homosexuality, for good and for ill. Tennessee Williams and the already-mentioned Truman Capote spring to mind; or Allen Ginsberg, exceptional among the writers so far named in that he openly declared his homosexual identification before Stonewall. I contend that the grouping of Baldwin, Sontag, and Vidal is a productive one with which to parse the relations between literary celebrity and gay politics because of their common, if individually complex, association with the notion of sexual liberation and because of the way in which that association entailed debate about what should be publicly permissible in terms of sexual representations and identities. In my view the careers of Capote and Williams do not yield the same kind of public sphere effects—which is not at all to say that they were cowed in their representations or their celebrity performances of queerness.[32] Ginsberg, by contrast, along with the other Beats and Beat-influenced writers like John Rechy, was invested in the putative outlawry of homosexuality, positioning it as an abject-yet-celebrated oppositionality; his 1960s work shows little interest in the idea of collective queer emancipation—though he was an early enthusiast for the radical gay cause in the immediate post-Stonewall moment.[33]

I don't suggest that Baldwin, Sontag, and Vidal in any way straightforwardly *endorsed* sexual liberation or gay liberation. Each writer in fact had important reservations about, or was openly critical of, these ideas; but their work also, in some cases inadvertently, richly elaborates possibilities of sexual liberation in general and homosexual emancipation in particular. I outline the specificities of each author's relation to these possibilities in the chapters that follow, but I need here to indicate what I mean by "sexual liberation." Throughout this book I use the term fairly loosely, to describe the assumption that the derepression of certain aspects of sexuality will have social and political benefits. I also use the terms "gay/lesbian liberation," or just "liberation," to indicate both the growing sense of the necessity and desirability of collective homosexual emancipation throughout the 1960s, as well as the social and political developments of the immediate post-Stonewall moment. My use of these terms is in some ways retrospective, as I occasionally use the words and ideas of gay liberationists of the 1970s to reflect on writing from the 1960s, but it also responds to contemporaneous ideas about the sexual revolution that were widely circulated in the media during the 1960s, as I outline in the next section. In one respect, importantly, my deployment of "liberation" is unusual and perhaps counterintuitive, in that while I give credit to its utopian inflection as an idea, I am more interested in its actual world-changing effects than its status as a desire. In this, as will become apparent, my account of liberation contrasts with a more thoroughly utopian tendency within queer theory, which, for all its rhetorical forcefulness and influence within the humanities, has changed little in the wider world of social relations.

Public Relations, Private Revolutions

The alignment of media representation and homosexual emancipation was noted by R. E. L. Masters in his preface to the 1964 paperback edition of *The Homosexual Revolution* (first published 1962), one of the many pop-sociological studies of the gay world that appeared in the preliberation decade. Masters writes that the increasing "overtness" of "homosexual behavior," "along with the broadening discussion of the problem and public tolerance of homosexuals has been in recent years almost exclusively a product of what might be termed 'public relations.'" There have been "no new scientific findings or breakthroughs that would serve to explain or produce our fast changing attitudes"; rather, these are explained by "full-blown discussions of the 'homosexual problem' in our mass communications and opinion-moulding media."[34] Itself a contributor to these discussions, Masters's book was an early entry in "an explosion in widely disseminated material on homosexuality" that took place during the 1960s, including coverage in the daily press, national magazines, fiction, drama, and film.[35] While the preponderance of this material concentrated on male homosexuality, lesbianism was an increasing focus of attention, receiving its own influential pop-sociological treatments in Ann Aldrich's studies of the New York lesbian subculture, written from a lesbian point of view, and the straight journalist Jess Stearns's *The Grapevine* (1964).[36] Along with more niche publications sometimes explicitly aimed at gay and lesbian audiences—including lesbian pulp fiction, physique pictorial magazines, and the journals and newsletters of the homophile organizations—mainstream coverage of homosexuality unwittingly contributed to the formation of gay political consciousness. As John D'Emilio writes of this period, "At the very least the growing discourse about lesbians and homosexuals strengthened a sense of belonging to a group, even when fear and guilt blocked any steps to act upon that awareness. For others, the new availability of information made the gay subculture of the nation's larger cities more accessible."[37]

As D'Emilio and others note, the emphasis on group consciousness and on subcultural formations was crucial, helping to dislodge the midcentury dominance of the psychoanalytic paradigm, which treated homosexuality as an individual maladjustment. However censorious or alarmist in tone, reportage on the homosexual world almost necessarily raised the possibility of emancipation, given the obviousness of antigay laws and attitudes and the solicitation by writers of the views of homophile groups like the Mattachine Society and the Daughters of Bilitis, which agitated for reform. Once "the sociological imagination" was applied to homosexuality,[38] terms like "liberation" and even "revolution" bubbled up. The title and general argument of Masters's *The Homosexual Revolution* was an early example of this trend; other titles taking up the theme included Roger Blake's *The Homosexual Explosion!* (1968), Eric Karlson's *The Homosexual Uprising* (1967), and Ken Worthy's *The*

New Homosexual Revolution (1967). Even though Masters disapproved of the ambitions of "the most militant of the homophiles," such as the admittance of homosexuals into the armed forces and that they should be allowed to express affection in public, he was also, as Martin Meeker notes, quite prescient about the "transformation of American sexualities and sexual subcultures" that followed the publication of his book.[39] An even earlier example of militant language was Seymour Krim's "The Revolt of the Homosexual," published in the *Village Voice* in 1959. Cast as a dialogue between a forthright homophile and an unsympathetic straight man, the article forecast a "beautiful future" in which "homosexuals are as proud to be what we are" as are heterosexuals in the present, a future arrived at, however, only after a "showdown" between the heteronormative dispensation and gay men who are "no longer going to accept your evaluation of us."[40] While *Categorically Famous* does not assume that there was anything historically inevitable about the emergence of gay liberation or the "authentic" gay and lesbian identities that were its concomitants, it does argue that possibilities of emancipation were strikingly anticipated in a wide range of media throughout the 1960s, including in the essays and fiction of Baldwin, Sontag, and Vidal. This work stood out in that it was authored by writers who had strongly homosexual orientations and who (their disavowals aside) had been on the receiving end of the assaultive homophobia of Cold War America; as is often pointed out, 1960s discussion of homosexuality was usually conducted by heterosexual voices, with "the passion of . . . aggrieved" gay men and lesbians largely unexpressed.[41] While none of the three authors considered "came out" as gay or lesbian in a way that would be legible in postliberation terms, and while none proposed a radical homophile politics, their widely disseminated representations of homosexuality nevertheless contributed to a growing sense of the legitimacy of homosexual lifeways—even if those representations lacked, or masked, the passion that we associate with the radical gay culture of the early 1970s.

As many have observed, political challenges to the entrenched homophobia of postwar America before 1969 for the most part appealed to the principle of citizen rights. It's true that, for all that it generated talk of "revolution," the growing conception of homosexuals as a marginalized or persecuted minority, analogous to Jews or African Americans, dovetailed with an established idea of rights-based reform. The understanding of the homophile movement—and other civil rights movements—as primarily "reformist" or "assimilationist," however, has the unfortunate effect of underestimating the courage of those involved in those movements and overestimating the amenability of the state to accommodating minority demands. Moreover, as several historians of sexuality have argued, "radical" and "reformist" tendencies coexisted in both the homophile movement of the 1960s and the liberation movement of the early 1970s, albeit in different degrees.[42] The emphasis on liberation in the politicization of gay and lesbian populations also needs to be connected to the promulgation of the idea of "sexual revolution" throughout the 1960s. The term, formulated by Wilhelm Reich in prewar Germany, arose out of his conviction that sexual repression was responsible for social ills and referred to the widespread changes necessary for derepression—such as eliminating the sexual double standard and allowing sexual experimentation by adolescents.[43] Beginning with the 1964 *Time* article "The Second Sexual Revolution," the term gained currency in the American mediasphere as a means of flagging the significant changes in sexual mores that were taking place.

For *Time*, it was a "second" revolution because it succeeded the earlier shift in sexual attitudes of the 1920s, "when flaming youth buried the Victorian era and anointed itself as the Jazz Age." While the first revolution was "led by the daring few," the second was much more widespread, leaving the youth of the 1960s "adrift in a sea of permissiveness, [with] little to rebel against."[44] *Time* betrays no inkling of the sexual rebelling that was yet to come, by second-wave feminists and homosexuals most notably. Indeed, the article scarcely mentions homosexuality, and while, on the one hand, this could be seen as a reflection of *Time*'s general conservatism, on the other, it is indicative of a general inclination to underestimate the place of homosexual emancipation in "the 1960s" that has persisted until recently.[45] In *Categorically Famous*, I argue that homosexuality actually was fundamental to the cultural shifts and the political effects collected under the differently weighted but overlapping rubrics of the "sexual revolution" and the "counterculture." In Chapter 4, I argue that Sontag's writing on camp and sexuality from the early and mid-1960s anticipates the unprecedented fusion of politics, lifeways, and unorthodox sexual styles that Theodore Roszak dubbed the "counterculture."[46] With coming out as its foundational political strategy, the gay and lesbian liberation movement that emerged around 1969 is rhetorically premised on the end of one kind of privacy and, thus, along with the women's movement, stands as an exemplary instance of the premise of the counterculture that the personal and the sexual are eminently political.[47]

The Anticategorical Imperative

Crediting terms like "liberation," "visibility," and "openness" with conceptual validity and political force, as I do in this book, of course puts my argument at loggerheads with some of the most cherished Foucauldian orthodoxies of queer theory, even though, as I've already intimated, *Categorically Famous* is also indebted to Foucault's insights about modern sexual subjectivity. While the detail of my differences with established positions in queer studies is worked out in the following chapters, a brief account of my guiding perspective is in order here. In volume 1 of *The History of Sexuality*, Foucault trenchantly argues against the notion that sexuality has been subjected to a historical repression. As is often noted, this critique of the repressive hypothesis should be understood in part as a takedown of mostly unnamed Freudian radicals (Wilhelm Reich, the Herbert Marcuse of *Eros and Civilization*, and Norman O. Brown), whose work had great influence on the discourse of sexual liberation.[48] While not denying that sex has been "prohibited or barred or masked or misapprehended," Foucault ultimately sees these "negative elements" as "only component parts that have a local and tactical role to play" in the transformation of sex "into discourse, a technology of power, and a will to knowledge."[49] For Foucault, famously, the "implantation" of perverse sexualities is a prime exemplification of this operation—an "encroachment of a type of power on bodies and their pleasures" that results "in the frozen countenance of the perversions."[50]

For the queer theory that has developed over the past three decades, this account of the frozen countenance of perversion has itself frozen into an argumentative approach that, at its most programmatic, sees the critique—or more accurately, perhaps, the *refusal*—of sexual categorization as both a necessary and sufficient conclusion. Eve Sedgwick, writing in *Epistemology of the Closet* (1990) on the cusp of the take-up of "queer" as a theoretical optic, sounded a monitory note about the critique of categorization, arguing that "to question the self-evidence of [the] opposition between gay and straight as distinct kinds of persons is not . . . to dismantle it." "Perhaps no one should wish to do so," she continues, given the "real power" for many people of "the nominative category 'homosexual,' or its more recent near-synonyms . . . to organize and describe their experience of their own sexuality and identity. . . . The durability of any politics or ideology that would be so much *permissive* of same-sex sexuality has seemed, in this century, to depend on a definition of homosexual persons as a distinct, minority population, however produced or labelled."[51] The massive influence of her book notwithstanding, Sedgwick's warning has not been well heeded. Sedgwick's connection between categorization and permissiveness (let alone acceptance) of same-sexuality dovetails with Foucault's account in *History of Sexuality* of the "reverse discourse" of homosexual identity, whereby "homosexuality began to speak in its own behalf, to demand that its legitimacy and 'naturality' be acknowledged, often in the same vocabulary, using the same categories by which it was medically disqualified."[52] But Foucault treats the reverse discourse only glancingly (in this text, at least), and queer theorists have followed his cue, largely discounting or disputing the liberationist insistence on the value of gay and lesbian visibility and audibility. Influenced by the antifoundationalist impulse of deconstruction as well as by Foucault, Judith Butler set out an (ironically) foundational critique of liberationist tenets in her 1991 essay "Imitation and Gender Insubordination," arguing that there "can be no transparent or full revelation . . . offered by 'lesbian' or 'gay.'" In a rhetorical move that has become a signature of queer theory, Butler asks whether the "infinite postponement of the disclosure of 'gayness'" is "*to be valued*, a site for the production of values, precisely because the term now takes on a life that cannot be, can never be, permanently controlled?"[53] In contrast with this utopian vision of an uncontrolled and uncontrollable subjectivity, *Categorically Famous* is interested, and invested, in the values that are generated by the assertion of counterdiscursive identity.[54]

For queer theory, the visibility of homosexuality that was crucial to gay liberation is rethought, in Lee Edelman's words, as "disciplinary inscription," an example of "the policial regulation of social identities." Introducing his generative study *Homographesis*, Edelman writes that his titular concept names, "on the one hand, the normalizing practice of cultural discrimination (generating, as a response, the self-nomination that eventuates in the affirmative politics of a minoritized gay community), and, on the other, a strategic resistance to that reification of sexual difference."[55] Here, affirmative politics are indicatively relegated to a parenthesis, as the work of "resistance" to the pejoratively dubbed phenomena of "normalizing practice" and "reification" that Edelman's book will prosecute is set in place. The prejudice of queer studies against visibility is perhaps most astringently summarized in Leo Bersani's assertion that "visibility is a precondition of surveillance, disciplinary intervention, and, at the limit, gender cleansing. . . . Once we agreed to be seen, we also agreed to being policed."[56]

In *Categorically Famous* I attempt to rethink the rethinking of visibility in queer studies and to argue for the value of categorizing persons. My approach aligns with some recent developments in queer studies and in critical theory more generally that indicate disenchantment with anti-identitarianism. For instance, in *The Limits of Critique* in a passage that in part responds to Butler's "Imitation and Gender Insubordination," Rita Felski argues that while the "fin-de-siècle critical theory" that this essay exemplifies decisively demonstrated that the language of identity "could be used to police, control, or exclude[,] . . . it hardly follows that attempts to speak of self, sexuality, or identity are automatically or invariably coercive."[57] Affirmations of identity, as Felski says, "serve differing ends and have countless uses." They may be characterized by qualification and hesitation as well as used "to bully, browbeat or exclude"; and they "can also forge new attachments and solidarities, renounce or reaffirm past histories, offer fresh angles of vision or reaffirm crucial but long-forgotten insights."[58] Tackling the knee-jerk antinaturalism of critical theory (her example is again Butler, this time *Gender Trouble*), Felski notes, "It is one thing to point out that certain ideas are bad and taken for granted. It is another to conclude that they are bad *because* they are taken for granted—in other words, that anything taken for granted is an agent of domination."[59] Similarly, in his work on "queer optimism," Michael Snediker argues that "in its attachment to not taking persons as such for granted, queer theory's suspicious relation to persons has itself become routinized, if not taken for granted in its own right," thus forfeiting to a damaging extent its capacity to generate new and, importantly, affirmative insights.[60] In *So Famous and So Gay*, a study that has particular affinities with *Categorically Famous*, in that it focuses on the paradoxical crossover of gayness and fame in the careers of Truman Capote and Gertrude Stein, Jeff Solomon also demurs at queer theory's routine preference for "subjectivity over personhood" and its concomitant "showcasing [of] negative affects over positive ones—negative affects that, unlike identity itself, are considered stable." The estrangement of normative identity on which queer theory prides itself has, for Solomon, the unfortunate effect of iterating the social estrangement of living gay and lesbian people and of "ignor[ing] the lived costs of incoherence."[61] A final coordinate for the theoretical tack of *Categorically Famous* is Christopher Castiglia and Christopher Reed's *If Memory Serves*, which brings a historical consideration of liberation to the critique of anti-identitarianism I have briefly outlined in the work of Felski, Snediker, and Solomon. Castigilia and Reed position themselves against queer theory's "unremembering" of the radicalism that liberationist identitarian politics enabled, arguing that the depredations of the AIDS crisis importantly if not completely account for the displacement of the "joyous, collective, idealistic, and socially situated possibilities of sexual liberation" by the " 'queer subject,' solitary and outside history," and shot through with "decollectivizing, shame-inducing, or ego-shattering death drives," which emerged in academic work on sexuality in the 1990s.[62] Working with Simon Watney's arguments in *Imagine Hope*, they note that the "anti-identity (and hence anti-communitarian) ethos of queer theory" reproduced "the competitive individualism of the Thatcher-Reagan period 'it ostensibly opposed.' "[63]

If Solomon casts queer theory's privileging of the unstable queer subject as paralleling the social pressures that make identity formation difficult for the queer individual, and Castiglia and Reed, via Watney, see it as unwittingly reinforcing neoliberal ideology, I want additionally to suggest that the fixation of queer theory on a queer subject who is "solitary and outside history" unfortunately repeats the dominant preliberation image of the homosexual as an isolated individual, unconnected to the collective and politicized experience that makes optimism possible. Along with Castiglia and Reed, then, I reject the queer-theoretical tenet that liberation is simply liberalization—entailing the capitulation or incorporation of minoritized subjects or desires—and assume the term's value as both a culturally productive idea and a descriptor of a set of actual historical developments. The attraction of queer theory to categorical uncertainty no doubt helps explain the concentration of queer literary studies on precategorical Victorianism and on early twentieth-century modernism, which tends to elaborate gendered and sexual fluidity. In contrast with what Christopher Looby calls this "utopian" impulse of modernism, midcentury literature tends, unpromisingly for queer critics, to take "the homosexual category of person for granted."[64] In *Categorically Famous* I am interested in the progressive, not necessarily utopian, implications of this category as they are worked out in literary terms.[65]

If I depart from some of the major positions of queer theory, like all the critics of the anti-identitarian position that I've just mentioned, I also draw on and share many of them. In particular, I find elaborations of the "affective turn" within recent queer studies galvanizing for the study of literary celebrity, a category that both focuses on authorial subjectivity and engages the transindividual nature of audience response. If, like others, I have reservations about the often ahistorical and pessimistic treatment of affects like shame, my argument is also informed by and contributes to this important strand of queer scholarship. *Categorically Famous* traces a kind of affective trajectory—beginning with shame, in fact—that is also a roughly chronological one. Focusing on the early 1960s and reaching back into the 1950s, Chapters 1 and 2 explore Baldwin and "celebrity shame" in his nonfiction and his fiction. Chapters 3 and 4 on Sontag tarry in the mid-1960s and are anchored by a discussion of the complex combinations of excitement and repulsion occasioned by her appearance on the cultural scene. Chapters 5 and 6 on Vidal both home in on 1968 and two key events in his career that are also, I suggest, key events in the making public of homosexuality—the publication of *Myra Breckinridge* and Vidal's "outing" by Buckley on live TV; Chapter 6 suggests that the latter event drew on and added to a social reserve of *embarrassment* around the publicization of homosexuality. The move from shame to embarrassment as it pertains to same-sexuality is in one sense a move from an account of affect focused on authorial subjectivity (Baldwin's shame) to an intersubjective one (audience embarrassment). But the move is also meant to pick up on historical developments. In tracing the work of Baldwin, Sontag, and Vidal, I am interested in part in unfolding the cultural shifts that made the expression of *gay pride* possible. I do not at all mean to suggest that there is a simple weakening of the affects generally attached to or generated by homosexuality across the decade (from shame to embarrassment). I assume the continuity and the intermingling of the various affects I've identified at both subjective and intersubjective levels. By focusing on particular affects at particular points in time, I mean rather to suggest the momentum of liberatory sentiment across the decade as it was routed through the celebrity effects of Baldwin, Sontag, and Vidal.

Neither claimants nor endorsers of gay or lesbian identity, Baldwin, Sontag, and Vidal might be seen as unpromising candidates for a study that emphasizes the cultural sway and political usefulness of those categories. I maintain, however, that, largely against their own wishes, they were caught up in and contributed to the movement toward liberation that consolidated recognizably contemporary gay and lesbian cultures and identities. Finding or substantially adding to their fame during a crucially transitional point in time with regard to American culture's relation to homosexuality—between the preliberation era of "the open secret" and the postliberation era of "openness"—the careers of these three writers help us understand the tensions and connections between queer identity and celebrity, not only during the 1960s but also in that period's extensive aftermath. If the "long 1960s," according to most estimations, concluded around 1974, the "identity politics" that the decade gave birth to is still very much with us.[66] In the small corners of the world that are the advanced capitalist West, there is a strong sense today, of course, of tectonic shifts in sexual identity politics, with much talk that the homosexual/heterosexual binary has lost its once-hegemonic capacity to organize people's understandings of the ways in which sexuality is lived. My inquiry here is guided by the suspicion that such talk may be premature—at least with regard to the logics of identity and coming out that gay and lesbian liberation put in place. As I suggest in this book's Afterword, turning briefly to present-day examples of queer celebrity, the headline-grabbing proliferation of gendered and sexual identities and even "fluid" nonidentities iterates the structure of the homo/hetero binary in ever-more-"refined" form, as well as attesting to the continued importance of acts of coming out. In its commitment to ideas of liberation, *Categorically Famous* does not, I hope, look back with unhelpful nostalgia on a seemingly distant period but asserts the ongoing relevance of notions of liberation and identity that were forged in that period and that were—and continue to be—importantly worked out in the production and reception of celebrity.

1 James Baldwin and Celebrity Shame

All art is a kind of confession, more or less oblique. All artists, if they are to survive, are forced, at last, to tell the whole story, to vomit the anguish up.[1]

I gagged, literally, and began to sweat, ran to the water cooler, tried to pull myself together, and returned to the office to explain the intention of my novel.[2]

I felt that [Eldridge Cleaver] used my public reputation against me both naïvely and unjustly, and I also felt that I was confused in his mind with the unutterable debasement of the male—with all those faggots, punks, and sissies, the sight and sound of whom, in prison, must have made him vomit more than once.[3]

THESE THREE IMAGES of involuntary alimentary expulsion attest, directly and indirectly, to the curious place of homosexuality in James Baldwin's career—as both central yet often unacknowledged, as audaciously represented yet hedged about with withdrawals and disavowals. In the first quotation, from "The Northern Protestant," a 1960 essay on Ingmar Bergman, Baldwin presents the artist's work as an act of compulsive confession, a vomiting up of personal anguish. For Baldwin, this confession entailed an "oblique" admission early on in his career of his own sexual queerness at a time when such admissions were courageous and dangerous. After earning critical success with a first novel drawing on his experiences as a boy preacher in Harlem, *Go Tell It on the Mountain* (1953), and a collection of essays, *Notes of a Native Son* (1955), Baldwin published *Giovanni's Room* in 1956, about a doomed love affair between two white men. This unanticipated change of direction for an acclaimed "Negro" writer at once rendered Baldwin a proto-visible homosexual, as I suggested in the Introduction, and, through its racial camouflage, interposed a distance between Baldwin as autobiographical subject and homosexual material, compounding the open secrecy that generally enveloped the midcentury queer author.

In the second passage, which comes from the introductory notes to his play *The Amen Corner* (1968), Baldwin describes his gagging reaction to an editor's suggestion that he radically alter his first novel—alter it so radically as to, in Baldwin's view, destroy it. While the overt reference is to the suggested excision of the religious elements of the novel, accounts of the drafting and publication of *Go Tell It on the Mountain* indicate that homosexuality may also have been at issue. The religious fervor of the semiautobiographical protagonist of the novel is closely related to his homoerotic attraction to another member of his church, and this relation was made even clearer in a discarded draft ending that, according to one of Baldwin's friends, he removed at the insistence of his editors.[4] In his introduction to *The Amen Corner* Baldwin presents the editor's suggestion that he take out the religious elements of *Go Tell It* as tantamount to the suggestion "that I burn the book."[5] The image recalls Baldwin's claim that his agent Helen Strauss had literally told him to burn the manuscript of *Giovanni's Room* because of its homosexual content (something that she denied).[6] The repetition of the image of book burning, I suggest, bolsters the possibility that the editorial reaction to the first version of *Go Tell It* had something to do with homosexuality. With *Giovanni's Room*, Baldwin would, on his own account, defy editorial censorship, vomiting up the truth of homosexuality "to survive" as an artist. As he described the writing of *Giovanni's Room* in a 1984 *Village Voice* interview, with his characteristic flair for self-dramatization, "If I hadn't written that book I would probably have had to stop writing altogether."[7]

But in the third passage we find Baldwin apparently repudiating the sexuality that he had previously been compelled to represent. The passage is from Baldwin's response in his book-length essay *No Name in the Street* (1972) to the Black Panther Eldridge Cleaver's homophobic attack on him in his book *Soul on Ice* (1968). Baldwin counters Cleaver's homophobia with some of his own, projecting onto the homosexual denizens of prison the debasement of maleness with which Black Power advocates in the late 1960s and early 1970s often charged him. Publicly shamed by Black Power leaders on the basis of his sexuality, Baldwin attempts to project shame outward, disavowing any connection with the "faggots, punks, and sissies" that he imagines Cleaver vomiting over.[8]

In this chapter and the next, I suggest that shame is intimately bound up with fame in Baldwin's celebrity career. Note that in his response to Cleaver, Baldwin states that he felt Cleaver had used his "public reputation" against him "naïvely and unjustly." At the same moment that he refuses identification with prison homosexuals, then, Baldwin indirectly acknowledges his status as one of the most famous proto-visible homosexual writers of the post–World War II period. Despite the predictions of his editors and agent, Baldwin's career was not ruined by the publication of *Giovanni's Room*. In fact, the novel sold well; and Baldwin's fame was cemented by the publication of his next novel, *Another Country* (1962), which continued his preoccupation with unorthodox sexuality. Thus, Baldwin transmuted the matter of homosexuality—defined as shameful by his culture—into literary success. But this transmutation did not involve a simple *denial* of the shamefulness of homosexuality, as the passage from *No Name* begins to indicate. Drawing on recent scholarship on the theoretical and political implications of shame, I suggest that shame was at the heart of both Baldwin's celebrity performance and his representation of homosexuality and that consideration of the operation of this affect helps us understand Baldwin's complicated relation to gay identity and the liberatory politics that formed around it. In this chapter I zigzag across Baldwin's oeuvre, traveling somewhat more widely historically than is the case in the other chapters, in part because Baldwin's account of homosexuality remains so consistent—or rather it remains, paradoxically, consistently ambivalent. Though the texts I cover are not all primarily autobiographical, I read them for their autobiographical resonances, following the example of Loren Glass, for whom autobiographical writing by famous authors brings into focus the operations of literary celebrity, in particular the emphasis on "individual authorial consciousness" that distinguishes literary fame from culture industry stardom.[9] Finally, I home in on an essay, "The Male Prison" (1954), published by Baldwin (to borrow the title of a well-known artifact of contemporary celebrity culture) "before he was famous"—or at least before the period of his mass-mediatized celebrity, which dates from the early 1960s. My focus on this early text is motivated by my interest in Baldwin's *ambition*. Exploring Baldwin's accounts of ambition here and elsewhere, I argue, helps us understand the interactions between fame and shame in Baldwin's career and in the reception of his career by his various audiences.

Shame on Display

Let me return to Baldwin's description of artistic confession as vomiting to begin to demonstrate the usefulness of shame as an optic through which to scrutinize the interrelations of homosexuality and career achievement for Baldwin. To vomit in public is, I would venture, for many people, in most circumstances, a shame-making event; at the least it can be read as a powerful image of shameful revelation. Baldwin's metaphor of vomiting in "The Northern Protestant" therefore suggests that artistic effort is potentially shame laden or derives from shameful experience. Shame is generally thought of as involving the accidental exposure of that which we would like to remain concealed, and this connection of shame with accident is called up by Baldwin's characterization of artistic confession as an involuntary physical response. Confirming Baldwin's choice of imagery, shame is indeed often figured as a particularly physical affect. As Jacqueline Rose puts it in a rather vomitous image, "Shame has a visceral quality about it. . . . People turn red with shame, are 'flooded' by shame, as though shame . . . brings the body too close to the surface, inner organs and liquids bursting through the dams of the mind."[10]

Baldwin insists that the writer must "tell the whole story"—no matter how compromising or unpleasant that story might be. This compulsion to tell about the potentially shameful, if it is perhaps peculiarly definitive of the artistic career, also indicates the way in which shame in general is intersubjective, and indeed theatrical. As Rose puts it, "Shame requires an audience. . . . Shame relies on the art of exposure, even if exposure is what it hates most, and most militantly struggles against" (1). Similarly, Ruth Leys comments that shame entails the "scene of exposure," "even if the scene is only an imagined one and the observer is not an external spectator but an internalized other."[11] Theatricality is also central to Eve Kosofsky Sedgwick's influential discussions of shame, which are particularly interested in the relation of shame to queerness. Drawing on the work of the psychologist Silvan Tomkins on shame, and deploying another visceral image, Sedgwick writes, "Shame turns itself skin side out; shame and pride, shame and dignity, shame and self-display, shame and exhibitionism are different interlinings of the same glove. Shame, it might finally be said, transformational shame, is performance. I mean theatrical performance."[12]

It is the theatricality of shame that underpins Jacqueline Rose's suggestion, in a rich meditation on the affective drives of celebrity culture, that "there might be an intimate, even passionate, connection between the cult of celebrity and shame" (201). The connection may be played out in the media performance of the celebrity as well as in the uses made of that performance by the audience: "Celebrity is often a ritual of public humiliation. Indeed, in relation to celebrity, shaming often appears to be the point. . . . Could it be then that celebrity is indeed our guilty secret, a veiled way of putting into public circulation certain things which do not easily admit to public acknowledgment?" (203). Rose's speculations link the sociologically oriented arguments of much celebrity studies, whereby "the celebrity . . . is an embodiment of a discursive battleground of the norms of individuality and personality," with the unconscious dimensions of celebrity consumption.[13] Celebrities, she suggests, "are the people required by us to embody or to carry the weight of the question: who are we meant to be performing to, or what are we doing when performing to an invisible audience? . . . Among other things, public celebrity might be an elaborate diversion from the complex, often punitive, audience inside the mind" (205). In this chapter and the next, I suggest that Baldwin's person and texts both exhibit the interlocking relations between shame and fame at the level of individual authorial consciousness and become a focus for the "guilty secret" of the Cold War audience's interest in homosexuality, something that in the 1950s and early 1960s does "not easily admit to public acknowledgment."

I have suggested that queer celebrity poses a challenge for celebrity studies' usual understandings of public and private relations and relations between stars and audiences. In the case of Baldwin, I find Sedgwick's work on shame particularly helpful for following the tangled threads of these relations. Sedgwick argues that shame at once isolates the shamed person under the spotlight of scrutiny and connects her to her audience, for shame is also "peculiarly contagious" (36). Think of the way in which the sight of a person making a shameful spectacle of himself—such as vomiting in public—may induce shame in us. Shame-making scenes, writes Sedgwick, make evident "the double movement" of shame: "toward painful individuation, toward uncontrollable relationality" (37). It is this double movement that, for Sedgwick, makes shame foundational to identity: "shame is the place where the *question* of identity arises most originarily and relationally" (37).

For queer people in particular, Sedgwick argues, shame is foundational and ineradicable: "The forms taken by shame are not distinct 'toxic' parts of a group or individual identity that can be excised: they are instead integral to and residual in the processes by which identity is formed" (63). We cannot simply scrub the connection between shame and queerness away, Sedgwick argues, but then neither should we want to do so, for shame is part of what gives queerness its political and cultural force. As she puts it, "Shame is simply the first, and remains a permanent, structuring fact of identity: one that . . . has its own, powerfully productive and powerfully socially metamorphic possibilities" (64–65).

In what follows I outline the ways in which the "double movement" of shame toward "painful individuation" and "uncontrollable relationality" can be seen to work in Baldwin's career in relation to ideas of homosexual identity and collectivity. Though Sedgwick's work is useful for Baldwin's understanding of shame, he did not exactly share her understanding of its productive effects. Baldwin was invested in efforts to eradicate shame even as he contradictorily registered its indelibility. In the late essay "Freaks and the American Ideal of Manhood" (1985), which provides his most extended autobiographical treatment of homosexuality, Baldwin writes that human existence is shaped by the judging "eye of the beholder," a process that begins with the judgment of our parents, followed by "the vast and claustrophobic gallery of Others . . . one's enemy or one's friend or one's lover." He goes on to say that while one can act to instruct the eye of the other "as to what to see" and thus keep "humiliation at bay," the presence of the judging eye "confirms the fact that humiliation is the central danger of one's life." "And since one cannot risk love without risking humiliation," Baldwin continues, "love becomes impossible."[14] This pessimistic peroration is at odds with Baldwin's more characteristic effort to instate romantic love as a transcendence of humiliation, of shame. The possibility that love might redeem the shamefulness of sex, and the shamefulness of homosexuality in particular, leads Baldwin to invest in the male couple and to abject the gay subculture, the focal point of liberatory sentiment and action. But if Baldwin turns away from the subculture and the liberation it enables, Baldwin's celebrity texts and person also make themselves available as touchstones for liberated gay culture. Thinking of how Baldwin's work may productively be related to sexual categorization goes against the grain of much of his work, as well as the criticism of it. In order to explain my position here, I move now to a discussion of Baldwin's account of racial and sexual categories, their overlaps and their distinctions.

Race Man/Man Who Loves Men

It is barely an overstatement to say that Baldwin launched his career by way of the critique of identity categories. Famously, in his essay "Everybody's Protest Novel" (1949), he attacked the treatment of race in the American novel—most scandalously in his erstwhile mentor Richard Wright's *Native Son* (1940)—as exemplifying American culture's fatal "passion for categorization, life neatly fitted into pegs."[15] First published in early 1949 in the French journal *Zero*, "Everybody's Protest Novel" announced Baldwin's "arrival" as a significant American writer when it was republished in the house journal of the New York intellectuals, *Partisan Review*, in June of the same year. If Baldwin made his name with this act of literary father killing, then the grounds of his attack were familiar for the liberal intellectual circles to which the essay was basically addressed. Evoking communication of the complexity of "our humanity" as the hallmark of the novel form's aesthetic success, Baldwin concluded, "The failure of the protest novel lies in its rejection of life, the human being, the denial of his beauty, dread, power, in its insistence that it is his categorization alone which is real and which cannot be transcended."[16] In the much less well-known essay "Preservation of Innocence," published the same year in *Zero*, Baldwin applied the same argument to "the problem of the homosexual."[17] A brief, somewhat unfocused piece that rehearses many of the claims about gender that will be more fully elaborated in "The Male Prison," "Preservation" critiques a handful of the "gay protest novels" that appeared in the immediate postwar years, including Gore Vidal's *The City and the Pillar* (1948), as "wholly unable to recreate or interpret any of the reality or complexity of human experience."[18] "It is quite impossible to write a worthwhile novel about a Jew or a Gentile or a Homosexual, for people refuse, unhappily, to function in so neat and one-dimensional a fashion. . . . A novel insistently demands the presence and passion of human beings, who cannot ever be labeled."[19]

Yet Baldwin's positions on the categories of racial and sexual identity contrast markedly, beginning with their different relations to politics. Baldwin consistently maintained that sexuality was a private affair; race, however, was for him eminently public, social, and political. This insistence on the privacy of the sexual experience as opposed to the public nature of racial identity was carried, as several critics have noted, in Baldwin's tendency largely to confine discussion of same-sexuality to his novels, whereas race was a consistent concern of all of his writing (novels, essays, plays, and so on).[20] To a certain extent, the difference of attitude can be explained by Baldwin's conviction, common to both sympathetic and unsympathetic commentators in the midcentury period, that homosexuality should be a private matter. Additionally, as Baldwin was in some ways a representative mid-twentieth-century liberal, it makes sense that for him the place for the discussion of homosexuality was the novel, regarded by liberal culture as the privileged venue for the exploration of the complexities of the private life.[21] (There is an obvious paradox here, in that the novel is also a public statement—an issue I take up in the next chapter.)

So race was political and public for Baldwin; and of course his mass-media celebrity largely derived from his capacities as an authoritative and eloquent speaker and writer on race. While Baldwin sometimes, particularly in his later career, denied that he saw himself as a spokesman for African Americans, throughout the 1960s he quite self-consciously fulfilled this role—or the role of the "race man," to use the vernacular African American term. The category of the race man, the prominent, successful African American male of the nineteenth and twentieth centuries who embodies "race consciousness, race pride, and race solidarity" overlaps with that of the celebrity.[22] Embodying the striving of the race, and exemplifying its ability to overcome second-class citizenship through his "aggressive demonstration of . . . superiority in some field of achievement," the race man is one version of the way in which the celebrity focuses the struggles over permissible and practicable identities within American culture.[23] Baldwin's inhabitation of the race man role, in his writing and in his public utterances, characteristically entailed the rhetorical adoption of a collective voice, in which the historical experience of African Americans is gathered together into his "I." For instance, in his 1963 *Time* cover story—one measure of midcentury celebrity status—Baldwin is quoted as speaking "not for himself but for all Negroes to all whites" when addressing a California audience: "I hoed a lot of cotton. . . . I laid a lot of track. I dammed a lot of rivers. You wouldn't have had this country if it hadn't been for me."[24]

The collective "I" of Baldwin's race man is also heterosexual and paternal (or avuncular), as the following collation of snippets from his speeches and interviews shows: "My son . . . my daughter, or my niece or nephew can't use a White waiting room in the deep South" (1965); "[white people] have to love my child as much as they love their child" (1970); "if my son or my nephew or my wife or my daughter walk into any room in the Western world, and nobody knows their name, she's just another nigger" (1984); "allow me the right to protect my women, my house my children" (1969).[25] As Justin Joyce and Dwight McBride note, in adopting the race man role, Baldwin assumes the "image of the black man as protector, progenitor and defender of the race," thus "masking his specificity, his sexuality, his difference."[26] However, if Baldwin's utterances as a race man tended to mask his sexuality through the insistent invocation of an imaginary heterosexuality and paternity, his unambiguous fictional explorations of homosexuality generated a climate of knowingness that undermined this status. For instance, Fern Eckman's statement in her 1966 portrait of Baldwin that "in his frail person, Baldwin embodies the paradoxes and the potentials of the integration battle in the United States" at once draws attention to his celebrity embodiment of collective racial striving and, through the reference to his "frail person," unsettles the putative virility of his race man persona.[27] More pointedly, the 1963 *Time* story states of Baldwin: "He is a nervous, slight, almost fragile figure, filled with frets and fears. He is effeminate in manner, drinks considerably, smokes cigarettes in chains, and he often loses his audience with overblown arguments."[28] As Lee Edelman notes, this characterization, "in its own fretful way, signifies nothing more nor less than 'Martin Luther Queen'" (the derogatory nickname for Baldwin that circulated during the 1960s and after), effecting through innuendo the direct identification of gossipy private speech that was interdicted in the mass media.[29] In subtle and not-so-subtle ways, characterizations like those of Eckman and *Time* undermine Baldwin's capacity to act as an African American leader, contaminating his enactment of the race man persona with insinuations of frailty, effeminacy, and homosexuality. But if knowing identifications and innuendo compromised Baldwin's race man status, it is nonetheless the case that Baldwin's deep investment in racial collectivity resulted in a powerful public presence. The *Time* profile states emphatically that Baldwin is "not, by any stretch of the imagination, a Negro leader," then goes on to contradict itself by detailing the high-profile activities that suggest he might without much of a stretch of the imagination be so regarded.[30]

There is a productive tension between Baldwin's commitment to the race man persona and his many forceful elaborations of race's artificiality. Baldwin's complicated relation to racial classification is evident, for instance, in the film *Baldwin's Nigger*, which records a 1969 talk he delivered at the West Indian Student Centre in London, capturing him in the full flight of his inspired speechmaking mode. After stating toward the end of the talk, "I don't really believe in race; I don't really believe in color," Baldwin is asked by an audience member why he continues to use the term "Negro" rather than "black." Visibly drawing himself back up into the oratorical stance that he had moments before relinquished to invite audience questions, Baldwin responds, in part:

> It was not I, nor any black man in America who invented the word "Negro." It was not I who wrote that on my birth certificate. It was not I who invented that language. I understand the purport of your question. . . . But you must understand too, that I cannot change my vocabulary overnight. I may agree with you, but we call, we've been called and call ourselves American Negroes, for all of nearly four hundred years. Now do you suppose, that because it angers *you*, that suddenly an entire nation is able to change its vocabulary?

Aware that the language of racial classification is, as he goes on to say, a "subtle effect of oppression," Baldwin nonetheless insists that one must "learn how to use those terms in order to survive and even to triumph."[31]

Despite his deconstructions of "race" and "color," then, Baldwin accepts the nomenclature of racial classification as not only historically inescapable but politically useful—a striking contrast with his view of sexual identity categories. In an indicative exchange with the bisexual English novelist Colin MacInnes in a BBC television broadcast from 1965, Baldwin is asked by MacInnes about the specificity of homosexual identity and the political identifications that may follow: "To what extent do you think a writer who may be bisexual or homosexual does identify himself with minority movements in a way a writer who is heterosexual would not? Do you think this plays an important part in the work of a writer of that description?" Baldwin replies that "those terms, homosexual, bisexual, heterosexual are 20th-century terms which, for me, really have very little meaning. I've never, myself, in watching myself and watching other people, watching life, been able to discern exactly where the barriers were."[32] Baldwin goes on to suggest that all sexual identity categories constrain human possibility, putting everyone into the same "desolate place" so that "a heterosexual who was miserable with his life and destroys his children and some poor lost creature thrown into the outer darkness of our society . . . match each other." MacInnes responds by suggesting the different relations heterosexual and homosexual individuals might have to the existing sexual hegemony: "I would have thought that the heterosexual despite his sense of loneliness and misery . . . would draw some slight consolation from the fact that he wasn't involved in yet another pressure. And . . . the homosexual might draw some curious satisfaction and passion from this clear identity of what he would assume was wrong with him." Baldwin rejects the point: "It seems to me, in the first place, that if one's to live at all, one's certainly got to get rid of the labels. It seems to me an incredible way to live, to glory in the fact that one is heterosexual because it proves that you're not something else, or vice versa."[33] While MacInnes gestures toward the power imbalance generated by the system of sexual categorization, Baldwin, demonstrating his characteristic lack of sympathy with subcultural expression, sets up a (false) equivalence between the homosexual and the heterosexual habitus.

Indeed, Baldwin's assertion of an equivalently "desolate" heterosexual and homosexual experience is belied by the overwrought language that he uses, here and elsewhere, when he engages gay subcultural identities and practices. In the exchange with MacInnes, not only does Baldwin identify the gay individual as "some poor lost creature thrown into the outer darkness of our society"; he also asserts that it is "what we call the sexual deviates, the sexual minorities" who "[reveal] most grotesquely" the "distrust we have of the affections and the flesh."[34] Baldwin's conviction of the grotesquerie of subcultural life is stridently elaborated in the narrator-protagonist David's (in)famous description of the effeminate patrons of the Parisian gay bar in *Giovanni's Room*, the "utter grotesqueness" of one of whom makes him "uneasy; perhaps in the same way that the sight of monkeys eating their own excrement turns some people's stomachs. They might not mind so much if monkeys did not—so grotesquely—resemble human beings."[35] Admittedly, this perception of "utter grotesqueness," the utterness of which is insistently and redundantly supplemented with the "grotesquely" inflected simile of the excrement-eating monkeys, is that of the sexually conflicted David. But David's notionally "unreliable" perception is only a heightened version of the view of subcultural life that can be found throughout Baldwin's writings. *Giovanni's Room*'s zoological metaphorics—bar patrons are not only like monkeys but "*les folles*," "screaming like parrots," looking "like a peacock garden," sounding "like a barnyard"—chimes with Baldwin's characterization of the subculture as *inhuman*.[36] In "The Male Prison," Baldwin writes that "today's unlucky deviate can only save himself by the most tremendous exertion of all his forces from falling into an underworld in which he never meets either men or women, where it is impossible to have either a lover or friend, where the possibility of genuine human involvement has altogether ceased."[37] This is a view amplified in *Another Country* in the gay character Yves's description of his forays into that underworld, which refigures inhumanity as mortality: "You do not meet many women in the places I have been; you do not meet many human persons at all. They are all dead. Dead."[38] Again, *Giovanni's Room* amps up this particular perception further, in David's hysterical view of another bar patron as "like a mummy or a zombie . . . something walking after it had been put to death."[39]

Grotesque, animal, inhuman, dead. Bearing these repeated patterns of imagery in mind, it is difficult to construe Baldwin's treatment of gay subcultural life as simply a valorization of sexual fluidity over the rigidity of "labels" or to view his treatment of sexual identity categories as isomorphic with his critique of "color." Yet these are the default positions of much recent Baldwin criticism, which finds in his treatment of racial and sexual identities anticipations of critical race theory and queer theory. Such criticism locates Baldwin as either, or simultaneously, pointing up the artificiality and limitations of identity categories or revealing their complex intersectionality.[40] The negative language with which Baldwin treats the gay subculture appears to be something of an embarrassment for many critics, who tend to gloss over it, to gesture toward autobiographical grounds for Baldwin's disaffection, or to elaborate overingenious arguments exempting these representations from homophobic affect.[41] But the evidence is stubborn. In a 1969 interview, in response to a rather insensitive line of questioning about whether he thinks homosexuality is a disease, Baldwin says, "If you fall in love with a boy, you fall in love with a boy. The fact that Americans consider it a disease says more about them than it says about homosexuality."[42] But he then continues, "When [homosexuality] becomes open, as it has here [in the United States], it becomes a disease. These people are not involved in anything resembling love-making: they're involved in some kind of exhibition of their disaster. It has nothing to do with contact or involvement between two people—which means that the person may change you."[43] Rejecting the collective "exhibition" of homosexuality for Baldwin goes hand in hand with rejecting the label of gay identity. Like Gore Vidal, Baldwin asserted that *homosexual* "is not a noun,"[44] and all humans are potentially bisexual. Quite unlike Vidal, Baldwin insisted that love has to be there for any sex to be meaningful. As he writes in "The Male Prison," "Sex is only sex. . . . There are few things on earth more futile or more deadening than a meaningless round of conquests."[45] To "use" another person sexually is one of the most debasing actions possible in Baldwin's fictional world. To quote from one representative depiction of a sexual encounter in his last novel *Just above My Head* (1979), "I was revolted when it was over . . . because I had used somebody merely as a receptacle and had allowed myself to be used merely as a thing."[46]

For Baldwin, love is imagined as something that might transcend shame. There is a consistent effort in Baldwin to differentiate merely physical acts of sex—in which shame and revulsion are closely linked—from sexual acts that are enriched by emotional connection. However, even when love informs a sexual encounter, shame hovers nearby. The description of one emotionally meaningful sexual act between men who become long-term lovers in *Just above My Head* is prefaced by a series of hypotheticals: "They might . . . wish never to see each other again. They might be ashamed—they might be debased: they might be forever lost."[47] While the danger of shame is averted in this instance, in *Giovanni's Room* shame is seemingly inextricably entangled with love. At the start of his affair with Giovanni, the narrator-protagonist David is exhorted by one character to "Love [Giovanni] . . . love him and let him love you. . . . You can make your time together anything but dirty, you can give each other something which will make both of you better—forever—if you will *not* be ashamed."[48] Yet shame and revulsion continue to characterize David's feeling toward Giovanni. Returning to Baldwin's favorite image of shaming compulsion, David says about Giovanni: "His touch could never fail to make me feel desire; yet his hot, sweet breath also made me want to vomit."[49] This statement is echoed in Baldwin's own statement in an interview, in which he defined a lover as a person who would willingly "hold me . . . if I am vomiting . . . if I am dying."[50]

If, for Baldwin, shame saturates both subcultural and loving versions of homosexuality, then, ultimately, I suggest, his work indicates that homosexuality cannot be kept apart from identity or from the subculture that harbors gay identity's counterdiscursivity. To illustrate, I turn to a passage from *Another Country* in which Eric, the book's main gay character, crosses Washington Square Park at night with some friends. In a heavy-handed moment that again makes the association of the subculture with "darkness" that Baldwin made in his exchange with MacInnes, the passage contrasts the square's "deserted" "children's playground" with "the darkness surrounding [it], in which the childless wretched gathered to act out their joyless rituals."[51] The passage is from Eric's point of view, and the narrator stresses that Eric's perception of the park arises out of the "melancholy and distaste" triggered by his return to New York and his reacquaintance with the mental torment of being homosexually identified that have been kept in abeyance by his time in France and by his love affair with a Frenchman, Yves. Yet Eric functions as a kind of surrogate for Baldwin in this novel, and, as I have already argued in relation to *Giovanni's Room*, it is not possible to neatly separate the horrified reaction to subcultural life displayed by his fictional characters from that found in Baldwin's interviews and nonfiction. In this passage, if the moralizing language of the free indirect discourse momentarily installs distance between Eric and "the childless wretched," the sentences that follow suggest his association with them. The thought of the wretched and their "joyless rituals" unleashes involuntary, shame-inducing memories that are once more likened to vomiting: "His life, his entire life, rose to his throat like bile tonight. The sea of memory washed over him, again and again, and each time it receded another humiliated Eric was left writhing on the sands. How hard it was to be despised; how impossible not to despise oneself!"[52] That Eric's confrontation with subcultural homosexual identity involves disavowal is made still clearer when, a page and half later, still walking through the square, Eric and his friends encounter "two glittering, loud-talking fairies." In response, Eric "pull[s] in his belly, looking straight ahead," avoiding the eye contact that would connect him to the fairies.[53] In Baldwin's novel the historical fact of urban queer identity disrupts the vision, offered earlier, of nonidentitarian homosexual love that Eric experiences in a self-consciously Edenic South-of-France setting with Yves (Eve). If Baldwin attempts repeatedly to abject the subcultural formations of homosexuality, those formations return repeatedly to his work, haunting it with the ineradicable shame that love cannot disperse.

Freakish Ambition

I have challenged the view that Baldwin's view of homosexuality is not homophobically informed. But I also want to affirm, following Sedgwick, the metamorphic possibilities that may be harbored in unpromising, shame-laden material, as in the case of many of Baldwin's representations of queerness. To approach this aspect of Baldwin's work, let's return to the traumatic circumstances surrounding the publication of *Giovanni's Room*. After Knopf, the publisher of *Go Tell It*, rejected *Giovanni's Room* on the basis of its homosexual content (Knopf apparently feared legal action), it was accepted by Dial in the United States and by Michael Joseph in the United Kingdom. As noted previously, the book sold well, and while reviews were, as they say, mixed, the book was not greeted with the "horror and loathing" with which Knopf responded, according to Baldwin in a 1984 preface to a reissue of *Notes of a Native Son*. "They would not, in short, publish it, as a favor to me," Baldwin recalls, continuing, "I conveyed my gratitude, perhaps a shade too sharply, borrowed money from a friend, and myself and my lover took the boat to France."[54] In Baldwin's account, Knopf is not mentioned by name but rather generalized as "Publisher's Row, that hotbed of perception."[55] The rejection by Knopf is made to illustrate the standoff between the integrity of the modern author and the aesthetic blindness of the commercial arm of literary production, despite the fact that *Giovanni's Room* was quickly picked up by competitors of Knopf. By eliding these specifics, Baldwin's account renders the fact that the book *was* eventually published an illustration of the triumph of courageous artistry over a timorous Publisher's Row. Admittedly, Baldwin's brief in this preface is to describe the genesis of *Notes of a Native Son* and to reflect on its significance to his career; it might be thought unfair to point up the occlusion of key details concerning the publication of *Giovanni's Room*. But my point here is not so much to expose Baldwin's self-mythologization as it is to suggest that the told-you-so sarcasm of this retrospect bespeaks a persistent woundedness regarding this novel that is paradoxically compounded with triumph. Baldwin's obsessive return, in this preface and elsewhere, to evocations of the "horror and loathing" of some editors and his agent (his repeated insistence that Helen Strauss suggested he burn the manuscript of *Giovanni's Room* is another example) indicates that shame was not erased by the victorious act of "confession" that was *Giovanni's Room* but lived on after it, even if in attenuated form.

In a contemporaneous rather than retrospective account of this period, the crucial point at which homosexual representation emerged in Baldwin's work is again represented as fraught with both triumph and abjection. The account comes from Baldwin's 1961 *Esquire* essay about his relationship with Norman Mailer, "The Black Boy Looks at the White Boy," included in Baldwin's second collection of essays, *Nobody Knows My Name* (1961).[56] The reference to homosexuality is implicit rather than, as in the case of the 1984 preface, obvious. But a careful reading of the autobiographical elements of the essay enables insight into the social and emotional forces at work in Baldwin's persona as proto-visible homosexual celebrity writer.

In "The Black Boy Looks at the White Boy," Baldwin writes that at the time he first met Mailer in 1956, he was at "the most dangerous point for any artist, his longest most hideous turning."[57] When he met Mailer, Baldwin had finished *Giovanni's Room*, though it was not yet published. The unnamed novel that he describes himself embarking on in the essay, then, is *Another Country*.[58] Baldwin represents himself as experiencing a crisis of artistic confidence as he is about to start writing his new novel; but I think we are certainly licensed to assume that anxiety about the reception of *Giovanni's Room* also had its part to play in his emotional state at this time, given the manuscript's reception by Strauss and others. In a paradigmatic statement of what Edward Said defines as the modern writer's need to forge an "aboriginal" career, in which "whatever work is in fact produced suffers from radical uncertainty at the beginning,"[59] Baldwin indicates in "Black Boy" that his earlier successes count for nothing: "The things I had written were behind me, could not be written again, could not be repeated" (273). But, in an equally typical statement of the driving ambition of the modern writer, Baldwin writes that "beneath" this crisis

> was that sense, that suspicion—which is the glory and torment of every writer—that what was happening to me might be turned to good account, that I was trembling on the edge of great revelations, was being prepared for a very long journey, and might now begin, having survived my apprenticeship (but had I survived it?), a great work. I might really become a great writer. (273–74)

If Baldwin's statements of career ambition here are in some ways quite typical of the midcentury male American writer of literary fiction, the nakedly confessional tone is perhaps unmatched (even by Mailer, the ostensible focus of Baldwin's essay). Homosexuality plays no overt role in this particular confession, but I suggest that it underpins it. Baldwin's crisis of artistic confidence is bound up, he tells us, with depression brought on by the end of a love affair. Suggesting the obsessive nature of his thought patterns at this time through a kind of stuttering repetition, Baldwin writes, "My private life had failed—had failed, had failed" (273). But this failure in love is imagined as forming the basis of artistic success. As Said argues, for the modern writer the "tyrannical domination" of the literary career means that "even the writer's personal life . . . [becomes] matter for the writing project"; it is this domination that for Said explains the strongly autobiographical inflection of much modern literature.[60] For Baldwin, if the homosexual "private life" ("What was happening to me") is rooted in shame, that foundationally shameful experience may be translated into greatness. The emotional and the vocational, the personal experience of psychic wounding and the public role of the celebrated author are brought together.

A little later in the essay, Baldwin returns to his artistic ambition, presenting it as a "revenge" against "power": "I know how power works, it has worked on me, and if I didn't know how power worked, I would be dead. . . . My revenge, I decided very early, would be to achieve a power which outlasts kingdoms" (279). Baldwin explicitly refers here to the social power of racial oppression, manifested for instance in the shaming and humiliation of segregated facilities.[61] But Baldwin's humiliations at the hands of power, as he tells us more straightforwardly elsewhere, were reactions not only to his racial identity but also to his sexuality. Indeed, for Baldwin, these two types of humiliation were interimplicated.

In *No Name in the Street*, Baldwin projects homophobic shame outward, dissociating himself from "faggots, punks, and sissies" as a defense against Cleaver's attack. But elsewhere in this text, moving away from the heroically masculinist rhetoric of Black Power, Baldwin describes himself as "an aging, lonely, sexually dubious, politically outrageous, unspeakably erratic freak."[62] This concatenation of self-deprecating attributes sets the idiosyncratic and anachronistic Baldwin persona apart from the young black militants with whom he otherwise sought to associate himself in *No Name* and in other publications and statements of the 1970s. And the shamefulness of his "sexually dubious" nature is central here.

It is surely his sexuality that in large part leads Baldwin to classify himself as a "freak"—a term that he takes up again in "Freaks and the American Ideal of Manhood" to describe those individuals, including himself, who depart from nationalist heteronormativity. Baldwin's perception of himself as a freak is also related to his physical appearance. He was short, slightly built, not conventionally good-looking—indeed, told from early on by his father that he was "ugly."[63] For Baldwin, these physical features were conflated with his queer sexuality and his racialization, as he makes clear in "Freaks." In that essay Baldwin acknowledges that he was called "sissy" during his upbringing in Harlem but stresses that it was his experiences as a young man in the supposedly tolerant environs of Greenwich Village that brought home to him the doubly shaming identity of the black homosexual, his existence as "the punch line of a dirty joke."[64] Deploying the discourse of freakery again, Baldwin states that of the "handful" of black people living in the Village in that period he "was decidedly the most improbable. . . . I don't think I felt absolutely, irredeemably grotesque—nothing that a friendly wave of the wand couldn't alter."[65] Yet Baldwin's shameful, freakish identity is the basis of his artistic ambition and creation—expressed as a vengefulness against the power that would oppress him, whether it be the publishers who reject that identity or a more abstract social power of racial and sexual hierarchies. In Baldwin's transmutation of his freakish, queer beginnings into the vengefulness of artistic success and fame, we have, I suggest, one example of what Sedgwick calls the "powerfully productive and powerfully socially metamorphic possibilities" that may emerge from shame.[66]

In "Freaks," Baldwin states that his experiences of racial and sexual diversity in Harlem meant for him "that all of the American categories of male and female, straight and not, black or white, were shattered, thank heaven, very early in my life. Not without anguish certainly; but once you have discerned the meaning of a label, it may seem to define you for others, but it does not have the power to define you to yourself."[67] Vividly evoking the foul miasma of racism and homophobia that clouded his life in the Village, Baldwin provides a compelling justification for his resistance to categorization, forcefully stated again in an interview toward the end of his life: "I was not born to be what someone said I was. I was not born to be defined by someone else, but by myself, and myself only."[68] Baldwin's resistance to sexual definition (different in kind, as we have seen, from his resistance to racial definition) is seemingly steadfast. Yet by self-identifying as a freak in "Freaks," in the earlier *No Name*, and elsewhere, Baldwin positions himself as close to those faggots, punks, and sissies with whom he refuses kinship in his response to Cleaver. Baldwin's perception of himself as a freak is not reducible to his sexuality, but by evoking the place of shame in his "painful individuation," as Sedgwick puts it, the perception brings him close to the homosexual identity that Baldwin refused. I turn now to Baldwin's early essay "The Male Prison," suggesting that there, unusually, the "painful individuation" of queer shame exfoliates into "uncontrollable relationality"—into a sense of connection to others, on the basis of shared queer shame and the social oppressions that enforce and reinforce that shame. Baldwin may have had good reasons for rejecting sexual labeling, but this essay indicates the positive effects that a sense of shared identity may unleash.

Connections

"The Male Prison," a review of André Gide's memoir of his wife, *Madeleine*, originally appeared in the *New Leader* in December 1954 under the title "Gide as Husband and Homosexual." Baldwin's retitling the essay for its appearance seven years later in *Nobody Knows My Name* indicates the resonance of its argument beyond the occasion of a response to Gide's book. In this essay, Baldwin sets out what is in many ways an astute and prescient reflection on American masculinity in the post–World War II period, arguing that culturally approved forms of gender confine men to a "prison" of emotional "isolation."[69]

Baldwin opens his essay by stating that Gide's memoir has impressed on him the necessity of a reevaluation of this author, whom he had formerly disliked. Baldwin notes that his "dislike of Gide—or, rather . . . the discomfort he caused me to feel"—is mainly due to Gide's not having "got over" his Protestantism and not having "come to terms with his nature," that is, his homosexuality. In other words, the things that Baldwin, as he puts it, must "confess" about his unease with Gide are emotionally charged, intractable aspects of his own life history.[70] Gide mirrors Baldwin, and it is this that causes the discomfort.

In a parenthetical, though lengthy, aside, Baldwin qualifies his unease about Gide's not having come to terms with his nature: "(For I believed at the time—rather oddly, considering the examples by which I was surrounded, to say nothing of the spectacle I myself presented—that people *did* 'get over' their earliest impressions and that 'coming to terms' with oneself simply demanded a slightly more protracted stiffening of the will)" (231).

The precise meaning of this statement is difficult to glean—it's unclear whether the "stiffening of the will" involved in "coming to terms" with one's "earliest impressions" means resisting them or simply accepting them as parts of oneself. It's also unclear whether "earliest impressions" refers to Protestantism or homosexuality, or both. With regard to homosexuality, however, Baldwin follows up this ambiguous passage with one that recommends not turning away from homosexual desire but keeping it private. Baldwin remarks that Gide's homosexuality "was his own affair which he ought to have kept hidden from us, or, if he needed to be so explicit, he ought to have managed to be a little more scientific . . . less illogical, less romantic" (231). This insistence on discretion, or at least the logical—presumably impersonal—presentation of homosexuality is, however, complicated by Baldwin's virtual confession of his own sexual freakery, his reference to "the spectacle that I myself presented." Here Baldwin seems to confess to the shaming theatricality of queer or proto-queer identity—despite his lifelong rejection of queerness *as* an identity. Protestantism could also be at issue here, as Baldwin's engagement with religion entailed the "spectacular" performer's role of the boy preacher. In fact, it is I think reasonable to suggest that in Baldwin's mind his period as a preacher and his homosexuality were to an important degree associated with each other. Religious feeling and homoeroticism are memorably brought together in *Go Tell It on the Mountain* and may have been even more explicitly so in the lost or destroyed early draft. And Baldwin himself related in his polemical essay *The Fire Next Time* (1963) that it was in part sexual confusion and guilt that brought on the "prolonged religious crisis" that resulted in his becoming a preacher at the age of fourteen.[71] But if Protestantism is at issue in the first two paragraphs of "The Male Prison," the possibility disappears from the essay after this as Baldwin's concerns shift more definitely to matters of gender and sexuality.

A moment of queer relationality, then, emerges from Baldwin's encounter with Gide, the formerly disliked other. While Baldwin rejected Gide's earlier work, he finds *Madeleine* compelling, indeed, in his words, "immensely humbling" (231). "To humble" of course means to reduce one's sense of self-worth, though the term has a more positive valence than its cognate (and close relative of shame) "humiliation." Gide's confession of what Baldwin calls his sexual "anguish" in *Madeleine* (compare his phrase for artistic confession, "vomit up the anguish") induces in Baldwin, on his own account, an affective response of self-abasement.

The autobiographical, first-person opening of the essay is followed by a discussion of the treatment of homosexuality and Gide's marriage in *Madeleine*, in which Baldwin adopts the standard impersonal voice of the essay or book review. Then, in the last two sentences, Baldwin modulates into a first-person collective voice: "We ought, for our own sakes, to be humbled by Gide's confession as he was humbled by his pain and make the generous effort to understand that his sorrow was not different from the sorrow of all men born. For, if we do not learn this humility, we may very well be strangled by a most petulant and unmasculine pride" (235). Baldwin here gives the gist of the essay: the necessity of escaping what he calls the prison of isolated masculine selfhood through a Forsterian project of connection with others.[72] In Baldwin's discussion of Gide, this connection is explicitly presented in heterosexual terms. Gide is acclaimed, because of his marriage to Madeleine, for "[keeping] open a kind of door of hope, of possibility, the possibility of entering into communion with another sex" (235). However, this affirmation of heterosexuality is premised on a critique of normative masculinity, that is, "the male prison." And underpinning this critique is Baldwin's identification with Gide: a connection in terms of shared homosexuality. Humbling or shaming in this essay becomes a positive mode of relationality, in spite of Baldwin's refusal of the very notion of queer identity. If Baldwin insists that Gide's homosexuality should have been kept private, or silent, the rhetorical moves of the essay work against this insistence, indicating a mode of bonding between one writer and another, one homosexual and another. In this respect the essay, published two years before *Giovanni's Room*, prefigures Baldwin's own career as a proto-visible gay writer.

The corollary of Baldwin's attempts to redeem sex by love is that, for Baldwin, homosexuality can be favorably represented only in its manifestation in the loving couple—or even though he refuses the concept of homosexual identity, in its manifestation in the gay *individual*, as demonstrated in my later discussion of *Another Country*. We could perhaps see Baldwin's valorization of the privatized intimacy of the loving couple played out in his relation to Gide—as a fraught but profound erotics of fellow feeling made possible through the relegation of subcultural manifestations of homosexuality, as he puts it here, to an "underworld" of the damned "where the possibility of human involvement has altogether ceased" (234). Yet Baldwin's moment of communion with Gide in this essay may also be read as a (pre)figuration of gay solidarity—a solidarity based on sexual orientation that operates across race, nation, and generation. Even as "The Male Prison" abjects the gay subculture, it gestures toward a shared categorical identity. As we've seen, Baldwin's repudiation of the idea of homosexual identity was in tension with the perceptions of others—not to mention his self-perception—that he exemplified a kind of queer personhood. For instance, "Martin Luther Queen" or the shameful persona of the "freak." But also: a black gay writer, the most *famous* black gay writer. Joyce and McBride note that "if Baldwin is undecided about his sexual identity, the one identity to which he seems firmly committed is his racial identity. . . . He understood that his efficacy as a race man was—in part at least—dependent on his limiting his public activism to racial politics."[73] But if Baldwin's unambiguous fictional explorations of homosexuality, along with a notable strain of camp performativity in his public persona, undermined his status as a racial representative in the eyes of many, they also opened up the possibility, however unwelcome or unintended for Baldwin, of "standing in" for a homosexual collectivity—as well as for African American homosexuals more specifically and, even more specifically, gay African American writers.[74] Writing in *James Baldwin Now* (1999), a foundational text of the current Baldwin revival, Marlon Ross notes the resonance of Baldwin's work for both white and black gay culture but warns that the "potential ghettoization" of Baldwin as black gay writer "contains assumptions against which his work struggles."[75] While I acknowledge the pitfalls of such ghettoization, I hope that my discussion has made clear the ways in which Baldwin's work may also speak to the positive effects of categorization, even if he himself continued to the end, on an overt level, to struggle against categorization. We can respect Baldwin's own account of himself while also respecting the uses made of him by various, overlapping audiences. Loren Glass suggests that literary celebrity "challenge[s] deeply held convictions about authorial inspiration and property in texts by appearing to cede creative agency and control to the mass audience and the literary marketplace."[76] Here I am suggesting that a particular "niche" version of this operation gives the celebrity image of Baldwin politically generative force. Despite his own disavowal of gay identity, by parlaying the shameful matter of homosexuality into literary fame, Baldwin was to become a crucial point of identification and aspiration for postliberation generations of gay and lesbian writers of all races, for gay and lesbian African Americans, for queers of all stripes.

2 Baldwin and the Celebrity Novel

IN HIS LARGELY FAVORABLE REVIEW of *Another Country* (1962), Lionel Trilling sounded a note of caution about Baldwin's fame, asking, "How, in the extravagant publicness in which Mr. Baldwin lives, is he to find the inwardness which we take to be the condition of truth in the writer?" The doyen of midcentury liberal literary criticism, Trilling assumes that the novel is the privileged venue for the exploration of the complexities of the private life and that, by extension, the successful novelist must eschew celebrity or "extravagant publicness" in favor of the cultivation of "inwardness," which we might gloss as a deep reflectiveness on his own interiority and that of others. For Trilling, the tension in Baldwin's career between publicness and inwardness results from his status as the only currently active "Negro" novelist "with a considerable body of work to his credit," who is also, both by default and willingly, "an increasingly public figure" who speaks for his "ethnic group."[1] But there was another element in Baldwin's notoriety, albeit one seldom addressed explicitly in media coverage: what I have called his proto-visible homosexuality. This chapter continues the investigation of the relations between Baldwin's celebrity embodiment of queerness and the formation of a recognizably contemporary form of politicized gay identity, homing in on *Another Country* and addressing in a less sustained fashion his other novel of the 1960s, *Tell Me How Long the Train's Been Gone* (1968). Using Trilling's question about publicness and inwardness as a starting point, I trace how Baldwin's novels, along with and as extensions of his queer celebrity persona, contributed to the making public of the ostensibly private matter of homosexuality that characterized the mediasphere of the 1960s—despite Baldwin's own official rejection of gay politics and his own career-long insistence that homosexuality should be a private, secret, or even unspeakable matter. Picking up on the previous chapter's discussion of the contradictory implications of Baldwin's account of homosexuality, I argue that Baldwin's novelistic affirmations of homosexual love involve intimations of social liberation that are in tension with his anticollectivist perspective. At the same time that they attempt to privatize homosexuality, his novels gesture, inadvertently and necessarily, toward its publicization and collectivization.

I turn my attention to Baldwin's novels in this chapter because, as exemplars of a mode in which the relations between public and private are held in particularly charged tension, they provide an apt focus for Baldwin's considerations of celebrity and of sexuality in the public sphere. In the previous chapter I noted that, in some ways, Baldwin's relegation of homosexuality to novelistic (rather than autobiographical or essayistic) representation is in keeping with the twentieth-century liberal culture to which, arguably, he subscribed throughout his career. If, for Baldwin, sexuality was a private affair, then it makes sense to explore it in the novel, the value of which derives from the depth with which it sounds the private life. But, as Trilling's question about publicness and inwardness indicates, Baldwin's celebrity status complicates this conception of the novel and the division of public and private on which it depends. Moreover, Baldwin himself, in his novels and elsewhere, displays an almost obsessive interest in the oxymoronic overlaps between public and private and between fame and sexuality.[2] While Trilling's question assumes the desirability of a strict division between publicness and inwardness, Baldwin's theorization and practice of the novel indicate their necessary interimplication.

I propose that Baldwin's two 1960s novels be thought of as "celebrity novels," a term I use not of course in the way that it is currently used—to refer to fictions, ghostwritten or otherwise, that are signed with the names of film stars, models, and other pop culture celebrities and that are launched onto the market as an extension of the brand of the celebrity in question. Rather, I use "celebrity novel" to signal the continuity between Baldwin's celebrity persona and his work. Taking my theoretical bearings from Joseph Roach and Leo Braudy, who emphasize the performative aspect of celebrity, and cued also by Baldwin's identification of art as confession, I regard *Another Country* and *Tell Me* as continuous with Baldwin's performance of his celebrity persona in the public sphere, in which the private matter of homosexuality is paradoxically bodied forth. In his remarkable book-length meditation on "It," the "certain quality, easy to perceive but hard to define, possessed by abnormally interesting people," Roach traces the continuities within celebrity charisma from the eighteenth century to the present.[3] In a much briefer but productively distilled reflection on celebrity, Braudy notes that "the relation between fame and celebrity or acting" means that the history of celebrity is a history of "the way the performer becomes the model for all human distinction."[4] Roach and Braudy refer mainly to film and stage stars and the ways in which their performances involve for the spectator an oscillation between celebrity image and the role they perform, but I argue here that this approach is germane for celebrity novelists as well, especially perhaps one like Baldwin, who had such a deep investment in performance. Avowedly a performer himself, Baldwin populated several of his novels with performer protagonists—celebrities or proto-celebrities, who also, not coincidentally, are homosexual or bisexual. Eric and Leo Proudhammer, the two main gay or bisexual characters in *Another Country* and *Tell Me How Long the Train's Been Gone*, respectively, may both be regarded as surrogates of Baldwin—Leo obviously so, Eric more obliquely, a distinction that has more than a little to do with their racial difference. Eric's whiteness and Leo's blackness necessitate reflection on the difference race makes to celebrity performance and homosexual embodiment, as well as the ways in which *Another Country* and *Tell Me* register the shifting racial politics of the 1960s. But while racial considerations indisputably complicate Baldwin's account of homosexuality, in what follows I move away from the intersectional emphasis of recent discussions of Baldwin's approach to identity to stress the ways in which homosexuality in *general*, as a transracial category, is felt by him to be intractable. While I am sympathetic to Marlon Ross's proposal that "it could easily be argued that *Another Country* is exactly a prolegomenon for a revolution that is (homo)sexual and racial simultaneously," I bring to the fore here the intimations of the homosexual, rather than the racial, elements of this revolution that the novel, uneasily, develops.[5] That homosexuality can to an important extent be understood in Baldwin's work, at least until the late 1960s, as a transracial category suggests another connection with celebrity, which, as Braudy writes, "emerge[s] from and reflect[s] peculiarly American contemporary—and historical—preoccupations with self-definition generally, cutting across gender, ethnic and racial difference."[6]

Because Baldwin's two 1960s novels configure relations between celebrity, homosexuality, and race quite differently, I counterintuitively devote greater attention to *Another Country* than *Tell Me*, a novel *about* celebrity. The most obviously autobiographical of Baldwin's works, *Tell Me* was, according to him, a novel about the problems of "surviving success" in America.[7] For mid- and late twentieth-century writers of literary fiction, the supposedly debasing associations of celebrity are conventionally a source of angst, giving birth to a subgenre of tortured fictionalized meditations on mass-mediatized fame, exemplified, for instance, by Philip Roth's cycle of Zuckerman novels; along with Norman Mailer's nonfiction novel *The Armies of the Night* (1968), *Tell Me* is one of the earliest examples of this subgenre.[8] Leo, the novelist's narrator-protagonist, is a stage actor who defines himself as bisexual (we can note in passing the recourse to an identity category).[9] The change of profession aside, many of the details of his life correspond to those of Baldwin's, including an upbringing in Harlem, an emotionally difficult time as a young man in Greenwich Village, and eventually, world fame as an artist and mediagenic voice of racial protest. Like *No Name in the Street*, the novel is marked by Baldwin's fraught relations to Black Power. The influence exerted on Baldwin by the macho and homophobic discourse of Black Power no doubt helps explain Leo's scornful references to white "faggots."[10] Yet, as Emmanuel Nelson and Douglas Field both point out, the novel subtly subverts Black Power ideology through its depiction of Black Christopher, a young militant who is Leo's lover.[11] Christopher is a sexy embodiment of racial liberation, but he does not figure sexual radicalism. Contrasting with his usual frankness from *Another Country* on, Baldwin draws a veil over the sexual aspect of the men's relationship, and there is no suggestion that Christopher or Leo has any engagement with the gay subculture. Indeed, subcultural expressions are very much marginalized in the narrative, meaning that *Tell Me* lacks the anxious, interrogative relations with homosexual collectivity that give *Giovanni's Room* and *Another Country* much of their troubling interest. The nomination "gay" bubbles up once in the narrative, indicating the increased public profile of the subculture, only to be dismissed by Leo as "incomprehensible vernacular."[12] Apart from those few walk-on white "faggots" and a typically disgusted account of anonymous sex in a cinema, representation of homosexuality is confined to the couple—to the discreetly rendered pairing of Leo and Christopher and the contrastingly fulsome description of the teenage Leo's erotic intimacy with his older brother (of all characters). The idea of homosexuality as a collective identity, in other words, is backgrounded in a text that is heavily inflected by Afrocentric politics.[13]

In *Another Country*, by contrast, homosexuality is central and problematic. The intractability of homosexuality for Baldwin is registered, I suggest, in a ratcheting up of the signature tendency toward inscrutability that distinguishes his prose style. Many celebrate Baldwin's style—prevalently understood as a melding of the syntactical complexity of Henry James and the ringingly authoritative tone of the

King James Bible. Yet Baldwin has also often been seen, particularly from *Another Country* on, as a frequently careless and undisciplined stylist, or—what amounts to much the same thing—as *over*writing.[14] While the recent Baldwin revival has hastened to defend him from these long-standing criticisms, here I am interested, up to a point, in taking them seriously and in unpacking the implications of Baldwin's "bad" style.[15] I suggest that Baldwin's characteristic complexity and afflatus go into overdrive when he turns his attention to the closely entangled categories of homosexuality and celebrity. Sexuality and charismatic artistry are deeply felt but often confusing matters for Baldwin, and attempts to come to terms with them in his novels tend to generate prose that is also deeply felt and confusing—but also richly interesting for what it indicates about the tangled relations between literary celebrity, novelistic practice, and homosexuality in the midcentury period. But first, to contextualize Baldwin's novelistic performance of celebrity, I turn to a consideration of his own stated relations to that category.

Charismatic Connections

At first glance, Baldwin's perspective on celebrity is consistent with that of the midcentury liberal culture represented by Trilling and with the early twentieth-century modernism that culture championed and in many ways continued. For the liberal/modernist perspective, celebrity is irredeemably associated with the debasing and inauthentic operations of commercialized popular culture, even though many modernist icons, such as James Joyce and T. S. Eliot, were themselves celebrities. For instance, in an early scene in *Tell Me*, the narrator-protagonist Leo Proudhammer likens the names of the stars on posters to "brand names like Campbell's Baked Beans or Kellogg's Corn Flakes. We went to see James Cagney because we had grown accustomed to that taste, we knew that we would like it."[16] This notion of standardized celebrity is itself standard in midcentury culture criticism, which inscribed the celebrity as a mass-produced, disposable commodity aimed at an easily manipulated mass audience. Extending Walter Benjamin's 1936 claim that "the cult of the movie star . . . preserves not the unique aura of the person but the 'spell of the personality,' the phony spell of a commodity," Theodor Adorno and Max Horkheimer in *Dialectic of Enlightenment* (1944) identified the "pseudo-individuality" of the culture industry star as "mass-produced like Yale locks, whose only difference can be measured in fractions of millimeters."[17] In his 1957 study *The Stars*, Edgar Morin likens the movie star to "chewing gum, refrigerators, soap, razor blades, and so on."[18] And while they're not straightforwardly critical, Andy Warhol's screen-printed multiples of the 1960s, in which repeated images of Marilyn and Jackie echo the seriality of the commodity form referenced in his prints of serried soup cans and Coke bottles, are a striking imagistic conveyance of this same idea. If midcentury critiques concentrate on pop culture celebrity, the putatively more elevated variety of literary fame was equally susceptible to such characterizations, with John Cheever, for instance, stating of his late-career celebrity, "I'm a brand name, like corn flakes or shredded wheat," and Philip Roth stating, "To become a celebrity is to become a brand name. There is Ivory Soap, Rice Krispies, and Philip Roth."[19] If Baldwin did not quite speak of his own mass-mediatized fame in such debasing terms, his comments on it often echoed those of other early and mid-twentieth-century celebrity authors of self-styled serious literature, presenting celebrity status as a form of self-estrangement in which media image displaced literary achievement. "When you become a celebrity," Baldwin stated in an interview in 1984, "[your] voice is magnified by multitudes and you begin to drown in this endless duplication of what looks like yourself" so that "the legend becomes far more important than the work."[20] Similarly, in *Tell Me*, Leo, during a period of illness that disrupts his celebrity career, leaving him free to "be [him]self," ruminates, "But who was this self? Had he left for ever the house of my endeavor and my fame? Or was he merely having a hard time breathing beneath the rags and rubble of the closets I had not opened in so long?"[21]

But Baldwin also qualified the conventional midcentury highbrow culture view of celebrity as empty, false, and commodified. The most striking of the instances in his nonfictional writing in which Baldwin moves away from the highbrow critique of stardom is the passage describing his boyhood identification with Bette Davis in his book-length essay on film and race, *The Devil Finds Work* (1976). Though Baldwin was often trenchantly critical of the ideological work of Hollywood, this position is complicated, in this passage above all, by his sense of how the film spectator's experiences of pleasure and recognition may be personally generative. Baldwin leads into his revelatory first sight of Davis on-screen in 20,000 *Years in Sing Sing* (1932) with an account of his father's attacks on his "ugliness." But the "rich" white movie star, the young Baldwin is astounded to see, is also "ugly," sharing his own ugly "pop-eyes"; moreover, "when she moved, she moved just like a nigger."[22] The sight of Davis, Baldwin writes, is a discovery "that my infirmity might not be my doom: my infirmity, or infirmities, might be forged into weapons"; for, he continues, "I was not only considered by my father to be ugly. I was considered by everyone who met me to be 'strange.' "[23] Baldwin recurs here to his "freak" persona, in which ugliness and "strangeness," which we can confidently if only partially gloss as gender nonconformity, are brought together.

This self-conception also turns up in the 1984 interview quoted earlier. In answer to the question, "Is the celebrity James Baldwin anyone that you know?," Baldwin answers, "Not really. . . . The celebrity is not exactly Jimmy, though he comes out of Jimmy and Jimmy nourishes that too. I can see now, with hindsight, that I would've had to become a celebrity in order to survive. A boy like me, with all his handicaps, real and fancied, could not have survived in obscurity."[24] As we have seen, Baldwin identified the "handicaps" of his sissiness or queerness—his general "strangeness"—as foundational to his art and fame. In both the account of the identification with Davis and in the reflection on his own fame from the 1984 interview, celebrity seems to function as a means of self-protection and self-affirmation, whereby putatively shameful aspects of Baldwin's "freakishness" are parlayed into charismatic qualities, and indeed into "weapons."

If Baldwin sometimes stridently insisted on his capacity for self-creation outside categories, elsewhere his account of identity formation points to their importance. What Edgar Morin in his pioneering study of stars and their audiences would describe as Baldwin's "projection-identification" with Davis is a particularly charged moment in this respect, in that it is an identification across the divides of race and gender that simultaneously points up the very real effects of those categories. Davis provides a model for self-imagination and self-construction that defies orthodox gendered and racial classifications, but it is the very divide between those classifications (male/female, black/white) that gives the projection-identification its enabling power. The moment is shot through with ambivalence and a sense of danger: "I sensed something menacing and unhealthy (for me, certainly) in the face on the screen," he writes; but, he concludes, "I was held, just the same, by the tense intelligence of the forehead, the disaster of the lips."[25] Registering the risk involved in this cross-racial and cross-gendered identification, Baldwin is nonetheless held by the possibilities inherent within it. The gay valence of this celebrity identification is fairly obvious, if unelaborated by Baldwin. Although Baldwin resists camp both as a subcultural expression and as a stylistic resource, in positing his identification with Davis as the primal source of what will become his flamboyant celebrity, he indicates his own closeness to camp.[26]

The kind of celebrity identity that Baldwin values is produced through the realization of artistic ambition, and there is for him always something freakish or strange about true artistry. It is true that Baldwin does not tend to use the term "celebrity," and we cannot easily set aside his many criticisms of the popular culture with which celebrity is associated. But his work is also notable for its fascination with the magnetic, embodied presence of the famous artist—the charisma that is arguably an important aspect of celebrity.[27] Baldwin singles out various charismatic artists, particularly certain jazz musicians, blues singers, actors, and novelists from the massed ranks of the midcentury celebrityscape, valuing their fame as socially meaningful—an evaluation that, as we have already seen in "The Black Boy Looks at the White Boy," he also extends to his own fame. To recap, in that essay Baldwin inscribes his ambition as a revenge against the white-supremacist (and, less obviously, homophobic) status quo. Ambition, realized in fame, is a form of artistic will-to-power that supersedes the social power that would keep him in place: "My revenge [against power], I decided very early, would be to achieve a power which outlasts kingdoms."[28] Baldwin here echoes the venerable trope of the capacity of literary art to outlast more worldly forms of fame (as in Shakespeare's Sonnet 55), but, given that the context emphasizes his struggle to "wrest from the world fame and money and love," I think the hyperbole of his statement works more as an articulation of his desire to realize ambition in the lived present than it does to convey investment in artistic immortality.[29]

For Baldwin, the charismatic artistry of actors and musicians has an effect that coincides with that of the successful novel. Both awaken in the atomized members of an audience or readership recognition of their common humanity, or "connection," a valorized term that Baldwin seems to have taken, somewhat indirectly, from E. M. Forster.[30] In a symposium at Hofstra College in 1961, Baldwin stated, "When I am writing a novel, I am writing about me and all of you, and the great difficulty is to discover what connects us. Something does connect us, and what it is is hidden. It is not science or prosperity; it is not to be found in any church so far as I know."[31] In what is in some ways a paradigmatic liberal humanist statement, Baldwin posits a shared experience that transcends and cannot be captured by or reduced to science, economics, or religion. This shared experience, conveyed through the novel, connects "us" to one another and to Baldwin himself. While this statement of Baldwin's about the mission of the novel certainly chimes with liberal tenets, I note here that rather than name this shared experience—say, as the human condition—Baldwin emphasizes the difficulty of accessing it, its hiddenness, its obscurity. I return to this emphasis on the obscurity of the private life presently, a return that will also, in part, be a return to the previous chapter's governing concern of shame. For now, I want to stay with the idea of connection and "connect" it to Baldwin's views of celebrity and charisma.

My suggestion that Baldwin's novels might be seen as an extension of his own charismatic celebrity performance is anticipated by Baldwin himself in some comments from 1962 about why *Another Country* became a best seller (thus furthering his celebrity). Written for an issue of the *New York Times Book Review* in response to a question put to authors of that year's best-selling books about "what they believe there is about their book or the climate of the time that has made it so popular," Baldwin stated that "people bought *Another Country* in considerably larger numbers than I imagined they would," and that he supposed the reason had to do with the fact "that many more people than are willing to admit it lead lives not at all unlike the lives of the people in my book." He continues, "I don't mean to compare myself to a couple of artists I unreservedly admire—Miles Davis and Ray Charles—but I would like to think that some of the people who liked my book responded to it in a way they respond when Miles and Ray are blowing."[32] Baldwin states, "I really do not, at the very bottom of my own mind, compare myself to other writers," but "I really helplessly model myself on jazz musicians and try to write the way they sound." *Another Country*, he intimates, approximates the "universal blues" of Miles and Ray, which imparts "not self-pity . . . but compassion" and which "tell[s] us something about what it is to be alive."[33] Although Baldwin concludes his reflections in this brief piece by referencing his literary hero Henry James, stating that when he writes, "I am aiming at what [James] called 'perception at the pitch of passion,'" his invocations of Charles and Davis may be understood, as David Leeming notes, as implicitly countering the many negative reviews of *Another Country*, which often attacked Baldwin's allegedly undisciplined composition and clumsy style.[34] By denying a relation to "other writers" and relating his novelistic practice to a tradition of African American musical expression, Baldwin marks his work as racially specific—an identification that he had previously actively resisted and that anticipates his gravitation toward Afrocentric cultural politics in the later 1960s and early 1970s. At the same time, the notion of a "universal blues" retains his conviction that successful artistry enables generalized human connection. Aligning his work with the blues, Baldwin reimagines the universal resonance of the novel form in terms of the celebrity performer's connection with his audience, a process that in turn connects audience members to one another. "Publicness" and "inwardness," to revert to Trilling's terms, as well as collectivity and individuality, are paradoxically entangled in this relation of artist and audience: the public elaboration of the nominal interiority of the blues makes possible a sense of shared humanity.

With regard to *Another Country* specifically, Baldwin stresses the novel's exposure of previously hidden or unacknowledged forms of life—the fact "that many more people than are willing to admit it lead lives not at all unlike the lives of the people in my book." Alluding to the sexual frankness of the book, with its multiple and multiply configured heterosexual, homosexual, and interracial affairs, Baldwin indicates that *Another Country* has fulfilled his idea of the responsibility of the novelist, defined by him in a 1961 interview as the "responsibility . . . to try to tell the truth as I see it—not so much about my private life as about *their* private lives," that is, the private lives of other Americans.[35] As I've intimated, however, Baldwin's own private life is not so readily dismissed from consideration of *Another Country*, in which sexuality, particularly homosexuality, is brought into alignment with charismatic talent and fame. Baldwin's explanation of the best-selling status of his celebrity novel with its scandalous treatment of race and sexuality lines up with Roach's suggestion of the ways in which "the driving motive of marginalized performers to attain celebrity mirrors that of the public to identify with and desire the excluded, the secret sharers of their fears and dreams," and also recalls Rose's suggestion that celebrity enables the "veiled putting into circulation certain things which do not easily admit to public acknowledgment"—with the important distinction that Baldwin prides himself as precisely *not* veiling his incendiary material.[36] However, by inscribing Baldwin's own sexuality only obliquely, the text does remain in a sense "veiled."

Another Country both thematizes and enacts the artistic ambition that was so important to Baldwin. The ambitions of several of the central characters to gain recognition through writing or performing variously grow out of, complement, or further complicate the turbulent emotional relations that are the more commonly critically examined aspects of the novel. *Another Country* is also arguably Baldwin's most ambitious novel, a sprawling work over which, in his own account, he expended much agonized labor over many years and which, as he related in a letter of 1968, he intended as a visionary critique of "the spiritual state of our country"[37]—an intention also hinted at in the novel's titular suggestion of a reimagined American nationhood. But if Baldwin seeks through *Another Country* to make a significant intervention in the public discussion of American identity, he does so of course by way of an exploration of private lives. In his *New York Times* piece, Baldwin implies he has been successful in achieving the goal that eludes the would-be novelist Vivaldo in *Another Country*: "With the same agony, or greater, with which he attempted to seduce a woman, he was trying to seduce his [characters]: he begged them to surrender up to him their privacy. . . . They were waiting for him to find the key, press the nerve, tell the truth."[38] If the truth of the private life is aligned here with heterosexual seduction, elsewhere in *Another Country* that truth is largely identified with male homosexuality, the libidinal and affective energies of which are distributed across a range of the male characters but centralized in the actor Eric. Seeking to make a definitive statement about "the spiritual state of our country," Baldwin does so by focusing on homosexuality, the least admissible kind of American private life.

Homosexuality at the Center

According to Baldwin himself, it is the American attitude toward homosexuality that renders it an apposite focus for his inquiry into the country's spiritual state. In Fern Eckman's 1966 biographical portrait of him, Baldwin states, "One of the reasons that homosexuality . . . occupies so large a place in *Another Country* is that it's an *American* phenomenon in that book—and in my experience." Baldwin refers to a distinctively American pathologization of homosexuality, contrasted here with the broad-mindedness of Italy, "where men kiss each other and boys go to bed with one another" and "no one is marked for life": "they grow up . . . and they have children. . . . No one ends up going to a psychiatrist or turning into a junkie because he's afraid of being *touched*."[39] *Another Country* is certainly critical of the pathologization of homosexuality, but in the figure of Eric it presents a character who, it seems, has successfully resisted pathologization. As many critics have noted, Eric is the least psychically troubled of the main characters and the only one who generates Baldwin's valorized quality of interpersonal connection—his sexual relations with both Vivaldo and Cass are revelatory or at least enabling for them, despite Vivaldo's nominal heterosexuality and the technical heterosexuality of Eric's involvement with Cass.[40] Reversing the marginalization of the homosexual that characterized the mid-twentieth-century novel in particular and American culture in general, Baldwin places him at the center and grants him unrivaled capacities of self-knowledge and understanding of others. (Of course, *Giovanni's Room* also made homosexuality narratively central, but the ambition and dimensions of *Another Country* amp up the audacity of the move.)

In his review, Trilling noted that Eric is the only character who seems to be "saved" and that his salvation seems to be linked to his sexuality:

> His homosexual tendencies, manifested in boyhood, had made life in a Southern town impossible; in the freer atmosphere of New York and Paris, he has been able to "accept" his homosexuality. He alone exists with a degree of dignity and direction—he is in possession of a *self*, as none of his friends is. How he achieved this fortunate condition is not made clear; presumably it has a connection both with his homosexuality itself and the moral straightforwardness and balance with which he confronted it.[41]

I don't want to suggest that Eric is simply redeemed and redemptive. The novel hardly ends optimistically for any of the American characters with whom he interacts, and the epilogue in which Eric's French lover, Yves, comes to rejoin him in New York, which seems to Yves to be "the city which the people from heaven had made their home" (416), if it is not straightforwardly ironic, is surely ambiguous, given the several hundred pages of grimly troubled emotional and sexual relations that have come before. Nevertheless, in his singular self-assuredness, Eric provides a salutary contrast with the heterosexual characters. Indeed, as Daylanne English has argued, it is heterosexuality rather than homosexuality that seems to constitute a pathological condition in the novel. Heterosexual relationships in the novel are unrelentingly unhappy, while the main homosexual relationship, between Eric and Yves, ends on a note of (admittedly uncertain) hope.[42]

This is not to say, of course, that Baldwin ignores or downplays the oppression of homosexuality. Far from "not ma[king] it clear" how Eric achieves his "fortunate condition," as Trilling claims, Baldwin specifies that Eric's comparative well adjustedness is the hard-won and precarious result of a history of struggle with the "terrors" and "fantasies" of his sexuality, in a long passage that is placed midway through the novel, thus literalizing the thematic centrality of homosexuality (no other character is presented with such an extensive backstory).

The passage is prompted by Eric's imminent return to New York from France where he has been living with Yves. The thought of his return "cause[s] many painful and buried things to stir in him . . . throwing his terrors into relief" (191). A fifteen-page aria of tortured and tortuous reminiscence and self-examination follows. In these pages, the terrors and fantasies of homoerotic desire are insistently associated with secrecy and unspeakability, but this association is contradicted by an equally emphatic identification of homosexuality as public, known, and performative. The passage is perhaps Baldwin's most intensive elaboration of the homosexual experience and its relations to the public/private divide, and close attention to it can help us further pick apart the complicated relations between homosexuality, artistry, and celebrity selfhood in Baldwin.

I say that the passage is both tortured and tortuous because although Baldwin is here concerned to specify Eric's sexual history, the specification is complex to the point of opacity. Trilling is wrong about Baldwin's efforts to elaborate the formation of Eric's "fortunate condition," but his assertion that Baldwin is not "clear" here coincidentally suggests the inchoate prose of the elaboration, which, as suggested earlier, emerges out of Baldwin's own conception of homosexuality as intractable. In an astute analysis of *Giovanni's Room*, Reed Woodhouse describes that novel as being "confused as it [is] complex," adding that "something about [Baldwin's] subject, something probably but not only about homosexuality seems to have so disequilibrized him that the novel is not a revelation but a dazzling concealment, a triumph, and a failure, of rhetoric."[43] These comments could also be applied to the central passage in *Another Country*. When he broaches homosexual sex and love, Baldwin often modulates his characteristically complex prose style into a new register of intricacy; this is one of the most notable yet oddly critically neglected aspects of his novels.[44] But as Woodhouse notes of *Giovanni's Room*, it is not only homosexuality that prompts these moments of rhetorical overdrive, in which Baldwin's syntax becomes both highly burnished and mysteriously dense. Something similar tends to happen in Baldwin's descriptions of heterosexual sex and in his representations of areas of experience that for Baldwin are adjacent to or that overlap with sexuality—in particular, in *Another Country* and *Tell Me* at least, the experience of charismatic performative artistry. Suggestively elaborating the interinvolvement of Baldwin's sexuality, his writing, and his performative persona, Woodhouse writes, "I do not think that it was possible for him . . . to make a surgically precise division between his homosexual self and his writing self. I do not think that this kind of 'control' was even interesting to him: does the preacher have 'control' over his sermons?"[45] With regard to the central passage from *Another Country*, it often becomes difficult in this passage (as in the novel as a whole and in most of Baldwin's novels generally) to distinguish the apparently authoritative voice of the narrator—what Woodhouse calls a "moral voice of great solemnity"[46]—from the free indirect discourse that we suppose approximates a character's (in this case, Eric's) thoughts.

The dense central passage toggles between figurations of obscurity and clarity, ineffability and nomination. Eric's terrors, we are told,

> were buried beneath the impossible language of the time, lived underground where nearly all of the time's true feelings spitefully and incessantly fermented. Precisely, therefore, to the extent that they were inexpressible, were these terrors mighty; precisely because they lived in the dark were their shapes obscene. And because the taste for obscenity is universal and the appetite for reality rare and hard to cultivate, he had nearly buried them in the basement of his private life. Or, more precisely, his fantasies. (191–92)

The passage's repeated invocation of precision ("Precisely, therefore"; "Or, more precisely") with its promise of a continually narrowing and clarifying focus, is at odds with the insistent imagery of darkness and inexpressibility and, indeed, the initial vagueness of the referent or referents. What are these terrors of Eric's that are so "mighty" and "obscene"? That's a rhetorical question, of course, as there is nothing surprising about the answer: the single category of homosexuality collects together these pluralized terrors.[47] However, the passage pointedly never gives homosexuality a name. It might be understood as one long resistance to "the impossible language of the time"; in a frequently quoted phrase, it concludes with Eric's refusal of the "hideously mechanical jargon of the age" (206).

But issues of naming, and the absent name *homosexuality* itself, structure the passage. Eric's terrors are "mighty" because they are "inexpressible," suggesting a damming up of repressed psychic energy—they live "underground where nearly all the time's true feelings" do; they are "buried beneath the impossible language of the time." If this imagery suggests the incapacity of available vocabulary to describe Eric's "true feelings," the relegation of these feelings to a burial place beneath "impossible language" also suggests the intimate relation of feeling and language—a "subterranean" theme of Baldwin's effort to imagine a homosexuality beyond labels.

The vagueness of the homosexual referent is dissipated as the passage modulates into two successive flashbacks recounting formative moments of homoerotic affect. In the first of these flashbacks, Eric, as a preadolescent "little boy," experiences bodily if not explicitly sexual intimacy with Henry, his parents' African

American handyman. In the furnace room of his house, Eric sits for many hours enfolded in Henry's arms, feeling for the first time "the chest and belly of a man" (193)—a scene that literalizes the metaphor from the beginning of the passage locating Eric's desire in "the basement of his private life," a metaphor that is itself an extension of the mentions of the "many painful and buried things," the terrors "buried beneath . . . impossible language." The secrecy of Eric's relation with Henry is thrown into doubt, however, by Eric's parents' possible knowledge of it, which, Eric speculates, is the basis for their eventual dismissal of the handyman. The separation from Henry catalyzes Eric's conviction that "everything he did was wrong in the eyes of his parents, and in the eyes of the world, and that, therefore, everything must be lived in secret" (193). The possibility of defensive recourse to a "secret life" is immediately undermined, however, as the narrator goes on in the next sentence to posit homosexuality as an open secret that is a "secret from the person who lives it and not at all a secret for the people he encounters," who "see his secrecy before they see anything else" and who "drag [it] out of him; sometimes with the intention of using [it] against him, sometimes with more benevolent intent" (193). But "whatever the intent," the "moment" (193) of exposure is "awful" and the "accumulating revelation is an unspeakable anguish" (194): again, "revelation" of the secret is aligned with unspeakability. In a psychoanalytically and deconstructively inflected reading of *Another Country*, Kevin Ohi argues that such treatments of revelation in the novel point to its impossibility—to the opacity at the heart of any revelation. For Ohi, the novel as a whole and this passage specifically stymie the reader's and the critic's desire for revealed "truth" (of homosexuality or any other secret). Largely setting aside the historical contexts of the novel, Ohi misses the ways in which Baldwin's figurations of obscurity and exposure in the passage negotiate with and draw on midcentury discourse on homosexuality rather than undo it.[48] By contrast, I read the passage as a textual wrestling with nomination and categorization. On the one hand, *Another Country* seeks to resist names and categories; on the other, it must acknowledge them. Like Baldwin himself, with his refusal of labels, the passage is caught up in and generated by the public system of sexual categorization.[49]

The notion of the inescapable publicity of the private life hinted at in the first flashback is amplified in the second one, which details the teenage Eric's first experience of homosexual lovemaking with a black boy named LeRoy with whom he is infatuated, after the two take a walk through their small Alabama town. Eric's experience of the affect circulating between him and Leroy is of "something unspoken . . . something unspeakable, undone, and hideously desired" (197). Though "this knowledge clamored in him . . . and everything in him was aching and yearning for the act, he could not, to save his soul, have named it" (198). However, in a further qualification, though "it had no name, no name for him anyway, . . . for other people, so he had heard, it had dreadful names" (198). Again, the invocation of unspeakability and unknowability is in tension with the system of naming so that even though Eric, hyperbolically, could not "to save his soul" have named his feeling, he has nevertheless "heard" that for others "it had dreadful names." The passage gestures here toward Baldwin's conviction of the specificity of desire (you never know who you're going to fall in love with), a specificity that resists social categories: "It had only a shape and the shape was LeRoy" (198). Yet even as it tries to reject and transcend the system of naming (in part through not naming names), the passage is centripetally pulled back into that system.

Adjectivally insisting again on the unspeakably secret nature of homoerotic desire, at the level of narrative event the passage now presents homosexuality as a quasi-theatrical spectacle. Eric is already under the suspicious surveillance of the townsfolk, both black and white, for being friendly toward LeRoy, and when he comes to collect LeRoy from his house on the day being described, "there was a snicker from LeRoy's porch, quickly muffled; a screen door slammed; every eye on the street was on them" (197). Later a car bearing six young white people known to Eric drives past them: "A great laugh came from the car, and the driver beat out a mocking version of the wedding march on his horn" (198).

Even as this central passage elaborates the private or secret nature of homosexuality, then, its two scenes of formative homoerotic experience suggest that to be homosexual is always to be seen and to be talked about. The subterranean liaison with Henry is apparently known about and discussed by Eric's parents; the "unspeakable" desire between Eric and LeRoy is knowingly seen by the townspeople. Homosexuality, the scene with LeRoy in particular indicates, is a kind of public performance, whether that performance is undertaken willingly or consciously or not. Eric's (and Baldwin's) resistance to the presumption of the dominant culture to name his desire is compromised by the cultural force of sexual categories. Even though the passage critiques the "hideously mechanical jargon of the age," it also indicates the inescapability and even, albeit glancingly, the sexually and emotionally positive potential of sexual categories. "I guess you know, now," LeRoy says, after "pull[ing] Eric against him, under the shadow of the leaves," "what they saying about us in this town." Eric "had *not* known what they were saying, or he had been unable to allow himself to know; but he knew now." "Well, if we've got the name, we might as well have the game," says Eric to LeRoy as a prelude to their lovemaking (199).

The implication, here and elsewhere in Baldwin's writing, that homosexuality is a mode of performance that always entails being seen and being talked about by an audience alerts us to the parallels between the homosexual and the celebrity outlined in the Introduction, and it is not coincidental, I suggest, that Eric's "dim notion of trying to become a movie star" is introduced into the scene with LeRoy in which he accepts his homosexual desire (197). Similarly, in *Tell Me*, a scene of incipient homoerotic affect involves the preadolescent Leo telling the adult man onto whom he has attached that he wants to be a "movie actor," something "he had never said . . . before."[50] The desire to act is in both novels nameable, in contrast with homosexual desire (*Tell Me*, as we've seen, refuses not only the "jargon" of medico-legal discourse but what it calls the "incomprehensible vernacular" of the self-nomination of "gay"). But my point here is that homosexuality and acting are in important ways fungible in these two novels, and this is, I think, indicated in *Another Country* by a late passage describing Eric's performance in a French film that the narrator and the other characters agree presages his future stardom. Seeking to convey Eric's charismatic artistry, the passage resorts to the rhetoric of ineffability that characterized the earlier treatment of homosexuality.

Ostensibly presented from Vivaldo's point of view, this moment in the text, like the central passage, adopts a forceful version of what Woodhouse calls Baldwin's "moral voice of great solemnity." The passage conflates Eric's talent with his physical presence, specifically his face, describing it as "a quality to which great numbers of people would respond without knowing to what it was they were responding. . . . It was a face which suggested, resonantly, in the depths, the truth about our natures" (318). Eric's face is "the face of a man," yet this masculinity is "defined, and made powerful, by something which was not masculine," which is "not feminine either, and something in Vivaldo resisted the word *androgynous*" (318). But even as this passage moves the description of Eric's talent toward the revelation of an ungendered, universal, and ineffable "truth about our natures," its initial association of his transfixing presence with gender confusion echoes the experiments with drag that are mentioned in the passage describing his sexual history, in which, as a boy, he appears "before his mirror by night, dressed up in his mother's old clothes or in whatever colorful scraps he had been able to collect, posturing, and, in a whisper, declaiming" (193). Here then, albeit briefly, is a third scene of formative homosexual identity, in which Eric's performative inclinations are rendered in terms of gendered and sexual ambiguity. If the later passage about Eric's film performance attempts to dissociate Eric's talent and charisma from this ambiguity, it distantly informs it, conflating the masculine, the "not masculine," and the unknowable.

The description of Eric's performance also recalls an earlier, extraordinary passage describing Ida's first singing performance in a nightclub and told this time ostensibly from Eric's point of view:

> She was not a singer yet. And if she were to be judged solely on the basis of her voice, low, rough-textured, of no very great range, she never would be. Yet, she had something which made Eric look up and caused the room to fall silent. . . . What she lacked in vocal power and, at the moment, in skill, she compensated for by a quality so mysteriously and implacably egocentric that no one has ever been able to name it. This quality involves a sense of the self so profound and so powerful that it does not so much leap barriers as reduce them to atoms—while still leaving them standing mightily, where they were; and this awful sense is private, unknowable, not to be articulated, having literally, to do with something else; it transforms and lays waste and gives life, and kills. (245)

As in the descriptions of Eric's performance and his sexuality, this description of Ida's talent is replete with invocations of ineffability. Ida's talent is "something," a "quality . . . that no one has ever been able to name," "private, unknowable, not to be articulated, having literally, to do with something else." But if the unknowable aspect of the central passage describing Eric's sexuality is in fact easily known, a precise description of what Ida's talent involves remains elusive. What *is* certain is that it involves an amplified sense of self: "a quality so mysteriously and implacably egocentric that no one has ever been able to name it." This quality, I submit, is "star quality," or "the X factor," or "It"—the charismatic "something" or "something else" that holds an audience. (Driving the point home, Baldwin has Eric tell Vivaldo after the performance, "Your girlfriend's got something" [246].) Ida's "something" echoes Joseph Roach's appropriation of Alexander Pope's couplet, "*Something*, whose Truth convinc'd at Sight we find, / That gives us back the Image of our Mind," to describe both the magnetic, unspecifiable quality of celebrity presence and the way it speaks to audience need.[51]

Egocentric though it is, Ida's embodiment of star quality or "It" is something that transcends the boundary of the self, that "transforms and lays waste and gives life, and kills," manifesting the awesome, simultaneously creative and destructive power of art. Baldwin here gestures to the significance of Ida's deeply personal and "private" performance for the collective body of the audience, recalling his description of the "universal blues" of Miles Davis and Ray Charles in his comments about the best-selling success of *Another Country*. The "sense of the self" involved in Ida's talent is "so profound and so powerful that it does not so much leap barriers as reduce them to atoms." Yet it "still leav[es] them standing mightily, where they were." Like the novel form according to Baldwin, Ida's charismatic performance paradoxically instates a sense of connection and imposes on her spectators a sense of the reality of their individuality—"the truth of their private lives."

Baldwin's descriptions of the charisma of Ida and of Eric chime with Roach's discussion of the performer with It as a "precarious center, at once self-expression and self-erasure," who stirs in the audience "inchoate urges, desires and identifications" that do not claim "anything so vulgar as a name."[52] But if the experience of charismatic artistry, for Baldwin and for others, resists nomination—or is collected together under the bare, mysterious nomination of "something" or "It"—I suggest that Eric's celebrity charisma, and Baldwin's as well, in fact speaks to "inchoate urges, desires and identifications" that, if they are not quite named, may be parsed. Usefully for my purposes, Roach's choice of "inchoate" evokes not only the tendency toward chaos in Baldwin's text ("chaos" is itself a favorite word of Baldwin's) but also *incipience*—the sense of something coming into view.

Despite the text's overt denials, there is an underlying homosexual and androgynous cast to Eric's charisma that is in tension with the insistence on its universalism. Eric's performance might thus be read as a sublimated version of Baldwin's own freakish, sissy performative persona.[53] If *Giovanni's Room*, with its central romance between white men, can be understood as a displaced confession of Baldwin's own sexuality, then *Another Country* continues the racial camouflage of that earlier text but also imbues Eric's experience of his homosexuality with a charge of self-acceptance unavailable to the protagonist David and even to the less uptight Giovanni. Given the multiple connections between Eric's performativity and his homosexuality that *Another Country* makes or implies, I think we are justified in seeing the description of his film acting as elaborating not only the power of art but also something like the essence of his character. Eric is a man but also not masculine, and not androgynous either—he is, it seems, a wholly new kind of man. The kind of man Eric is, I suggest, is the prototypical liberated gay man, a man lurking within the increasing media coverage of homosexuality that characterized the 1960s—a man whose relation to orthodox gendering remains uncertain, troubling. When Trilling wrote about Eric, he noted that "he has been able to 'accept' his homosexuality"; the scare quotes around "accept," I suggest, don't simply indicate Trilling's homophobia but a more general cultural skepticism about the possibility of such acceptance—a skepticism that would be increasingly challenged as the 1960s went on.[54]

Eric models the liberated gay man in his refusal of the dominant medico-legal paradigm of homosexuality. The central passage, with its tortured torsions in relation to the homosexual name, reaches the following conclusion:

> [Eric's] life, passions, trials, loves, were, at worst, filth, and, at best, disease in the eyes of the world, and crimes in the eyes of his countrymen. There were no standards for him except those he could make for himself. There were no standards for him because he could not accept the definitions, the hideously mechanical jargon of the age. He saw no one around him worth his envy, did not believe in the vast, grey sleep which was called security, did not believe in the cures, panaceas, the slogans which afflicted the world he knew; and this meant that he had to create his standards and make up his definitions as he went along. It was up to him to find out who he was, and it was his necessity to do this, so far as the witch doctors of the time were concerned, alone. (206)

The passage inscribes Eric as anachronistic in his resistance to Cold War culture ("the vast, grey sleep which was called security") and to the "standards" and "definitions" that that culture attaches to homosexuality above all. His relation to these standards and definitions is contingent and oriented toward the future: "He had to create his standards and make up his definitions as he went along. It was up to him to find out who he was." Daylanne English has recently argued that in *Another Country* Baldwin "anticipates and exceeds" the influential notions of queer temporality elaborated in Lee Edelman's *No Future* and José Esteban Muñoz's *Cruising Utopia*. She reads the closing pages of the novel that reunite Eric and Yves in "the city which the people from heaven had made their home" as an intimation of queer utopia that is rooted in the here and now of queer relationality. Thus, for English, Baldwin's queer-affirmative vision, in which "same-sex desire or queerness marked by dynamism and by nonstandard temporalities" is privileged over heterosexuality supplies a riposte to Muñoz's claim that "queerness is not here yet. . . . We have never been queer. . . . Queerness is essentially about the rejection of a here and now and an insistence on potentiality or concrete possibility for another world."[55] Additionally, it is in Baldwin's work, she argues, "with his version of a queer utopia, that we can find an interruption in what Lee Edelman would term 'pro-procreative prejudice,' that is, state-interested promotion of conventional forms of human sexuality and relationships."[56] My argument here is close to English's, but rather than see moments of the text that privilege homosexuality as anticipating queer futurity, I want to tie them more closely to the historical context of the novel's publication, in which gay liberation is the emergent or anticipated moment. Despite their distinct, not to say adversarial, positions, Edelman and Muñoz's work has in common the fixation on an uncategorizable, untamable queer subjectivity, free of the exigencies of history, that I have proposed is influentially limned in Butler's "Imitation and Gender Insubordination." By contrast, Baldwin's text, through the figure of Eric, engages with a proto-liberatory mode of thinking that is embedded in the historical struggle through which gay personhood, as we now understand it, emerged.

In his defiance, Eric presages or parallels liberationist discourse. In one final demonstration of the importance and inescapability of the system of naming, he claims, like the "homophile" or "gay" activists of the 1960s, the right to forge his own definitions and standards in opposition to the "hideously mechanical jargon" promulgated by the accepted authorities, contemptuously dismissed as "witch doctors." However, for Eric, unlike those activists, alternative definitions or names have no collective context. His self-affirmation and self-definition are things he must do "alone." Baldwin's usual aversion to gay collectivity—his confinement of positive representations of homosexuality to the individual or the couple—here results in his reinscription of one of the key images of the discourse of the "witch doctors" against which he ranges himself: the homosexual as isolated individual. Yet, as we saw briefly in the discussion of the Washington Square Park scene, the novel is also preoccupied with gay collectivity. Like *Giovanni's Room* before it, *Another Country* indicates the impossibility of disentangling the homosexual individual and the homosexual couple from subcultural embodiments. Unlike the earlier novel, however—and here it marks a historical shift—*Another Country* also inadvertently gestures toward the gay collectivity's public emergence as a potentially liberated and liberatory force. Though Baldwin tries to reject the subculture, the supposedly strictly personal liberation embodied in Eric is informed by and refers back to it.

Chaos

The richly suggestive confusion of Baldwin's position on homosexual collectivity is most apparent in the central passage with which I have largely been concerned in my reading of *Another Country*. Before returning to that passage, though, I briefly focus again on the Washington Square Park scene. As noted previously, Eric's disavowal of his relation to the gay subculture is made clear when he, Ida, and Ellis pass "two glittering, loud-talking fairies" and Eric "pull[s] in his belly, looking straight ahead," avoiding the eye contact that would connect him to the fairies. If the description of the fairies as "glittering" and "loud-talking" conveys a flamboyant performativity that Eric himself does not exemplify, it is significant that at the moment of encounter Eric is talking to Ellis about his acting career in France: "'I did a couple of things for American TV. . . . And I saw a lot of theater . . . it was very good for me.' The birds of paradise passed; their raucous cries faded" (253). Recurring to the avian metaphorics ("*les folles*") with which the effeminate homosexuals of Paris are described in *Giovanni's Room*, this brief passage juxtaposes Eric's own cathexis onto acting with the embarrassing antics of the fairies, an association of homosexuality and performance also carried in the reference, earlier in this scene, to the "childless wretched . . . act[ing]out their joyless rituals" in the park (251). Once again, the public aspect of homosexuality is rendered as performance—and once again the figure of the liberated homosexual individual is associated with the disavowed subcultural manifestations of homosexuality.

The walk-on role of the two fairies uncannily anticipates *Life*'s famous photo-essay of 1964, "Homosexuality in America," a landmark in mass-media coverage of the subculture.[57] Probably best known today for its coverage of the San Francisco leather scene and its gay macho style, the essay also includes a photo of two fairies walking through what appears to be Washington Square Park, shown from behind, captioned, "Two fluffy-sweatered young men stroll in New York City, ignoring the stare of a 'straight' couple. Flagrant homosexuals are unabashed by reactions of shock, perplexity, disgust" (Figure 1). Or maybe *Another Country*'s anticipation of this tableau is not so uncanny. If in its depiction of homosexuality, *Another Country* was in some ways a daring book that extended the audacity of *Giovanni's Room*, in other ways the tropes through which it figures homosexuality line up neatly, even predictably, with the treatment of the gay subculture in the early 1960s print media. The often baffling complexity of Baldwin's prose describing the gay underworld is juxtaposed with an account of the homosexual and his ways that was gaining increasing currency, and becoming increasingly conventional, in the mediasphere. Paralleling *Life*'s identification with the gaze of its "'straight' couple," commentary on the fairies in *Another Country* by another straight couple, Ellis and Ida, follows the encounter (Eric is conspicuously silent). Ida says, "I feel so sorry for them!"; a "grinning" Ellis responds, "Why should you feel sorry for them? They've got each other"; and Ida continues, "A couple of the waiters on my job are like that. The way some people treat them—! . . . I like them, I really do. They're very sweet. And, of course, they make wonderful escorts" (253). Ida's attitude correlates with popular nonfictional takes on homosexuality from the period, such as Jess Stearns's *The Sixth Man* (1961) and Helen Gurley Brown's *Sex and the Single Girl* (1962), which disclosed that a gay man could be "a girl's best friend."[58] I don't mean to say, of course, that the novel *endorses* Ida and Ellis's condescension here. Rather, I mean to suggest that the novel participates in the tropology of gay life that emerges in the early 1960s at the same time that it works in the central passage, through the poetic and gnomic complexities of Baldwin's prose, to develop an uneasy and somewhat inadvertent utopian rhetoric of the idea of sexual liberation that journalism and pop sociology set out in more pedestrian terms. This utopian rhetoric feeds into the passionate liberationist discourse that was to emerge by the decade's end.

In the central passage, Eric moves from recollections of his childhood and adolescence to reflections on his sexual encounters within the gay underworld. The passion and imprecision of the prose deepens, a movement reflexively forecast in the identification of the experience of loveless sex with men as "chaos":

> On the day that Yves no longer needed him, Eric would drop back into chaos. He remembered that army of lonely men who had used him, who had wrestled with him, caressed him and submitted to him, in a darkness deeper than the darkest night. It was not merely his body they had used, but something else; his infirmity had made him the receptacle of an anguish which he could scarcely believe was in the world. (204)

The hyperbolic insistence of the imagery ratchets up the sense of homosexuality's intractability. Baldwin recurs to his often-used trope of "darkness" to describe the gay world, but it is here extended into "a darkness deeper than the darkest night"; and the anguish of homosexuality is of a kind that Eric "could scarcely believe was in the world." Superadding to the portentousness of the passage, in a return to the image of the army ("of lonely men"), Baldwin alludes to that favorite of woe-saying speechmakers and editorialists, Arnold's

Figure 1. The gay subculture on display ("Homosexuality in America," *Life*, 26 June 1964, 68–69). Bill Eppridge/© Estate of Bill Eppridge.

"Dover Beach": "And [Eric] thought of these men, that ignorant army. They were husbands, they were fathers, gangsters, football players, rovers; and they were everywhere. Or they were, in any case, in all of the places he had been assured they could not be found" (204).

In contrast to the "glittering" and (per *Life*) "flagrant" fairies of the square, the men mentioned here are normatively masculine and closeted. Absent from subcultural venues such as bars, these men nevertheless engage "furtively" in the subcultural institution of public sex, "in an empty locker room, on an empty stairway or a roof, in the shadow of a wall in the park, in a parked car" (205). The unobviousness of these men chimes with the nonfiction exposés of the 1960s, which sensationally disclosed that homosexuals do not necessarily conform to the easily identifiable mode of the fairy; they are everywhere, unsuspected.[59] As Stearns, in his best-selling pop-sociological text, was moved to italicize: "*Homosexuals can be anybody*."[60] And the cruising and public sex that Baldwin outlines here were also mainstays of the 1960s print coverage of the gay world.[61] Of course, one way of viewing these men in *Another Country* might be not as homosexually identified men at all but as "trade," a view seemingly confirmed when the passage goes on to state, "It could not be said that they were attracted to men. They did not make love, they were passive, they were acted on. The need seemed, indeed, to be precisely this passivity, this gift of illicit pleasure, this adoration" (205).[62] Barry Reay has argued that the widespread equation of homosexuality with effeminacy at this time meant that many normatively masculine men who desired or engaged in sex with other men did not understand themselves as homosexual. However, in contrast with Reay's account—typical of the sexual relativism of queer studies, which rejects the notion that such men are self-deceiving and in need of liberation into gay identity—Baldwin goes on to identify his "army of lonely men" as "perishing" from "lack" of "affection," acting on their homoerotic desire "out of poverty and in the most tremendous ignorance" (205). While he does not of course prescribe the accession for these men into gay identity as their salvation, Baldwin projects an alternative possibility that parallels liberationist rhetoric: "The dark submission was the shadow of love—if only someone, somewhere, loved them enough to caress them this way, in the light, with joy! But then they could no longer be passive" (205).[63] Like the gay liberationists to come, Baldwin rejects the passivity of trade as a form of self-deception or self-hating, and while his imagery of homosexual caresses "in the light, with joy" most obviously instates his quasi-religious conviction in the sanctifying, shame-defying power of love, the imagery of illuminated openness also anticipates the liberationist rhetoric of decloseting. In contrast to the argument of Reay, and in concert with nonfiction accounts of the early 1960s—both those from a homophile and those from a heterosexual standpoint—Baldwin imagines these men as in need of a kind of consciousness raising, even if he steers clear of the idea that homosexual identification is meliorative.

The utopian possibility of a homosexuality exposed to light and to love, is, however, immediately ruled out, as the narrator reminds us of the state of these men:

> Chaos. For the great difference between these men and [Eric] was also the terms of their connection. He saw their vulnerability and they saw his. But they did not love him for this. They used him. He did not love them either, though he dreamed of it. And the encounter took place, at last, between two dreamers, neither of whom could wake the other, except for the briefest and bitterest of seconds. Then sleep descended again, the search continued, chaos came again. (205)

Baldwin's standard downbeat account of loveless sex between men is here complicated by the rich confusion of his rhetoric. The encounters between Eric and the army of lonely men, the narrator tells us, are characterized by use rather than love and entail chaos, by which seems to be meant the emotional torment associated with homosexual desire (though the uncertainty of reference here is part of my point). But within this chaos is also the possibility of "connection." Occasionally, the narrator tells us, "When the liaison so casually begun survived the first encounters . . . a kind of shy affection began to force itself up through the frozen ground, and shame abated." But then, "chaos more than ever ruled. For shame had not so much abated as found a partner. Affection had appeared, but through a fissure, a crevice, in the person, through which, behind affection, came all the winds of fear. For the act of love is a confession. One lies about the body but the body does not lie about itself; it cannot lie about the force which drives it" (206).

The account of Eric's adult sexual history constellates shame, love, compulsion, and confession—elements that I have indicated echo throughout Baldwin's work. But I think it is impossible, here or elsewhere, to satisfactorily parse the relations between these elements. The passage from *Another Country* is not just complex—it is confusing and obscure. As in *Giovanni's Room*, shame and homosexual love appear to be inextricable. First we are told affection makes shame abate, yet then the narrator corrects himself: "shame had not so much abated as found a partner."

Here, it seems, homosexual love no less than shame is an involuntary confession of that which one would prefer to remain hidden (presumably because of its taboo nature). Yet in spite of my best efforts to unpack this passage, ultimately, for me at least, it collapses into incoherence: Is the "force" that drives the body love or sexual compulsion? Are the two to be differentiated here, or do they collapse into one another? The passage does not seem to me to be able to decide these questions: in describing chaos, it becomes chaos itself. But this chaos of feeling is also proffered as a mode of communion. Even as the men in the passage are torn apart from one another, they are in a state of "connection."

Coda: An Army of Lovers

There is another moment in this long central passage that mixes the idea of communion and the idea of isolation, but here the language is succinct rather than confused. And it is another moment that resonates with the exposés of the gay world in the 1960s mass media. I am thinking of Baldwin's description of the hidden gay world as an "army of lonely men," a phrase that might have come from the jacket copy of one of the pop-sociological texts of the decade. The phrase posits homosexual identity as ambiguously positioned between lonely singularity and community. According to Baldwin, this army is ignorant, flailing about in a state of chaos. But the image of the army also calls up the idea of organized, collective aggression. In tension with his own conviction about the necessary privacy of homosexual expression, Baldwin here inscribes homosexuality as not only public but as potentially liberated, as potentially militant.

Fast-forward to 1971 and we find this potential realized in the lesbian liberationist poem "Sappho's Reply," by Rita Mae Brown. Voicing aggressive liberationist sentiment, the brief lyric concludes with the line "An army of lovers shall not fail" (militancy is also wittily signaled in the title for the collection from which the poem comes, *The Hand That Cradles the Rock*).[64] If Baldwin became a proto-visible gay celebrity, Brown was one of the first famous out lesbians and became an important spokesperson on the national stage for the militant rhetoric of liberation that, I have suggested, is gestated, albeit in ambiguous phrasing, in Baldwin's novel. A prominent figure in the early liberation movement, Brown achieved crossover status with her lesbian bildungsroman *Rubyfruit Jungle* (1973), which moved her into "the world of major publishing houses, mainstream publicity, and widespread notoriety."[65] Initially published by New York University Press to modest sales, *The Hand That Cradles the Rock* was reprinted by the independent feminist publisher Diana Press in 1974 and, "boosted by the huge success" of *Rubyfruit Jungle*, became a best seller for them.[66]

Admittedly, it is something of a wrench to move from *Another Country* to Brown's poem, not only because Baldwin was, at best, uninterested in the political organization around sexual identity in which Brown was passionately involved. Baldwin's preoccupation with male homosexuality contrasts with his silence about lesbianism. He provided no fictional representations of it, and, as far as I know, did not even ever mention it in his public comments.[67] Yet Baldwin and Brown's common, if differently inflected, image of the army indicates the way pre- and postliberation conceptions of gay life thread together. In the next two chapters I turn to Susan Sontag, an indirect predecessor of Brown in her modeling of queer female celebrity. If Baldwin in his persona and his fiction presented a strong version of proto-visibility, Sontag represented the ambiguous fascination of a celebrity persona at once highly visible and obscure, at once queerly sexualized and impersonal. But while Baldwin's representation of sexual love as a mode of transcendence inadvertently gestures toward the language of sexual liberation, Sontag represents a more explicit (though not unwavering) commitment to the idea that sexuality and liberty are "twin subjects."[68] Despite her public reticence about lesbian identity, Sontag helped pave the way for the prideful lesbianism that was one offshoot of the sexual openness of the 1960s.

3 Susan Sontag's Impersonal Stardom

IN THE PHOTOGRAPH BY HARRY HESS that adorns the back dust jacket of her first novel, *The Benefactor* (1963), Susan Sontag is shown from the breast area up, in three-quarter profile (Figure 2). Her body is turned to the viewer's left, but her head is inclined slightly rightward, and her steady gaze is directed to the right. Her face is made up, unsmiling. She is dressed in several layers of dark clothing: a leather jacket or coat, its collar turned up, is worn over a woolen or fabric jacket, the collar of which is also turned up; a scarf wrapped around her neck leaves only a tiny sliver of throat exposed. The dark clothing matches her dark hair, and while both hair and clothing stand out from the background, this is also generally dark, though some striations of light or half-light break up the darkness, with the brightest one, a diagonal to the extreme right of the picture, echoing and reinforcing Sontag's determined stance. Glimmers of light also show up on Sontag's hair, at the crown of her head, and on the leather coat—around the breast, at the shoulder, and on the collar. It is Sontag's face, however, that most decisively breaks up the portrait's tenebrous composition, with the other shards of light serving to enhance rather than distract from its radiance. Lit to glow, Sontag's face seems to hover in the darkness, though it too ultimately recedes into the black, with a shadow on her left cheekbone melting indistinguishably into her dark hair. In its otherworldly radiance, her face has the inhuman perfection of a statue—or a glamour portrait of a female Hollywood star. Specifically, the Hess portrait references or resembles classic studio portraits of the 1930s in its use of "dramatic 'Rembrandt' lighting, highly contrasted areas of light and shadow that seem to sculpt what they reflect." As in the Hess portrait, this lighting "create[d] forms and shapes accenting or highlighting facial features," with "background shapes . . . often arranged to throw the star presence into high relief."[1] The interplay of light and dark, and solidity and indistinction, constitutes Sontag as an alluring enigma.

Figure 2. Back dust-jacket portrait of Susan Sontag by Harry Hess, *The Benefactor* (New York: Farrar, Straus and Company, 1963).

Evoking long-standing metaphorical connotations of chiaroscuro, the pattern of contrasts and overlaps between light and shade in the photograph suggest both mystery and clarity; "chiaroscuro," the *Oxford English Dictionary* tells us, has a figurative use meaning "partly revealed and partly veiled." The layers of dark clothing protectively or defensively shield Sontag's body up to the top of the neck, suggesting a literally buttoned-up self. Yet the tiny sliver of exposed throat mitigates this shielding, providing a sexualized frisson; and while the lighting lends an alien quality to her beautiful face, her direct, calm gaze at the camera seems to solicit the spectator. The image is at once suggestive of sexuality and of its withholding.

I begin with this image because I think it epitomizes what I call Sontag's star effect. To refer to Sontag as a "star" is a cliché or truism of commentary on her, but I want in this chapter to take the idea of Sontag's stardom seriously, working with and against film star studies to develop an account of Sontag's queer iconicity. Sontag's star effect was not confined to her many glamorous portraits, of which the Hess photograph is the first widely circulated one, but was also produced by her press coverage more generally, her many interviews, and her writing (or at least the media reporting of her writing). The Sontag star effect solicits eroticized audience attention in the very act of seeming to repel it through her vaunted "impersonality." The effect is produced by the overlap between the general operations of star construction and the impersonal aloofness of her prose. Through the queer allure of her image and her groundbreaking 1960s essays, Sontag helped promote unorthodox sexual identities and attitudes, even as she avoided association with lesbianism.

Summarizing Sontag's critical style, Angela McRobbie states that there is in it "hardly a trace of her own personal voice, not a trace of gender, of place, or of preference."[2] This characterization does not register the flirtation with the autobiographical—and with the sexual—that flickers through and tempers the otherwise austerely deindividualized style of Sontag's essays. The tendency to read Sontag's essays as a kind of veiled life writing has become an established approach to her work; indeed, at least insofar as the essays function as a kind of intellectual autobiography, this critical tendency was accorded Sontag's own imprimatur. In her prefatory note to the paperback edition of her first essay collection, *Against Interpretation* (1966), Sontag states that "in the end what I have been writing is not criticism at all, but case studies for an aesthetic, a theory of my own sensibility."[3] Later, in an essay on Walter Benjamin from 1978, she wrote, "One cannot use the life to interpret the work. But one can use the work to interpret the life"; and critics have deployed this aperçu as a license to probe Sontag's work for its autobiographical resonances.[4] Sontag herself noted in a 1984 interview that her essays from the 1970s and 1980s on Benjamin, Elias Canetti, and Roland Barthes were "portraits that are in some sense self-portraits."[5] She rejected psychologizing interpretations, however, stating in "Singleness," an essay from 1995, that "my books are not a means of discovering who I am either; I've never fancied the ideology of writing as therapy or self-expression."[6] But the first person always hovers tantalizingly behind the collective "we" and the depersonalized "one" that are the dominant pronominal forms of her essays—as her own statements on her work indicate, acknowledging and then withdrawing the first-person presence in a kind of fort/da game with her readers (it is Susan Sontag in the first person who rejects the idea that her books can enable us to "discover" who she is). Sontag's work neatly illustrates Sharon Cameron's point that "impersonality (as a practice, as an ethic, as a representation), since it is undertaken by persons, [can] only be contradictory by definition."[7]

Moreover, while McRobbie's claim that Sontag's prose bears not a "trace" of gender is true in that Sontag rarely enfolds the experience of femininity within her writing, consideration of Sontag's star effect means that her prose cannot be hived off from her photographed and very definitely gendered image. Sontag, rather than Vidal and Baldwin—and arguably more than most other literary celebrities—deserves serious consideration in relation to the discourse of stardom not so much because she was much photographed (Vidal and Baldwin were equally if not better-known well-known faces in the 1960s) but rather because of the way in which photographic representation of her exceptional good looks draws on the tradition of what Laura Mulvey famously defined as the to-be-looked-at-ness of the female film star.[8] Additionally, my argument is informed by what Edgar Morin in his pioneering study *The Stars* (1957) calls the "feminine character" of the "star system." Morin argues that " 'mythification' is effected primarily upon female stars: they are the most 'fabricated,' the most idealized, the least real, the most adored. In present-day social conditions, woman is more mythic than man as both subject and object. She is more of a star than a man."[9] Leaving to one side Morin's somewhat dated phrase making, I think it is fair to say that, in line with his argument, there was a mythic quality attached to Sontag that does not apply to the male literary celebrities examined in this book. A female intellectual possessed of youth and beauty, Sontag seemed to burst out of virtually nowhere onto the early 1960s New York literary scene. Like the movie star, she was produced and received as a somehow "unreal" being. As her onetime friend, the experimental novelist Alfred Chester described a fictionalized surrogate of her in his novella *The Foot* (1966), she was "very beautiful . . . unhistorical, classless, like a movie star, like a woman in a movie."[10] Hollywood historians note that the fantastic glamour of the 1930s studio portraits was displaced in the war years by more "down-to-earth" images of stars. There is, then, something anachronistic and therefore appropriately noteworthy about Hess's photographic announcement of the *lusus naturae* Sontag's arrival.[11] However, Sontag was hardly universally idealized or adored; instead, her sudden appearance was greeted with a complex mix of often sexist expressions of fascination and dismay. The ambivalence of response generated by Sontag's anomalousness forms an important strand of this chapter's discussion. It is an ambivalence that is tied to an intuition of Sontag's queerness and to the way she disseminated queer affect. Sontag generated ambivalence in part because she embodied it in her relations to her own celebrity and to her own queerness. In what follows, I begin by unpacking the construction of Sontag as a star and her own relations to the category of celebrity. I then focus on her reception in the 1960s, particularly among the New York intellectuals, who variously figure as her mentors, peers, and adversaries, to demonstrate how gender and, concomitantly, sexuality figured in her celebrity. Finally, I turn to her 1960s essays, making a case for how her revisionary aestheticism, with its valorization of antipsychological artworks conveyed in a seemingly impersonal style, can be seen in fact to promote and elicit the sexual interest that is one of the key effects of stardom.

Star Authors

The construction of Sontag as a star began with the publication of *The Benefactor* and the Hess image, which her publisher Farrar, Straus and Company chose to feature on the back cover in place of an impressive array of endorsements from the likes of Hannah Arendt and Kenneth Burke.[12] But this initial effort to trade on the power of Sontag's image was abortive; *The Benefactor*—a decidedly unautobiographical and cerebral first novel, set in a despecified France and North Africa in the 1930s and 1940s, indebted to European novelistic modernism, and narrated by a sixty-one-year-old male—proved a flop. Instead, Sontag rocketed to media notoriety the year after with "Notes on 'Camp,'" published in *Partisan Review*. The journal had a circulation of less than ten thousand, but the essay went on to an afterlife in less rarefied media outlets, with *Time* publishing a summary of it in December 1964, thereby precipitating the mainstreaming of camp and cementing Sontag's stardom. Her other essays of the 1960s, anthologized in the landmark collections *Against Interpretation* (1966) and *Styles of Radical Will* (1969), which extended Sontag's interest in cutting-edge, unsanctioned, and popular cultural forms (for instance, Happenings, science-fiction movies, and underground cinema, as well as camp) can in retrospect be seen as shepherding in what is now called "postmodernism" and what was named at the time the "New

Sensibility," a phrase coined by Sontag in a polemical essay about the shifting grounds of art and artistic appreciation, "One Culture and the New Sensibility" (1965), that formed the closing salvo of *Against Interpretation*. Commentary on the New Sensibility, which became almost as ubiquitous as discussion of camp in the second half of the 1960s, frequently tied it to the erotic edginess of the counterculture (one review of *Against Interpretation* referred knowingly to the "New Sensuality").[13] Eventually, the term was repurposed by Herbert Marcuse in *An Essay on Liberation* (1969) to signal the unprecedented fusion of politics, aesthetics, and eroticism that characterized the counterculture, or what Marcuse called the "rebellion of the young intelligentsia."[14] Marcuse's use of "New Sensibility"—which does not seem to have been noted by commentators on either Marcuse or Sontag—politicizes it, while Sontag was clear about what she saw as the "apolitical" nature of the art she collected under the term.[15] However, Sontag's commitment in her early and mid-1960s work to the apolitical aspects of both art and eroticism is complicated by her sense of the liberatory energies they harbor, and in this way her writing anticipates the countercultural politics celebrated by Marcuse. As I detail in this and the following chapter, Sontag, the New Sensibility's celebrity spokesperson, to some extent invited and to some extent was unwillingly swept up in the "liberatory" openness around sexuality—including queer sexuality—that characterized the 1960s. However, while Sontag was widely associated with shifting attitudes toward same-sexuality, she was not herself identified as lesbian.

In this respect Sontag contrasts with the other two writers central to this book. While for Baldwin and Vidal, diplomatically inexplicit or snidely innuendo-laden references in the media to their "personal lives" only thinly veiled their embodied interests in same-sexuality, the secrecy around Sontag's lesbianism was, for most of her career, not as much open as deep. Sontag's brief marriage at the age of seventeen to the University of Chicago sociologist Philip Rieff, with whom she had a son, David, secured her for many years a nominal public identity as a heterosexual. It was not until the 1990s that Sontag's sexual affairs with women were widely bruited, and it was not until 2000, when an unauthorized biography by Carl Rollyson and Lisa Paddock was about to appear, that Sontag preemptively half-acknowledged her same-sexuality, stating in an interview in the *New Yorker*, "That I have had girlfriends as well as boyfriends is what? Is something I never thought I was supposed to say since it seems to me the most natural thing in the world."[16]

The posthumous publication of selections from Sontag's journals, particularly the first volume, covering the period from 1947 to 1963—from her adolescence in Los Angeles to her early years in New York—provides a startling, even shocking contrast with the reticence of her essays and interviews. In the journals, Sontag is unstintingly frank about her erotic relations with women, her fascinated engagement with the queer subculture, and her identification as a lesbian. The journals indicate the extent to which her lesbian "sexual ambitions," as she put it in a 1948 entry when she was fifteen, were bound up with her intellectual ambitions.[17] In 1959, in a Reichian moment, she writes: "The orgasm focuses. I lust to write. The coming of orgasm is not the salvation but, more, the birth of my ego. I cannot write until I find my ego. The only kind of writer [I] could be is the kind who exposes himself."[18] In another entry, from a few days later, she echoes Baldwin's description of how he forged the "infirmity" of his queerness into a "weapon": "My desire to write is connected with my homosexuality. I need the identity as a weapon, to match the weapon that society has against me. . . . Being queer makes me feel more vulnerable. It increases my wish to hide, to be invisible—which I've always felt anyway."[19] As the journals suggest, for Sontag, queer sexuality lies at the heart of her contradictory desires to expose herself and to hide within writing. These contradictory desires were played out in a career as a celebrity writer who eschewed talk of her own same-sex desire. I argue in this chapter and the next that Sontag, like Baldwin, used queerness as a weapon—a subtle and subversive weapon, but a weapon nonetheless—against the orthodoxies of midcentury American culture.

The dialectic of exposure and hiddenness set out in her journals supports the argument I make here, but my focus is of course on Sontag's published work. Lesbianism is not entirely absent from this work—and I conclude this chapter by looking at a striking instance of its presence—but its expression is fugitive, and it tends to be routed through references to the gay male subculture.[20] Sontag's textual engagements with same-sexuality provide an interesting preliberation instance of the tendency for lesbians to invest in the gay male subculture. This investment, I suggest, was not merely an aspect of Sontag's personal history—a "pattern of association with male homosexuals," as she put it in a 1968 journal entry[21]—but exemplifies how gay male culture, as the most widely publicized version of queerness, may help form other queer identities through cross-identification. While it would be inaccurate of course to say that lesbianism was not publicized in the midcentury period, or that it did not have its own distinctive styles of visibility (notably, butch/femme), it attracted significantly less media attention than gay male life. As the more publicized culture, gay male culture has been and continues to be an object of investment for queer women; in Sontag's case, this investment was connected to fascinations with the sexual institutions and the artistic and intellectual trappings of metropolitan gay culture. Taking up these fascinations in more detail in the next chapter, I argue that they prompted and became the focus for her interests in the sexual revolution.[22] If Sontag was not associated with lesbianism, across the various components of her celebrity—in her writing, in her photographs, and in the commentary of others—she projected an erotic glamour that had a decidedly queer cast.

It is the unusual substantial commentary on Sontag that refrains from mentioning her widely circulated image, and many critics tend to align or conflate her portraits and her writing. For instance, in his idiosyncratic appreciation *Sontag and Kael* (2004), Craig Seligman argues that the "reserve" of Sontag's writing "added piquancy to the fact that, as her photographs told you if her prose didn't, she was an unabashedly sexual being." "But," he backtracks, "her prose *did*," going on to cite a passage from Sontag's 1961 review of Norman O. Brown's *Love's Body*, in which she invokes "the revolutionary implications of sexuality." Trying to keep writing and portraits distinct, Seligman ultimately collapses them, in the process also entangling impersonality and eroticism. Sontag's effect, Seligman decides, is "hard-to-get," which, he observes, "is a classic element of allure." Sontag's "mystery . . . *is* her charm"—an erotic style that is "Garboesque, almost."[23] The pileup of qualifications and repeated recourse to italics attest to the complex and intense erotic affects that the Sontag persona generates for many. In Theodore Solaratoff's earlier characterization from 1967, the paradoxical energy animating Sontag's hard-to-get persona is treated more warily: "Like the celebrity that Miss Sontag appears to court with her left hand and disclaim with her right, her critical stance somehow manage[s] to be both matter-of-fact and outrageous: a tone that gets under the skin in much the same way that those dust-jacket photographs of her—poised, striking, vaguely sinister—either seduce or repel."[24] Bringing together Sontag's celebrity, her critical voice, and her photographed image through a series of linked comparisons, Solaratoff points to the combined contribution of all three aspects of her fascinating, uncanny effect. In her under-the-skin strangeness, she "either seduce[s] or repel[s]"; or, as the parallelism with the description of her critical voice ("both matter-of-fact and outrageous") encourages us to extrapolate, she is *both* seductive and repellent.

These ambivalent responses to Sontag parallel the effects of celebrity parsed by Sharon Marcus, who notes that "the contradictory personae of celebrities in turn often elicit contradictory stances from publics, whose feelings veer between attraction and repulsion, contempt and envy, derision and admiration, and identification and disidentification."[25] The ambivalent affective nimbus of the star is conceptualized by Judith Brown as "glamour" and Steven Shaviro as "allure." While Brown's argument relates specifically to stars of Hollywood's 1930s "Golden Age," and Shaviro's to contemporary "postcinematic" stars, the characteristics described by both indicate continuities in formations of celebrity over the twentieth century and beyond. Brown notes affinities between the style of Hollywood glamour and "the modernism that favors blankness, the polished surface, the stance of impenetrability"—for instance, in a studio portrait of an "otherworldly" Jean Harlow that, like the photographs of Sontag according to Solaratoff, "simultaneously beckon[s] and repel[s] the viewer."[26] Further parallels between movie star glamour and avant-garde aesthetics are evident for Brown in the paradigmatic case of Garbo, who in her on-screen image "enacts one of literary modernism's central principles, the extinction of personality."[27] At the same time, the movie star is taken to embody "personality," the early twentieth-century category defined by such flashy features as "charm, magnetism, and fascination," which nudges aside the older "morally-freighted" concept of character.[28] While the charismatic force of personality often generates a sense of proximity to the person projecting it, Brown notes that the glamorous celebrity, the epitome of personality, in fact takes "personality to an impersonal extreme," becoming a site of "rich audience identification based on the limited information made available by the media." The celebrity does not finally offer access to "human warmth" but is constituted as a "coolly aloof and beautifully coiffed personality, hovering over the multiple indignities of life on the ground."[29]

If Brown's account of modernist glamour helps us pick out the parallels between Sontag's "coolly aloof" image and that of the movie star, Shaviro's discussion of allure elaborates the fascination that such distance engenders. Shaviro draws on the work of the philosopher Graham Harman on this concept:

> Allure is the way in which an object does not just display certain particular qualities to me, but also insinuates the presence of a hidden, deeper level of existence. The alluring object explicitly *calls attention* to the fact that it is something more than, and other than, the bundle of qualities that it presents to me. . . . The object becomes alluring precisely to the extent that it forces me to acknowledge this hidden depth.[30]

Extending Harman's concept to celebrity, Shaviro continues: "When a pop star or celebrity allures me, this means that he or she is someone to whom I respond in a mode of intimacy, even though I am not, and cannot ever be, actually intimate with him or her. What I become obsessively aware of, therefore is the figure's distance from me. . . . Such a figure is forever unattainable."[31] Allure thus describes the paradoxical combination of strangeness and intimacy that characterizes our experience of the star, and that, I argue here, is mobilized in particularly compelling form by Sontag's impersonality.[32]

The erotic component of allure remains implicit in Shaviro's account. Perhaps the most fully worked-out account of the overlaps between the discourse of celebrity and the discourse of sexuality is that of Richard deCordova in his study of early twentieth-century film stardom, which he develops from the observation that at a certain point in the formation of the star system, the question of popular film actors' "existence outside [their] work in film became the primary focus of discourse" about them, with the private lives of the actors "constituted as a site of knowledge and truth."[33] Drawing on Foucault, deCordova notes that the star system, and twentieth-century culture in general, "equates identity with the private and furthermore accords the sexual the status of the most private, and thus the most truthful locus of identity" (140). This similarity between the star system and the modern regime of sexuality is more than one of "discursive strategy": "the very modes of knowing the star, or investigating the truth of his or her identity, are linked to and part of a broader strategy of deploying sexuality in modern times" (141). Although deCordova acknowledges that audience interest in stars includes desire for information about their nonsexual lives, he argues that "the intensity of our involvement, [and] the fanaticism of the fan" are best explained by the way in which "the star system engages us in the very processes through which our society constitutes sexuality as an object of knowledge and fascination" (143). In a passage that chimes with Shaviro's account of allure, deCordova notes that "the truth of the star is never more than partially visible: it demands an orientation beyond that which can be simply seen" (145). If the star is obviously in important ways an image—photographed, filmed, mediatized—that image impels a desire on the part of the audience for the truth of the secret, sexual self behind that image, so that the star effect is constituted through a "play of surface and depth" (130).

DeCordova's acute analysis is especially helpful for my discussion of Sontag's ambiguously sexualized star image. However, general claims about audience interest in the private lives of public figures as constitutive of celebrity status are complicated by the phenomenon of queer stars in the preliberation era, during which time the media could not or did not usually directly comment on the homosexuality of public figures. The desire for knowledge and truth about the private life of the queer celebrity may certainly impel public and media interest during this period, but the homosexuality of that figure cannot be definitely acknowledged—in the mass media at least. Instead (to modify the "star" metaphor), celebrity homosexuality constitutes a kind of dark sun around which an asteroid ring of innuendo and indirection orbits. But, at least in the case of literary stardom, it is not only the audience that is captivated by the star's sexual self; star authors, too, are invested in their sexuality and typically compelled to articulate it through their writing, even if only in guarded terms. Building on Loren Glass's insight about the difference that the emphasis on "individual authorial consciousness" makes to literary celebrity, I suggest throughout this book that this emphasis generates the preoccupation with same-sexuality in the work of Baldwin, Sontag, and Vidal.

Glass's point about the difference of literary celebrity from culture industry celebrity is an invaluable one, and it cautions us against simply equating the Sontag effect with the effect of a Hollywood star. But a consideration of Sontag also paradoxically complicates the distinction that Glass makes between literary and cultural industry celebrities—paradoxically, because if Sontag is one of the celebrity writers who most easily invites comparison to movie stardom, she is also notable for the steadfastness with which she denied her own star status. Another avatar of the New Sensibility, Marshall McLuhan, noted in *Understanding Media* (1964) that "with print, the private life became of the utmost concern to readers. . . . [Print] projects the author at the audience as the movie did."[34] Like Turner, deCordova, and other celebrity scholars, McLuhan highlights the audience interest in the private lives of particular kinds of public figures but suggests continuities between the elevated realm of literature and the mass medium of cinema. His observation, with its suggestive scrambling of chronology, whereby cinema appears to precede print, points to the potential for celebritization within the figure of the modern author, undermining the cordon sanitaire between literary fame and culture industry celebrity. As Leo Braudy discusses, from the early-modern period "immortal" literary (or artistic) fame has been distinguished from other more worldly forms of fame achieved by monarchs and military leaders.[35] As recognizably modern forms of celebrity begin to take hold from the eighteenth century, literary fame continues to be positioned as an alternative and privileged form of renown, even though writers furnish many of the most notable examples of early celebrity—the heavily commodified and mediatized image of Byron is perhaps the most well-known example.[36] By the mid-twentieth century, the idea of literary fame premised on the uniquely authoritative perspective of the author still has force, but disentangling it from the operations of celebrity culture is increasingly difficult, if not impossible. I have argued that Baldwin's stated desire in "The Black Boy Looks at the White Boy" for a "power which outlasts kingdoms" appeals to the notion of transcendent literary fame even as it invokes the strictly contemporary category of celebrity (a wresting from the world of "fame and money and love") that the twentieth-century literary career potentially activates.[37] Numerous scholars have argued that the figure of celebrity both symptomatizes and promotes a given culture's emphasis on the category of the individual so that "process[es] of individualization and celebritization can be seen as interdependent, mutual indexes of each other."[38] A wide range of arguments has posited the figure of the author, too, as epitomizing and even prototypically instantiating modern notions of the individual.[39] Thus, the author, as one of the key exemplars of individual uniqueness (realized in his or her unique artistic expression) is, as McLuhan suggests, a prime source for celebritization. But, as noted previously, the perceived disconnect between individual authorial consciousness and mass-mediatized fame creates tensions for those who become star authors. As Joe Moran notes, American star authors have "repeatedly nagged away at the subject of their celebrity as though compulsively tonguing a sore tooth,"[40] with many engaging in tortured fictional meditations on their fame, which then loop back into their celebrity personas.[41] Authors like Baldwin and Vidal (and Mailer and Roth and Cheever, to name a few others) may not have been happy about their association with celebrity, but they acknowledged it.

In marked contrast with these other midcentury authors, Sontag took an unreconstructed position on the literary fame/celebrity distinction and always disingenuously insisted on her own distance from the machinery of publicity. In a 1989 interview, for instance, after more than twenty years of a highly publicized career, Sontag insisted "with considerable annoyance" that "my life is entirely private. My interests are not that of a pop celebrity" but that "still, the legend" of her active pursuit of publicity "goes on." Disavowing her own investment in publicity, Sontag directs our attention to her devotedness to art and to the pantheon model of literary fame: "My only interest is in literature and doing work that, if I have the talent and the energy and the devotion to accomplish it, will be a permanent part of literature."[42] Sontag's pronouncements of faith in the immortal canon certainly became more forceful in the last two decades of her life, as she recoiled from what she and others saw as the leveling effect of a triumphant postmodern media culture (an effect for which she was ironically sometimes held partly responsible). But her refusal to engage with her own celebrity status is consistent throughout her career.[43]

Alongside such pronouncements, however, we need to register Sontag's own attachment to the category of stardom, manifestations of which suggest or make explicit the parallels between the author and the star for which I have been arguing. Something of a professional fan who preferred to write about artists she admired, Sontag on occasion presented herself as starstruck. Discussing her teenage obsession with literature in an interview from 1995, she remarked, "Writers were as remote to me as movie stars."[44] Movie fandom, as a figure for intense affective investment, also informed Sontag's 1969 essay "Trip to Hanoi," in which she wrote that being in North Vietnam "absurdly resembled meeting a favorite movie star, one who for years has played a role in one's fantasy life, and finding the actual person so much smaller, less vivid, less erotically charged, and mainly different."[45] A collector of movie stills, Sontag attested at length in a 1967 journal entry to the "role" of stars in her "fantasy life": "I love *them*. . . . I admire them; they make me happy. . . . They're a playful version of the sublime company to which I aspire." The distinction between "playful" and "sublime" companies of eminence here is unsettled by Sontag's inclusion of Kafka among the listed names of the stars adorning her walls: Garbo, Dietrich, and Bogart.[46] In this "Dear Diary" moment, Sontag admits to an aspiration in which literary stardom is not easily distinguished from movie stardom and in which desire is not meaningfully separable from identification. As Wayne Koestenbaum notes, "Stardom was one project she pursued"—both in others and in herself.[47]

Picking up on Sontag's investments in and iteration of the figure of the movie star, it is not surprising that Seligman should reach for a Garbo comparison. To communicate the surprise she generated when she arrived on the 1960s cultural scene, he picks another figuration of stardom, or rather starletdom, inadvertently reinforcing the male chauvinism that underpinned the surprise: "A million B pictures have cast a starlet as the female scientist on the expedition, to throw in some sex appeal. Sontag doesn't give the lie to those characters; she *validates* them."[48] But the often sexist or misogynist responses to Sontag also invoked an unseemly or unsettling sexuality of a kind rarely associated with the starlet. It is the co-implication of gender and perverse sexuality in Sontag's star image that I now bring to the fore.

Dark Lady

The so-called New York intellectuals, the group with which Sontag was most closely associated in the early years of her career, provided some of the most intense, and intensely worried, responses to her arrival, in part because they felt that her work, and the wide acclaim it received, signaled the decline of the influence of the older generation of intellectuals and the political and aesthetic values they shared. Sontag's relation to the established New York intellectuals was ambiguous—she was to some extent fostered by them, publishing much of her early work in their house journal *Partisan Review*, and she professed respect for some of them. In her self-fashioning as a critic, she also "owe[d] a great deal to the New York model of the free-floating intellectual," which "significantly influenced her conceptualisations of intellectual generalism and engaged cultural criticism, her presumptions of critical autonomy, and her commitment to the essay form."[49] But the essays collected in *Against Interpretation* are, as Liam Kennedy notes, "littered with very deliberate provocations" regarding the critical positions and cultural tastes established and endorsed by older intellectuals such as Lionel Trilling, Irving Howe, and Alfred Kazin, and Sontag's effort to map the New Sensibility in this book would "prove a partial yet influential guide to the breakup of the liberal critical consensus."[50] If in her early essays Sontag seemed to announce a dramatic shift in American intellectual and cultural life, so too did the glamorous femininity of her much-circulated image contrast with the old-school masculinity of the New York intellectuals with their suits, ties, and short hair.[51]

Norman Podhoretz gave voice in his 1967 memoir *Making It* to the unease that Sontag's arrival generated, even as he tried to contain it through sexist condescension. Coining an epithet that simultaneously pointed to Sontag's sexually alluring enigma and undermined her as a mere "repeat," Podhoretz dubbed her the "Dark Lady of American Letters—a position originally . . . carved out by Mary McCarthy in the thirties and forties."[52] Mustering the full force of pre–Second Wave male chauvinism, Podhoretz elaborates that this position was vacant because "Miss McCarthy" had "recently been promoted to the more dignified status of *Grand Dame* as a reward for her long years of brilliant service. The next Dark Lady would have to be, like her, clever, learned, good-looking, capable of writing family-type criticism as well as fiction with a strong trace of naughtiness."[53] "The ante on naughtiness having gone up by the 1960s," however, "it was not nearly enough . . . for a bluestocking to confess to having slept with The Man in the Brooks Brothers Shirt" (the allusion is to McCarthy's once-shocking short story of 1941); "in an era of what Sherry Abel has called the 'fishnet bluestocking,' hints of perversion and orgies had to be there."[54] Hints of perversion indeed: for all the rebarbativeness of Podhoretz's characterization, with this phrase at least Podhoretz gets at the queer affect of Sontag's persona—the unsettling suggestion of sexual unorthodoxy carried both in Sontag's interest in her 1960s work in sexually radical texts and topics and in her uncanny beauty.

That there was felt to be something sexually untoward about Sontag's persona was also evidenced in the disgusted—and disgusting—comments of another New York intellectual, Philip Rahv, to her putative predecessor Mary McCarthy, that Sontag's ascendancy meant that "perversion is in" and that "above the girdle, the girl is a square."[55] Similarly evoking the specter of Sontag's perversity, but in order to (somewhat backhandedly) praise her, John Barth characterized *The Benefactor* in one of the unused blurbs solicited by Farrar, Straus and Company as "damned disquieting, queer, [and] un-American." Voicing the tongue-in-cheek view that "clearly it was not composed by any Miss Susan Sontag, whose existence I doubt in any case," Barth exaggerated the sense of Sontag's "queer" uncanniness into an assertion of the impossibility of her very being.[56]

But perhaps the most forceful attempt from the period of Sontag's initial notoriety to make unthreatening her *Unheimlichkeit* is Irving Howe's description of Sontag in his essay "The New York Intellectuals" (1968) as "a publicist able to make brilliant quilts from grandmother's patches."[57] The damning energy of this putdown—which conflates the supposedly worthless and feminized activities of publicity and handcraft in its identification of Sontag's writing as an unoriginal patchwork (however meretriciously "brilliant") of the already written—indexes the intensity of the anxiety that motivates it. One of a slew of critical responses from the Old Left to the counterculture and the New Left that appeared in the mid- to late 1960s, "The New York Intellectuals" is a passionate defense of the values promoted by Howe and his peers against the encroaching New Sensibility—a defense that, as James Penner notes, is "anchored in gendered binary oppositions," with the rationality and masculinity of the New York intellectual version of high modernism pitted against the irrational and feminizing tendencies of the prototypical postmodernism of the period (Warhol, camp, etc.).[58] Howe singles out Sontag as a particular focus for his disapprobation of the emerging "Dionysian" spirit of the 1960s. She is a New York intellectual who has, as he punningly puts it, "gone over to the other camp" of the New Left and the counterculture, allegedly abandoning the established standards of taste and reinventing herself as an undiscriminating pluralist.[59] In one of many phrases from his essay that conflate the New Sensibility with sexual license, Howe writes that Sontag "has proposed a cheerfully eclectic view. . . . Now everyone is to do 'his thing,' high, middle or low."[60] Both of the New York intellectuals and not of them, she "employs the dialectical skills and accumulated knowledge of intellectual life in order to bless the new sensibility as a dispensation of pleasure, beyond the grubby reaches of interpretation."[61] But if Howe's reduction of Sontag to quilt-making "publicist" is a clear attempt to domesticate Sontag's sexualized uncanniness, the energy with which she is attacked suggests that the queer difference that Sontag made was not easily mastered.

Sontag famously proclaimed in the title essay of *Against Interpretation* that "in place of a hermeneutics we need an erotics of art," but responses to her persona indicate that erotics and hermeneutics are not easily separated.[62] Eroticized interest in Sontag's persona is actively invited by the seemingly cool and impermeable surface of her prose. In another of the perhaps surprisingly common comparisons of the writer and the movie star, Morin states, "Like the writer, the star admires herself, adores herself."[63] While I don't wish to charge Sontag with the stereotypically feminine narcissism that informs Morin's statement, I do think that it points usefully toward the strain of self-eroticization in Sontag's writing and how this inflects her celebrity mystique.[64] In the next section, I follow the established approach of "interpreting" Sontag's writing as a kind of life writing but open up new lines of inquiry by considering the ways in which her writing feeds into her star persona. I read her according to her own aesthetic principles, proposing that her essays are not only engagements with art but artworks themselves. Her impersonal style I take to be (as she puts it in "On Style") "the signature of the artist's will"; but her essays are also, I suggest, as she says of artworks, "living, autonomous models of consciousness," which can be "virtually independent of the volition of [their] maker."[65] Picking up on a point from my discussion of Baldwin, I maintain there is no clear distinction between Sontag's performance as a celebrity intellectual and what she once called the "literary performance" of her essays.[66] Sontag herself in *Against Interpretation* explicitly identified stardom and artwork, defining Delphine Seyrig in Alain Resnais's film *Muriel* (1963) as an exemplary star performer who "doesn't simply play (or even perfectly fill a role)" but "becomes an independent aesthetic object in herself."[67] The essays, as authorial expressions, bear the trace of her sexual interests in ways that work against her willed guardedness, and they solicit investigation that is erotically oriented.

As components of her star persona, Sontag's 1960s essays demand or invite "an orientation beyond that which can be simply seen," to requote deCordova, that is at odds with her own professed devotedness to style, surface, and aesthetic form. Indeed, Sontag in her 1960s writings veers between investment in form and—admittedly less frequent—recourse to the idea of hidden or buried content, in ways that not only speak to the complexity of her thinking on aesthetics but also reflexively register the "play of surface and depth" that deCordova says defines the star effect—and that is also the effect generated by the modern author.

Masked Voice

The chapter "Going to the Theater, Etc." in *Against Interpretation* is a little-discussed section of a much-discussed text. The result of a short-lived engagement during 1964 as *Partisan Review*'s theater reviewer that, according to Sontag in an afterword in a 1996 reissue of the book, she "had accepted against [her] better judgment," this chapter is, she states there, "the only thing in the collection I don't like at all."[68] In accepting this role Sontag was literally replacing Mary McCarthy, who had served as the *Review*'s theater reviewer for twenty-five years. Sontag's dislike of the engagement, and her quick relinquishment of it, indicates her determination to refuse to "imitate" McCarthy and to forge her own intellectual identity.[69] As an "about-town" response to the ephemeral cultural life of New York that obliges Sontag to deal at some length with works that do not hold her interest or that she actively dislikes, the chapter is indeed quite out of place in relation to the other essays, which she styles in her 1966 preface to the paperback edition as "meta-criticism," the elaboration with "passionate partiality" of "*problems* raised for me by works of art, mainly contemporary."[70] But if this chapter is disavowed by Sontag herself and passed over by commentators on her work, I suggest here that part of it—a less-than-positive review of the 1964 premiere production of Baldwin's *Blues for Mister Charlie*—helps illuminate the complicated relation to same-sexuality that energizes Sontag's 1960s work.

This particular review sits awkwardly with the other commentaries of the collection not only because it is negative but also because it constitutes the book's most flagrant departure from the title essay's strictures "against interpretation." Sontag's take on Baldwin's play is markedly a "task of interpretation" that is "virtually one of translation"—an act of "excavation" that "digs 'behind' the text to find a sub-text which is the true one."[71] The review (which is paired with one of LeRoi Jones's *Dutchman*) commences with a generalization about the mask, "that ancient device of the drama," which is "a peculiarly effective, shorthand way of defining virtue and vice" (150). Sontag continues that "'the Negro'—once a grotesque, a figure of folly" is "fast becoming the American theater's leading mask of virtue" (151). But if "the Negro," according to Sontag, is supposed to be the mask of virtue in Baldwin (and in Jones), the review of *Blues*, as it continues, modulates into a different account of indirect representation, identifying "a rather complex displacement of the play's true subject," which is "perhaps the origin of what seems forced, hysterical, unconvincing" in it (154). "The truth," Sontag writes,

> is that *Blues for Mister Charlie* isn't really about what it claims to be about. It is supposed to be about racial strife. But it is really about the anguish of tabooed sexual longings. . . . It has, in short, a psychological subject. The surface may be Odets, but the interior is pure Tennessee Williams. What Baldwin has done is to take the leading theme of the serious theater of the fifties—sexual anguish—and work it up as a political play. Buried in *Blues for Mister Charlie* is the plot of several successes of the last decade: the gruesome murder of a handsome virile young man by those who envy him his virility. (155)

In thus identifying the "buried" truth of "sexual anguish"—or as she goes on to put it, changing metaphors, the "veiled homoerotic hang-ups" (155) of the play—Sontag at once violates the precept of her polemical title essay and iterates the standard modern assumption that sexuality is the substratum of human identity. That our culture, to return to deCordova's phrasing, "equates identity with the private and furthermore accords the sexual the status of the most private, and thus the most truthful locus of identity," is an assumption that we also of course saw mapped in Baldwin's work in the previous chapter.

For Sontag, "tabooed" homosexual "longings" are awkwardly and unconvincingly masked by *Blues*'s ostensible concern with "racial strife," so ultimately it is a psychological rather than a political play—Tennessee Williams rather than Clifford Odets. This submerged "psychological"—that is, sexual—aspect of Baldwin's work, according to Sontag, explains its appeal to a large white audience: "Baldwin's plays, like his essays and novels, have undoubtedly touched a nerve other than the political. Only by tapping the sexual insecurity that grips most educated white Americans could Baldwin's virulent rhetoric have seemed so reasonable" (153). Conceding that Baldwin is right about the role that "sexual attitudes" play in race relations—resulting simultaneously in a symbolic emasculation of black men and "its converse, treating the Negro as a mere object of lust"—and that he makes this point straightforwardly and forcefully in his essays, Sontag implies that in *Blues* and in his "last novel" (*Another Country*), Baldwin manifests his own sexual insecurities, or "homoerotic hang-ups," burying these under the narrative surface of his work so that "the racial situation has become a kind of code or metaphor for sexual conflict" (155).[72]

I am not particularly interested in pointing up the contradictions in Sontag's approach to interpretation in this passage, or in *Against Interpretation* more generally (as critics pointed out from early on, there's a whole lot of interpreting going on in this text, despite its official stance "against" that activity—interpreting that does, however, in its prioritization of aesthetic form, mark a salutary difference from the standard moralizing approaches of the day). Nor am I interested in judging the persuasiveness of Sontag's account of Baldwin's play. Rather, my focus is on the way her review establishes parallels between the depth model of interpretation and the depth model of sexuality. Sontag indicts Baldwin with conflicted responses to homosexuality, but her own work, beneath its seemingly implacable impersonality, indicates comparable tensions.

In identifying sexuality generally and homosexuality particularly as psychological rather than political issues in her review of *Blues*, Sontag affirms the conventional midcentury view that homosexuality is a personal matter, without political repercussions—a way of thinking that we have already seen played out in our discussion of Baldwin's novels. For both Baldwin and Sontag, despite their significant differences, race is eminently "political," while sexuality is "psychological." Sontag's overt opposition to psychology and psychologizing (the disdain for the "psychological subject" of Baldwin's play as "pure Tennessee Williams" is hard to miss) is a key feature of her critical armature—evident, for instance, in her frequent attacks on Freudian interpretation throughout the 1960s and in her championing of the antipsychological French nouveau roman. As Phillip Lopate has argued, however, a careful reading of Sontag's work reveals a perplexingly complex attitude toward psychology, "ranging from outright hostility to accommodation."[73] In line with this complexity, Sontag conceives of sexual identity both as psychological depth and performative surface.

If Sontag in her review of *Blues* uses metaphors of masking and veiling to frame her interpretation of how racial strife smuggles in sexual anguish, elsewhere in her 1960s work she deploys the figure of the mask to convey a diametrically opposed account of homosexuality and of identity more generally, whereby the notion of psychological essence is dismissed in favor of an understanding of personhood as pure performance. In *The Benefactor*, the homosexual character Jean-Jacques and friend of the narrator Hippolyte discourses on the centrality of masks to all social life: "the masks of one's job, one's class, one's citizenship, one's opinions. The masks of husband and wife, parent and child, master and slave. Even the masks of the body—male and female, ugly and beautiful, old and young." But while "most men, without resisting, put [their masks] on and wear them all their lives," homosexual men do not, for "homosexuality . . . is a kind of playfulness with masks. Try it [he urges Hippolyte] and you will see how it induces a welcome detachment from yourself."[74] Here Sontag mobilizes a notion of sociality as theatrical—a notion that has a long genealogy but that is aligned here with a homosexual literary tradition extending from (at least) Oscar Wilde to Jean Genet (and beyond) and that is also observable in gay subcultural attitudes, as Sontag will go on to elaborate in "Notes on 'Camp.'" While the heterosexual majority take their masks to be the truth of their selves, the double consciousness of the homosexual minority enables them to see through the fraud of authentic identity. Recognizing that life (even the body) is performative, homosexuals engage in a self-conscious "playfulness with masks"—what Jean-Jacques goes on to call "the homosexual parody."[75] The Wildean echoes are clear: Wilde wrote in "The Critic as Artist" that "man is least himself when he talks in his own person. Give him a mask and he will tell you the truth," and he wrote another essay called "The Truth of Masks."[76]

Wilde is of course the dedicatee and tutelary spirit of "Notes on 'Camp,'" but Wildean aestheticism also explicitly and implicitly informs Sontag's other central arguments in *Against Interpretation*. The title essay, which opens the book, has an epigraph from Wilde that announces Sontag's commitment to surface reading: "It is only shallow people who do not judge by appearances. The mystery of the world is the visible, not the invisible." In the following, equally polemical, essay "On Style," she argues: "Even if one were to define style as the manner or our appearing, this by no means necessarily entails an opposition between a style that one assumes and one's 'true' being. . . . In almost every case, our manner of appearing *is* our manner of being. The mask is the face" (18–19). Even when Wilde or other gay writers are not explicitly mentioned, Sontag's aestheticism is shot through with homosexual cultural reference—for instance, through repeated references to the venerable metaphor of the mask.

But at the time that Sontag came to prominence, the mask also had a meaning for gay men and lesbians that differed somewhat from the Wildean use of the metaphor. In *Masked Voices*, his study of letters to the homophile *ONE* magazine during the postwar, preliberation period, Craig Loftin argues for the aptness of the mask metaphor rather than the figure of the closet to describe Cold War homosexual experience, drawing on the use of the metaphor by the correspondents themselves, as well as its ubiquity in contemporaneous subcultural expression. For Loftin, the mask metaphor restores agency to the gay men and lesbians of this period in the definition of "their own sexual identities," while the closet metaphor "implies that gay people consciously denied their authentic selves," casting them as "lonely, scared, invisible, helpless victims."[77] For Loftin and others, the use of the closet metaphor by contemporary scholars ironically affirms the dominant Cold War homophobic discourse of the isolated individual.[78] The mask, in contrast, represents "an adaptive negotiation with a hostile society": "Situational passing as heterosexual—that is, wearing the mask—was not a denial of their authentic selves, but instead provided gay people with the necessary security that allowed them to consciously identify as homosexual and participate in a subaltern, camouflaged public sphere. Passing, ironically, brought their homosexual identities into sharper focus."[79] Though passing or masking in this account clarifies homosexual identity, thus indicating the imbrication of mask and face, the way in which the metaphor was used nevertheless points to the conviction of an authentic personhood behind the mask, as illustrated in an image from a *Mattachine Newsletter* cover from 1959 discussed by Loftin, in which a man seen from behind enters a venue of the "subaltern, camouflaged public sphere" of the gay world—a bar, or an apartment in which a gathering is being held—leaving his mask on a hat rack outside the door along with the masks of other venue attendees (Figure 3). My point here is not to catch out Cold War homosexuals in a "naïve" belief in authentic selves but rather to suggest the way in which the use of the mask metaphor in the postwar era indicates the consolidation of the liberationist conception of a gay self in need of emancipation, a conception that would be further developed with the emergence of the closet metaphor in the 1960s (for all that this metaphor can sometimes work to reinstate a conception of homosexuals as isolated victims).[80]

Sontag's use of the mask metaphor in "On Style," with its stress on a lamination of mask and face, appears to be at odds with this conception and to evoke the older, Wildean attitude. However, she leaves open the possibility of delamination

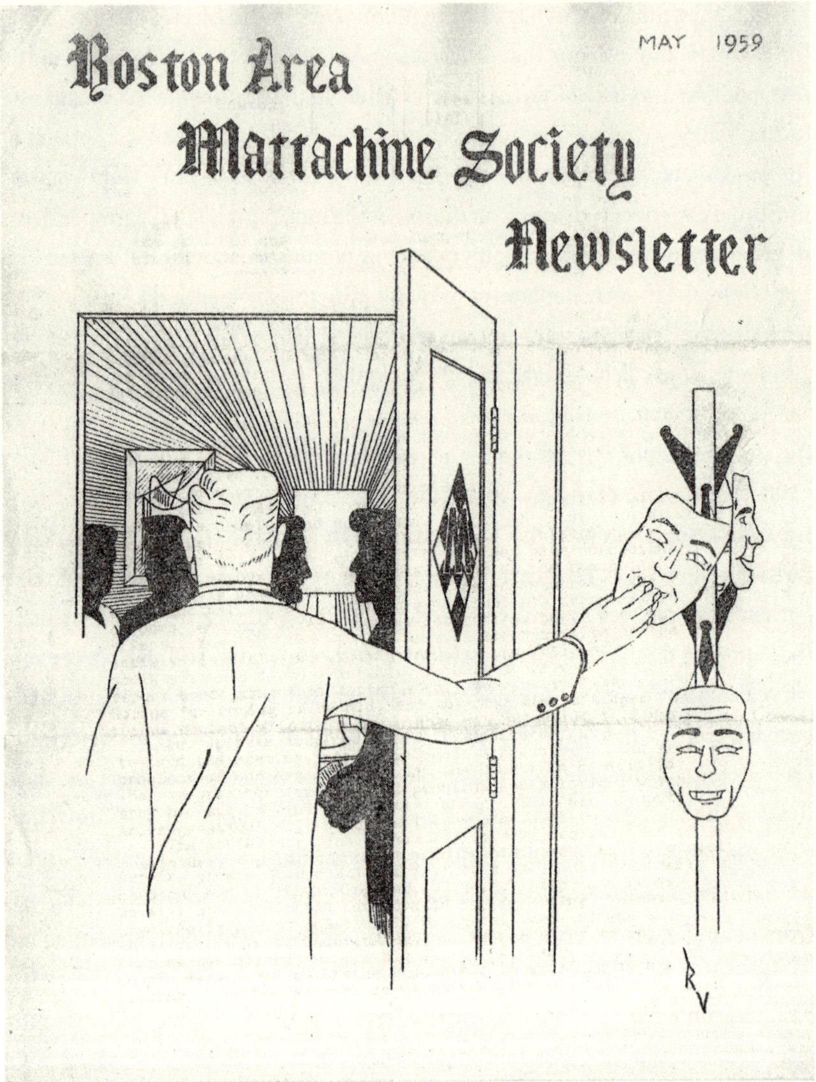

Figure 3. Cover of *Boston Area Mattachine Society Newsletter*, May 1959. Courtesy of ONE Archives at the USC Libraries.

in her odd and unelaborated concession that the disjunction between mask and face is possible but "extremely rare." Though she made her name with a revival of Wildean aestheticism, as my discussion of the theater review indicates, Sontag in fact tends to shuttle between depth and surface reading, between a stress on the hidden or the opaque and a stress on the evident or the transparent—a move that is intertwined with her own fort/da game of acknowledging and withdrawing her autobiographical presence from her writing. Sontag's use of the mask/face metaphor and other, related figures of depth and surface, and opacity and transparency, I suggest in the next section, aligns with or activates the possibility of a specifically lesbian meaning that indicates the closeness of her writing to other print media representations of the lesbian category.

Sexual *Persona*

Sontag returns to the figure of the mask in her second collection of essays, *Styles of Radical Will*, in an essay on Ingmar Bergman's film *Persona* (1966). The film centers on the relationship between a successful actress, Elisabet, who has suddenly ceased speaking and fallen into a state of near catatonia, and a young nurse, Alma, charged with caring for her. As the film progresses, Alma appears increasingly to take on the confusions of her patient, while Elisabet appears to regain her strength of mind. A landmark of 1960s European art cinema, *Persona* is replete with key defining features of that cinematic genre or style, including formal experimentation, an intense psychodramatic scenario, and—by the standards of the English-language cinema of the day—a notable erotic frankness. Of these three aspects, Sontag unsurprisingly privileges the film's formalism, gathering the other two beneath it. Challenging the common critical interpretation of the film as a "psychological chamber drama" involves for Sontag a downplaying of the erotic—as we have seen, the psychological and the sexual are fungible categories for her—but the erotic, and particularly the lesbian erotic, nonetheless importantly informs, and troubles, her account.[81]

Sontag does not deny the psychological dimension of *Persona* but stresses that psychologizing explanation of motives (especially with regard to the enigma of the actress's silence) are consigned by Bergman to "a relatively minor place" so that ultimately the film "takes a position beyond psychology—as it does, in an analogous sense, beyond eroticism." The film, she concedes, "certainly contains the materials of an erotic subject," "above all in the connection between the two women . . . which, in its feverish proximity, its caresses, its sheer passionateness (avowed by Alma in word, gesture, and fantasy) could hardly fail, it would seem, to suggest a powerful, if largely inhibited, sexual involvement" (131). Having raised this possibility of represented lesbian eroticism, Sontag rejects it, arguing that "the most purely sexual episode in the film" is the famous scene in which Alma recounts to Elisabet the "shameful secret" of her experience in an orgy on a beach with another woman and two men. For Sontag, the "violent sexual atmosphere" of this scene is generated by Alma's narration and has "nothing to do with the 'present' of the film and the relationship between the two women." Sontag concludes that Bergman has moved beyond the somewhat similar structure of his earlier film *The Silence*, "in which the love-hate relationship between the two sisters projected an unmistakable sexual energy," achieving in *Persona* "a more interesting situation by delicately excising or transcending the possible sexual implications of the tie between the two women" (132). For all the persuasiveness of Sontag's analysis, I venture that here it is perhaps Sontag carrying out the delicate act of excision. Despite the undoubted effectiveness of the "orgy" scene, the erotic intensity of many of the interactions between the two women is surely what gives the film much of its unsettling power—a power attested to, despite her subsequent excision of it, in Sontag's reference to the "charged, trancelike physical contact between the women" (130), as well as in her registration of "feverish proximity. . . caresses. . . sheer passionateness." In the very act of dismissing lesbian eroticism, Sontag lingers over it, presenting this ostensibly uninteresting interpretive possibility through an appositional aggregation of excited-sounding adjectives and nouns. (In her discussion of the orgy scene, Sontag also ignores the way Alma's narration is generated out of and affects the eroticized "present" of the relation between the two women; Elisabet's reaction shots are as important to the effect of the scene as Alma's speech.)

Sontag's account of the film bears reading in terms of the metaphor of the mask that the film calls attention to it via its title. *Persona*, as Sontag notes, is the Latin word for the mask worn by an actor, from which the English word "person" derives: "To be a person, then, is to possess a mask" (136). Sontag warns against a reductive interpretation of the film to a "story" about the relations between polarized opposites—"a patient and a nurse, a star and an ingenue, *alma* (soul) and *persona* (mask)" (130). "Such reduction to a story means, in the end, a reduction of Bergman's film to the single dimension of psychology" (130), repressing the formal complexity that actively resists this reduction, carried in the film's enigmatic narrative opacities (its utter confusion of "fantasy" and "reality") (128–30) and in its self-reflexive references to the technology of filmmaking (136–42). What I am suggesting, however, by highlighting Sontag's disavowed attention to lesbianism in her discussion of the film, is a masking of psychology, or lesbian erotics, by attention to form.[82] I do not claim to read Sontag's thoughts; rather, I read "Bergman's *Persona*," like the artworks Sontag favors in her 1960s criticism, as an "autonomous individual creation" that escapes her attempts to control it, even as the essay is, as she writes of the artwork, "an objectifying of the [authorial or creative] will."[83] If, as Sontag argues in "On Style," artworks must be understood as both "autonomous models of consciousness" and "dependent historical phenomen[a]," I suggest here that her own essay on *Persona*—qua artwork—brings together these two aspects in its admittedly fleeting modeling of lesbianism. Opening up lesbian possibility, the essay takes its place, however briefly, among the increasing number of media texts that chart an open lesbian identity. Moreover, the autonomy that for Sontag distinguishes the artwork, or at least the interesting artwork, operates here in such a way that *Persona* can be seen as commenting on Sontag's own commentary. Elisabet, the enigmatically mute star actress mirrors the star author Sontag, who is mute on the matter of her same-sexuality. In Elisabet's "powerful, if largely inhibited, sexual involvement" with Alma, however, the lesbianism that the star author Sontag does not publicly acknowledge is exhibited.

If her essay on *Persona* untypically leaves space open for consideration of lesbianism, Sontag's more usual silence on the matter can also be construed as a kind of speaking or communication. This is a point that she herself implies in "The Aesthetics of Silence," the opening essay of *Styles of Radical Will.* In this essay, Sontag moves between, and brings together, the avant-garde artworks that are her explicit concern (including, again, *Persona*) and the human subject: "A person who becomes silent becomes opaque for the other; somebody's silence opens up an array of possibilities for interpreting that silence, for imputing speech to it" (16). She continues, "The way in which opaqueness induces spiritual vertigo is the theme of Bergman's *Persona*," where Elisabet's decision not to speak can be viewed as both "a wish for ethical purity" and "a means of power, a species of sadism, a virtually inviolable position of strength from which she manipulates and confounds [Alma], who is charged with the burden of talking" (16). But, Sontag goes on to argue via a brief reading of Keats's "Ode on a Grecian Urn," "the opaqueness of silence can be conceived more positively, as free from anxiety." The "silence of eternity" invoked by the "Ode" intimates a utopian space, "prepar[ing] for a thought beyond thought, which must appear from the perspective of traditional thinking and the familiar uses of the mind as no thought at all—though it may rather be the emblem of new, 'difficult' thinking" (17). On the one hand, Sontag's account of silence in *Persona* points to the inevitably fraught nature of human relations; on the other, her account of Keats points to an aestheticizing, utopian impulse that transcends and remakes those relations through an expansion of consciousness (a consistent theme of Sontag's aesthetics). Whether considered in terms of its negative or its positive aspects, "silence keeps things 'open,'" as Sontag puts it elsewhere in the essay (20).

As we saw in the Introduction, it is the positive or utopian aspects of opacity or silence that structure Judith Butler's admonitions regarding the liberationist emphasis on coming out in her now-canonical 1991 essay "Imitation and Gender Insubordination." Butler argues: "Being 'out' always depends to some extent on being 'in.' . . . Being 'out' must produce the closet again and again in order to maintain itself as 'out.' In this sense, *outness* can only produce a new opacity." Butler rhetorically asks whether this "infinite postponement of the disclosure of 'gayness' . . . [is] to be lamented" or whether it is "*to be valued*, a site for the production of values?"[84] It is my argument in this book that queer theory, rather than consistently produce new "values" out of the infinite postponement of the disclosure of gayness, has come to take postponement to be a political value in and of itself. The critique of the category of gayness, while a salutary move that enabled much productive work during the early days of queer studies, has now been so incessantly rehearsed that its analytical force has been dulled. All too often, the demonstration of the instability of gayness forms both the founding assumption and the end point of queer argument. Moreover, the speculative and utopian projections that emerge from this premise (as in Butler's deconstruction of outness), once exciting, have become vapid in the decades-long process of their recycling. Its gaze fixed on the "beyond" of queerness, queer theory has scanted the positive values that inhere in open expressions of politicized gay and lesbian identity—indeed, it has repressed its own indebtedness to gay liberation, given that queer theory is liberation's direct, if distant, descendant.

If we consider Sontag's assertions about silence in relation to lesbian eroticism, as I have been arguing we are licensed to, her statements might on first glance be thought of as in accord with Butler's. Silence, says Sontag, like Butler about opacity, keeps things open. But her statement that "somebody's silence opens up an array of possibilities for interpreting that speech, for imputing speech to it," points to the possibilities of interpretation from "outside" the person rather than the personal agency from within opacity that is implicitly invoked by Butler. Rather than utopian possibility, or rather than *only* utopian possibility, Sontag's impersonal silence points toward the "dependent historical phenomenon" of lesbian categorization. If little to no innuendo about lesbianism per se gathered around Sontag in the 1960s, her perverse aura at least made room for that ascription or enabled the possibilities of queer recognition or self-recognition; this no doubt partly explains the "idolization" of her by many gays and lesbians in the years before her same-sexuality became widely known. Edmund White, in his account of meeting her in the 1970s, notes that she had "been my idol for many years," while Terry Castle writes that before meeting her in the 1990s, she had "idolised Sontag literally for decades."[85] It's probably needless to say that both writers go on to elaborate the feeling of letdown, but also attachment, that follows on meeting the "actual person"—as in Sontag's analogy of the movie star and North Vietnam in "Trip to Hanoi." As a star author, Sontag was introjected into the fantasy life of others, inviting this operation, paradoxically, through her own impersonality. As she put it in "The Aesthetics of Silence," in an observation indicating the importance of the psychological that she elsewhere downplayed, "Psychologically, distance often is linked with the most intense state of feeling, in which the coolness or impersonality with which something is treated measures the insatiable interest that thing has for us" (26).

4 From Camp to Counterculture

> Difficult to define a sensibility. Some years ago (1964) I wrote essay on camp, as test study in the idea of sensibility. Far from being a proponent. . . . My original choice was "morbidity." (From the neo-classical statues of Canova to the mummy art of the Capuchin catacombs of Palermo and Siracusa (Sicility [*sic*]) and Gaunjuato [*sic*] (Mexico). When that didn't work, I turned to "camp." To define the sensibility of Diane Arbus plunges me back into my original subject.
>
> Elliott Stein, eminence grise of many artists (me, Kenneth Anger)—underground cult founder of this taste: freaks, twins, Siamese twins, s-m, art nouveay [*sic*], voodoo art, camp, baroque, Strauss operas, Damia & Frehel & Milly, Romaine Brooks, cancer exhibit in Medical Museum in London, Tod Browning movies, Zumbo effigies in Glore, "Symbolist" art (de Knopff), Times Square sex book shops, black magic, motorcycle cults, *Justice* weekly. Elliott's room at the Hotel Verneuil in Paris was the 1960's. You could come into his room in the late 1950's and see the 1960's, see the future. Like the "magic box" ~~in Demian.~~[1]

THIS TYPEWRITTEN NOTE, held in Sontag's archive and dated in her hand "Nov 1972," appears to be work toward an essay or a speech on Diane Arbus, whose 1972 posthumous retrospective at New York's Museum of Modern Art was the germ of one of Sontag's most celebrated and controversial works, *On Photography* (1977).[2] Framing this early, fragmentary attempt to work through her interest in Arbus in the terms of that other celebrated and controversial text, "Notes on 'Camp,'" Sontag fixes on her friend the gay film historian and critic Elliott Stein (1928–2012), whom she met in Paris in the 1950s—"eminence grise of many artists (me, Kenneth Anger)" and "underground cult founder" of the camp sensibility. Or rather, she fixes on his room at the Hotel Verneuil, which houses or registers Stein's catholic range of outré tastes (freaks, s-m, art nouveau, Strauss operas, Times Square sex books shops, and so on), thus portending "the 1960's." Although Sontag elsewhere dismissed the perception of twentieth-century history in terms of decades, here she reproduces the idea that the 1960s represents a dramatic cultural shift—one in which for her, here at least, camp and sexual dissidence are fundamental.[3] One of the most widely contested claims in "Notes on 'Camp'" is that "the camp sensibility is disengaged, depoliticized—or at least apolitical."[4] Yet Sontag's position on the relations between gay culture and liberatory politics is more complex than this single, much-cited phrase suggests. In her 1960s work, Sontag both elaborates a view of gay subcultural expression as apolitical and aestheticized and discloses an investment in sexuality itself—and arguably queer sexuality above all—as a form of freedom.

Fragmentary though it is—a torn half-sheet of paper consisting of a bare nine sentences—Sontag's note at once attests to the centrality of camp to her intellectual and personal formation and manifests a characteristic strategy of disavowal. The project to speak on Arbus is framed in the terms of the project of "Notes on 'Camp'"—defining a sensibility—with the very wording echoing the earlier essay. The opening sentence fragment, "Difficult to define a sensibility," is a shorthand version of the statement in "Camp" that "a sensibility (as distinct from an idea) is one of the hardest things to talk about" (275). It is as if Sontag cannot at this stage get to Arbus except through the terms that camp provides; in fact, she does not get to Arbus at all, with the photographer's presence displaced by the clutter of Stein's room.[5] Sontag here more or less states that Stein's room was a primary source for "Notes on 'Camp,'" a datum of Sontag's career that figures importantly in the long-submerged, recently reclaimed history of Sontag's interactions with gay men and the gay subculture. If the absorbing miscellany of Stein's Paris room served as a model for what Terry Castle calls the "cataloguing mania" of that essay, here the description of the room itself returns to that compulsive listing, instituting a feedback loop between room and essay—an apt image of what her critics (and here Sontag herself) have insisted is the centrality of camp and "Camp" to her oeuvre.[6] Yet if camp is Sontag's "original subject," she was, she specifies, "far from . . . a proponent" of it. This Janus-faced position characterizes Sontag's attitude toward camp throughout her career. Famously or infamously, the essay begins with an announcement of ambivalence: "I am strongly drawn to Camp, and almost as strongly offended by it." "That is why I want to talk about it and why I can," Sontag continues. "For no one who wholeheartedly shares in a given sensibility can analyze it. . . .

To name a sensibility, to draw its contours and to recount its history, requires a deep sympathy modified by revulsion" (276).

The overkill of that modifying "revulsion" has been taken by many gay-affirmative critics to indicate the "phobic de-homosexualization of camp" that the essay as a whole performs.[7] Offended by Sontag's stance of (partial) offense, these critics characterize the essay as excising the gay presence from camp. Though the gay critique of the essay emerged early in the liberation period, it took on particular intensity (and particular intensity of offendedness) during the first flush of queer theory, reaching an early boiling point with D. A. Miller's 1989 essay "Sontag's Urbanity," with critics subsequently often simply citing Miller's essay "to proceed as if Sontag's homophobia had been proved beyond doubt."[8] More recently, after Sontag's lesbianism has become widely known, the essay has been reassessed as (a somewhat covert or "coy") assertion of homosexual identity, if not of the revolutionary cultural politics of the 1960s itself.[9] Sontag herself stated in a 1975 interview that "the diffusion of camp taste in the early '60s should probably be credited with a considerable if inadvertent role in the upsurge of feminist consciousness in the late 1960s," as camp's ironic attitude toward gender helped "undermine the credibility of certain stereotyped femininities," thus promoting the "depolarizing" of the sexes.[10] Unsurprisingly, given my arguments about Sontag up to this point, I incline toward the view that the essay feeds into a progressive sexual politics. This is not to claim Sontag as a gay liberationist *avant la lettre*. The distancing from gay culture in "Camp" (and elsewhere) is real, but so is the identification—and I argue here that identification outweighs distancing. The balance of feeling is carried in the presentation of Sontag's key term. While the title "Notes on 'Camp'" indicates that its topic is dubious enough to require handling with the tongs of scare quotes, the essay itself awards it an honorific initial capital, "as if it were a proper noun like Dadaism or Renaissance, formally elevating a subversive sensibility to the status of a style."[11] In the essay Sontag identifies camp as "one of the three great creative sensibilities," along with "high culture" and "extreme states of feeling, represented in much contemporary avant-garde art" (287). Bold at the time, given the critical consensus on the unassailability of seriousness, Sontag's elevation of camp has been characterized by gay critics as appropriation—a depoliticizing transformation of a mode of solidarity among preliberation urban gay men into a "wholly aesthetic" (287) sensibility that Sontag then claims for her own. Miller takes particular exception to Sontag's statement that "if homosexuals hadn't more or less invented Camp, someone else would" (291); the act of severing camp from gay men "thus performed," Miller argues, "someone else could invent Camp, and who better than the author of this manifestly inventive and authoritative essay?"[12] The index to the collection *The Poetics and Politics of Camp* (1994) actually cross-references Sontag with "appropriation."

Although I maintain that charges of appropriation are overblown, they do nevertheless get at something about Sontag's complex relations with the urban gay subculture, which she alternately drew on, promoted, defended, and disavowed. Ironically, Sontag's perceived erasure of gay men from the history of camp prompted liberationist sentiment. As Fabio Cleto argues, "Despite its likely (or declared) intentions . . . the very publication of Sontag's piece" and the subsequent mainstreaming of camp taste gave rise to "a counter-process . . . in which the reclaiming of camp and the constitution of a confrontationist identity went in concert."[13] Inscribing within its pages the "ethnicity model" of gayness, "Camp" helped consolidate gay identity and has continued to act as a rallying point around which (usually disgruntled, occasionally delighted) gay critics enact that identity. At the same time that it disseminated the idea of ethnic gayness, "Camp," along with other Sontag essays from the 1960s, helped promote the emphasis on the polymorphous that would be a countervailing, but arguably equally important, aspect of the cultural politics of gay liberation. In what follows, I argue that Sontag, like other celebrities, helped "co-ordinat[e] the ideas, choices and actions of large numbers of people"[14]—in this case, specifically in relation to sexual dissidence. First, to flesh out the complex relations between gay culture and Sontag's celebrity career in the 1960s, I interpret her friendships with two gay writers, Stein and Alfred Chester, exploring how they enabled her career and also how their lesser fame was alternatively boosted and blocked by Sontag. I then turn to a reading of "Notes on 'Camp'" and its reception, arguing that what one hostile critic called the "celebrity" of camp taste that the essay unleashed discloses the intertwinement of male homosexual culture and mass-mediatized fame in Sontag's career specifically.[15] Extending the previous chapter's account of the interplay between surface and depth in Sontag's star image, I reflect on how the essay's dialectic of partly visible, partly hidden authorial personhood both feeds into and works against a nascent gay politics. Picking up on the liberatory hints within "Camp" and other essays, I consider how Sontag as celebrity intellectual helped disseminate ideas of sexual revolution and consequently set the coordinates of what came to be known as the "counterculture."

Names

Let's begin by returning to Elliott Stein and his room. In Paris and, from the late 1960s, in New York, Stein continued the role of influencer attested to by Sontag, becoming a generative, if somewhat obscure, figure in American film culture, a "critic's critic" who never published a book but who helped shape the taste of many better-known writers throughout his long career as a reviewer and programmer.[16] In an intriguing coincidence for this book's argument, Stein's career as male muse extends, according to some reports, to the work of Baldwin, with his Paris room supposedly inspiring the chaos of the eponymous *Giovanni's Room*. If these reports are accurate, Baldwin's rendition of the room as a squalid mess might be seen as supporting the claim I made about Baldwin's repudiation of camp (in his writing, if not in his public persona); the affect of claustrophobic horror invoked in Baldwin's novel by Giovanni's *chambre de bonne* is a marked contrast with the mix of disconcertion and fascination that characterizes Sontag's response to Stein's room.[17] My view of Sontag's response is not only an extrapolation from her attitudes in "Notes on 'Camp' "; disconcertion and fascination also structure the lengthy description of the room of the homosexual character Jean-Jacques in *The Benefactor*. Clearly modeled on Stein's, the room is jam-packed with "exaggerated, trivial, and vulgar artifacts," including "a Boy Scout hat, an *art nouveau* mirror with a snake design, a beaded lamp, a piece of cemetery statuary, a circus poster, a set of marionettes representing Bluebeard and eight wives, a white-and-green wool rug with the shape and design of an American dollar bill."[18] The passage prefigures Sontag's essay not only in its "cataloguing mania" but also in Hippolyte the narrator's professions of confusion and rejection. Hippolyte is mystified about why Jean-Jacques, who has "scrupulous judgement in all the arts," should collect such objects and notes, with a characteristically Sontagian gesture of disavowal, that "I did not share these enthusiasms" (54). The attention lavished on Jean-Jacques's "strange treasure" (53), however, indicates that attraction is mixed in with repudiation. Read retrospectively, it is as if the passage is gearing up for the essay. In response to Hippolyte's confusion, Jean-Jacques states that "you will never understand, but sometime I will explain it to you anyway" (54), forecasting Sontag's attempt to think through camp taste.

Stein's role as the inspiration for "Notes on 'Camp' " was unambiguously asserted by the American composer and diarist Ned Rorem in his memoir *Knowing When to Stop* (1994): "Susan Sontag told me, circa 1966, that Elliott's room, no less than his pince-sans-rire rhetoric was the chief source for her 'Notes on

Camp.' . . . Since there is no record of Susan telling this to anyone else, I'll give Elliott credit where it's due."[19] Although Sontag's drafted note suggests that she at least considered putting Stein's influence on record, Rorem's statement chimes with the persistent insinuation across Sontag commentary that she appropriated from, or failed to give due acknowledgment to the influence of, the gay men with whom she fraternized—a charge also made, as we've seen, in regard to the broader context of the gay subculture with relation to "Notes."

The influence of experimental American novelist and essayist Alfred Chester (1928–71) has been similarly figured as insufficiently acknowledged, with Chester's influence on Sontag claimed as an alternative origin of "Camp." In a brief reminiscence of Chester, Ira Cohen describes Sontag as "a onetime friend to whom Alfred gave the secret of Camp."[20] And Chester's memorialist and champion, the poet Edward Field, asserts in his memoir *The Man Who Would Marry Susan Sontag* (2005) that Sontag's "ideas for the essay largely came from discussions she had had with [Chester] about W. H. Auden's article on Oscar Wilde," which had appeared in the *New Yorker* in 1963.[21] The Auden piece is actually a sober assessment that barely touches on Wilde's camp aesthetic; though Chester's attitudes and theatrical persona may have played their part in Sontag's conception, Stein does seem a more likely immediate influence. But I'm wary of overstating the influence of Stein, or of anyone else. While Stein may have provided the initial impetus, Sontag's extensive working notes on the essay testify that "Camp" appeared only after an intense period of independent research.[22] When one reads through the memoirs of Rorem and others, the cloud of implications of appropriation can tend to obscure the extent to which the essay is, in Miller's words, "manifestly inventive and authoritative."

Chester was for a time a close friend of Sontag's and a key facilitator of her early career. Sontag met him in 1958 in Paris through her then-lover Harriet Sohmers. Back in New York, Sohmers, Sontag, and Chester, together with Sohmers's new lover María Irene Fornés (who subsequently became Sontag's partner), became an inseparable quartet at cultural events and Greenwich Village parties during the early 1960s. As the interchanges of lovers suggest, the four-way relationship was emotionally complex, with the talented but troubled Chester thriving on the attentions of, and the intrigues between, these three glamorous lesbians yet also inclined temperamentally to foment fallings out. Chester, then enjoying a brief period of notoriety in the New York literary world, helped Sontag by introducing her to other well-known writers and editors, but he became increasingly mistrustful of her. Conflicted in his own relation to fame, he was both disgusted by and envious of Sontag's careerist drive and her accession to celebrity.[23] Leaving his own chance for celebrity behind, Chester moved to Tangier in 1963, where he associated with the circle around Paul and Jane Bowles and where Sontag paid him a disastrous visit in 1965. Chester, suffering a psychotic break, became convinced that Sontag wanted to steal his Moroccan boyfriend, then later proposed marriage to her.[24] His erratic behavior put Sontag in fear of him, "afraid even of physical attack."[25] The Tangier episode put an end to their difficult friendship. Yet Chester retained a presence in Sontag's emotional and artistic life. In 1989 Sontag rejected Edward Field's requests to write anything for a collection of republished work by Chester yet noted that she felt "moved and sad" whenever she thought of him.[26] More ambiguously, Sontag lifted Chester's title for a never-completed novel, *I, Etcetera*, for her 1978 collection of short stories.[27]

In 1966 the writer and publisher Richard Kluger, unaware of the rift between Sontag and Chester, asked her to supply a blurb for Chester's novel *The Exquisite Corpse*, which Kluger, then beginning a stint at Simon and Schuster, had, in his words, "stuck his neck out for."[28] Although Kluger had accepted Sontag's refusal to write an endorsement, he went ahead and included a more general statement about her admiration for Chester on the dust jacket. After seeing an advance copy of the book that had been sent to her close friend, the poet and translator Richard Howard, Sontag successfully requested that Simon and Schuster remove the reference to her from the jacket. In 1967, in the aftermath of this to-do, Kluger wrote Sontag a letter, copied to Roger Straus; to the literary agent Candida Donadio, who often advised Sontag on business matters; and to Richard Howard. In it he recorded her refusal to blurb the book as taking the form of "saying something like, 'I am tired of playing den mother to America's homosexuals.' " He set out a vindication for his having included Sontag's name on the jacket—she had expressed her admiration of Chester to Kluger in conversation, and she had written a letter to the *New York Times Book Review* praising Chester in 1964—and expressed disappointment that the beginning of his career in publishing had been marked by her "undeserved rebuke" of him.[29] In a letter replying to Kluger, Sontag stated that she wanted to "say . . . a couple of things, for the record, since there now seems to be a 'record' and one being distributed in a number of copies." She objected to the "line of reasoning" that led him to conclude "that, while I would refuse to support *this particular book*, I would not mind being the only critic mentioned who admires Alfred's *entire work*." She also stated that she saw his repetition of her "flippant remark about homosexuals" in a "public letter" as "nothing less than malicious."[30]

That Sontag saw herself—or saw others as seeing her—as a den mother to the collective body of America's homosexuals indicates the importance of pre-Stonewall gay male culture to Sontag's formation as a celebrity intellectual. And that Sontag saw Kluger's putting her "flippant remark" on the "record," in a "public letter," as "malicious," indicates how deeply, and contrarily, her anxieties about her association with gay men ran.[31] In her writing Sontag registered, albeit subtly, her indebtedness to gay culture and helped promote its distinctive profile, most famously in "Camp." As I will show, and in marked contrast with the view of her taken by queer theorists in the 1990s, in the 1960s Sontag was generally understood as a defender of camp and therefore of homosexuals. The evidence for this understanding was not confined to the famous essay. The 1964 letter to the *New York Times Book Review* mentioned by Kluger, for example, was prompted by a damning, homophobic review by Saul Maloff of Chester's book of short stories *Behold Goliath*. Praising the stories as "ingeniously fashioned and intelligent" and pronouncing "at least half" of them "beautiful achievements," Sontag scored as "impudent" the way that Maloff's "aversion to homosexuality makes him feel he has the license to lecture [Chester] as to how to handle 'this treacherously difficult theme.' "[32] Yet Sontag also disliked being too closely identified with the gay world, and this partly explains her subsequent uneasiness about her breakthrough essay, or at least its organizing concept. In her letter to Kluger, Sontag took particular exception to his copying-in of Howard, which she described as "in extremely poor taste"; Howard's only connection with the matter, as Sontag states, was that he had shown her the copy of Chester's novel with her name on the jacket, but the fact that Howard was gay explains her strong words, the charges of malice and poor taste.[33] Apparently wanting no longer to be associated in the public mind with gay men, Sontag nevertheless was alarmed that her expression of that desire, however flippant, should be made known to a gay man who was emotionally and intellectually important to her.

Accumulating Attention

In his letter Kluger stated that he had hoped Sontag would reconsider her initial refusal to blurb Chester's book, "though I knew you were tired of having your name batted around by so many people for so many reasons."[34] By 1966 Sontag was a celebrity on the cultural scene, meaning, as Kluger intimates, that she had little control over the wide circulation of her name in the public sphere. Yet as a celebrity, Sontag also wielded the power of endorsement, of supplying or not supplying her imprimatur to the work of others. In choosing in this instance to withhold her name, removing an endorsement from what turned out to be his last book published during his lifetime, Chester's own name was arguably more certainly relegated to obscurity.[35] In his novella *The Foot* (completed 1966, published 1970), Chester took a kind of revenge on his famous former friend, fictionalizing her as two characters, both called Mary Monday, who figure the split between person and image. The burlesquing of Sontag's famous name is the least part of Chester's "maniacal dissection" of her celebrity persona.[36] Mary is subjected to various sexual indignities, and there are references to her "ass" and her "vastly hairy, silky, black" "cunt."[37] In a metafictional moment, the narrator effectively creates Mary before the reader's eyes, recalling Chester's instrumental role in securing Sontag's New York fame and phantasmically reversing the relations of influence and patronage that were in place between the two writers by 1966.[38]

Sontag's status as a name—as a sought-after endorser, as an authority to be appealed to, or as a prominent figure to be repudiated—indicates her considerable capital in the "attention economy." Formulated as an idea by the political scientist Herbert Simon, and subsequently taken up by social scientists, cultural theorists, and business strategists, the attention economy refers, in Simon's words, to how an "information-rich world" creates "a poverty of attention."[39] In such a world, as the social theorist Georg Franck puts it, celebrity is "simply the status of being a major earner of attention."[40] With regard to the practice of celebrity endorsement in relation to the attention economy, Robert van Krieken notes that it "illustrates the self-reproducing 'perpetual motion' character of attention capital": endorsements both enhance the reputation of the endorsed person or product and further publicize the celebrity's own name.[41] A similar process is at work when the name of the famous person gets "dropped" by a lesser-known author or artist, expanding the attention-getting capacity of an artwork, memoir, or interview (and, again, making a small addition to the famous person's fame). The gossipy mention of Sontag ("Susan Sontag told me . . . ") by the inveterate name-dropper Ned Rorem is exemplary; the primary appeal for many readers of Rorem's diaries and memoirs is the intimate glimpses they afford of literary and artistic celebrities rather than an interest in Rorem himself.

Building on Franck's definition of celebrity as "simply the status of being a major earner of attention," van Krieken argues that "attention can be thought of as a form of risk-capital, where risk taking can lead to massive windfalls which can then be converted with new projects into even more celebrity (attention) capital."[42] This understanding of attention might productively be applied to Sontag's career as a celebrity intellectual renowned for spectacular changes of position and riskily provocative pronouncements (her announcement that "communism is fascism with a human face" in 1978, her insistence on the "courage" of the 9/11 hijackers, and so on).[43] Identifying Sontag with the risk-taking strategies of celebrity culture described by van Krieken attributes to her a calculatedness or even a cynicism that is not customarily applied to discussions of literary fame. But if we accept that Sontag was "driven," an allowance for calculation on her part can surely be made. There was, I'd suggest, a fair amount of conscious risk taking involved in Sontag's publication of "Notes on 'Camp,'" though with the difference from the other moments of her career that I've just singled out that the essay was not written by a celebrity but was instead the "breakthrough" that saw Sontag vaulted from relative obscurity into the brightly lit arena of international media attention. Sontag didn't necessarily seek or expect the kind of mass-mediatized fame that the essay brought; but she did, I suggest, court controversy through the essay's provocative position taking. The provocation is conveyed in Sontag's statement, twenty years after its publication, that "Camp" "really was written for Lionel Trilling. I wanted him to read this essay and think about something besides Matthew Arnold."[44] This statement retrospectively throws down the gauntlet not only to Trilling but implicitly to the New York intellectuals collectively, indicating that Sontag sought an "accumulation" of attention, as van Krieken would put it, via her articulation of an unsanctioned aesthetic perspective—though as we'll see, Sontag insisted that the attention she sought was confined to the readership of *Partisan Review*.[45] If "Camp" made Sontag's name, it made it in circles in which she claimed she had no interest. Structured by ambivalence toward its object, "Camp" itself became an object of ambivalence for Sontag, generating a force field in which uneasy feelings about media fame and homosexuality were intertwined.

In "Some Notes on 'Notes on Camp,'" a highly speculative, richly suggestive reading, Terry Castle argues that Sontag's "uncomfortable" relation to her essay in the decades following its publication is a defensive response to its "private content," the "tumultuous world of feeling" that is inadequately masked by its "cool, analytic, supposedly educative pose" and gestured toward in the essay's "cataloguing mania."[46] In a conjecture compatible with the claim I made earlier about how Sontag's veiled autobiographical references have tended to elicit flashes of fellow feeling in gay and lesbian readers, Castle writes, "I can't help but feel she wants both to reveal herself—the books she has read, the films she's seen, the personalities she has encountered, what she thinks is funny, what she thinks is sexy, what she thinks is dumb, *who she is, in other words*—and to seduce her imaginary reader into some corresponding self-revelation" (22). If other readers have found Sontag's writing (and "Camp" in particular) insufficiently confessional, Castle makes a case for the essay, "viewed in hindsight," as "part of a coy, yet now-unmissable 'coming out' " (29). The paradox of a coy coming out captures the interplay of surface and depth, of withdrawal and accessibility that I have argued characterizes Sontag's queer star persona. Additionally, Castle's response to Sontag's essay, and to Sontag's persona more generally, returns us to Roach's account of the way in which the celebrity image reflects back to the audience their own needs and desires.

Castle notes insinuations of queer feeling that Sontag's earlier gay critics missed or scanted: for instance, the fact that the essay's opening sentence—"Many things in the world have not been named; and many things, even if they have been named, have never been described"—might be read as referring autobiographically to Sontag's lesbianism as well as to the camp sensibility and the fact that almost all of the actresses whom she associates with camp (Garbo, Barbara Stanwyck, Tallulah Bankhead, Edwige Feullière) "were either lesbian or bisexual in inclination or noted for playing lesbian characters. She might as well have been semaphoring her sapphic tastes via such a listing" (30). Sontag's gay critics have seldom duly acknowledged that, her opening caveats aside, the essay is almost entirely uncritical—positive where it is not studiedly neutral (and the very studiedness, can, as Castle argues, be read as not-too-convincingly masking attraction).

Castle speculates that Sontag later "repudiated" camp and "Camp" because the essay was too obvious about her own sexuality and because it symbolically registered the "fierce emotions" of "pain, fear, abandonment, [and] rage" (30) rooted in Sontag's "family romance" (26), which Castle sees as typifying queer childhood experience. Proposing that "a childhood sense of 'slight' " is "part of camp's psychic underpinning," Castle notes that "it is hardly surprising that the camp sensibility should flourish among gay men and women" (30). Compelling though Castle's reading is, she perhaps overstates the deflective "contempt" that Sontag felt for the essay (31). It's true that Sontag indicated that she was "over" "Camp"—and camp—almost as soon as the essay was published. The headline for a 1966 feature on her in the *Columbia Owl*—"A Bored Susan Sontag: 'I Think Camp Should Be Retired' "—sums up the attitude she struck in the wake of the essay's notoriety (while also of course trading on that notoriety).[47] But the record of Sontag's later comments on the essay indicates its continuing, if conflict-ridden, importance—for instance, in the note from her archives and in her 1975 comment that the diffusion of camp contributed to "the upsurge of feminist consciousness in the late 1960s."

The conflict is clearly set out in Sontag's response to the inevitable question about camp during a 1984 Q&A session with William Gass's students at Washington University. Sontag states that she wrote the essay "when I was young and naïve, and didn't know what happened to serious work that got flashed on the wide screen of the media." The essay, she avers, "was meant for the very small audience" of *Partisan Review*, the magazine that had been the object of her adolescent dreams:

> I dreamed about growing up and moving to New York and writing for *Partisan Review*, for a magazine which had at most ten thousand readers. Those were all the readers I wanted to have—until I was dead of course [laughter]. . . . The essay was destined for people who read Hannah Arendt and Lionel Trilling and R.P. Blackmur. As a matter of fact, it really was written for Lionel Trilling. I wanted him to read this essay and think about something besides Matthew Arnold. . . .
>
> But the essay became something else, a hot tip in the world press. And so it became unusable. I love that essay; I think it's one of the best essays I ever wrote. But ideas can be ruined. Words can be ruined.[48]

Here, at a distance of twenty years from the publication of "Camp," Sontag does not dismiss or disavow the essay but professes her love for and pride in it. It has been "ruined" because it was taken up and debased by "the media," by which she means of course the "mass" media—a little magazine like *Partisan Review*, with its select readership, is exempted from the taints of commerce and publicity attached to more widely read and viewed texts. These 1984 comments are to an extent in accord with comments she made closer to the time of the essay's first appearance. In her interview with the *Columbia Owl* Sontag insisted, "I made a particular use of the word 'camp' and then other people started using it in ways that had nothing to do with me or the way I used it. If I had to do it all over again, I don't even know if I would write the essay. If I did I would certainly try and have it published in a more obscure journal."[49] And in a 1967 interview with Nora Ephron, she said, "I [used] that essay to rescue the word from a clique use, and instead it broadened to a public use more vulgar than before. I had no idea it would become what it did. If I'd wanted a lot of people to read it, I wouldn't have printed it in *Partisan Review*. I discovered you can't choose your audience."[50] As all three sets of comments indicate, "Camp" came for Sontag to stand for the operations of media fame. It's not, I think, an overstatement to say that Sontag displaced her feelings about celebrity onto the essay so that her occasional professions of rejection then work to disavow not only the "tumultuous world" of queer feeling, as Castle argues, but also the role of "pop celebrity" that Sontag felt was being thrust upon her and that she contrasted favorably with good kinds of fame—being known by the fit audience though few who read *Partisan Review* while she was alive, on the one hand, and Parnassian posthumous fame, on the other. There is, however, probably an element of disingenuousness in Sontag's position here, chiming with the disingenuousness with which she treated her stardom generally, in that *Partisan Review* had a well-established influence beyond its small readership. As Trilling noted in 1966, the New York intellectuals, and by implication *Partisan Review*, were "bound by organic filaments to groups less culturally fluent. . . . The great communications industries do not exactly rely for their content and methods upon the class of New York intellectuals, yet journalism and television show its effects."[51]

Sontag's admission that she used her essay to "rescue the word ['camp'] from a clique use" might be read as evidencing the charges of the "de-gaying" and appropriation of camp leveled at her by Miller and others. The address to Trilling might seem to support this reading, with Sontag presenting the practice of camp reading for consideration and possible assimilation by Trilling and his confreres. But such an interpretation misses, of course, Sontag's uneasy relationship with the New York intellectuals. There is something barbed about Sontag's offering up of queer taste to the resolutely heteronormative and routinely homophobic world of the New York intellectuals, and if Trilling characteristically treated Sontag's provocation with serene indifference, the appalled responses of Howe and others indicate that the barb had its effect.

In his discussion of the literary dedication, Gérard Genette states that he "know[s] of no example of a work addressed to one person and dedicated to another" and notes that "in the realm of works of passion, in any case, that situation could prove quite interesting."[52] If we agree with Castle that "Camp" is to be understood as a work of passion, in which the tumult of queer feeling is inadequately masked by its cool, pedagogical posture, the essay's bifurcated structure of address/dedication is indeed "interesting" for what it indicates about Sontag's publicization of gay subcultural expression. The essay's dedication to Wilde, the famous homosexual martyr of the modern era, might be read as an act of homosexual solidarity—albeit an indirect one. The covert address to Trilling, meanwhile, puts a homosexually inflected cultural practice in his face (and in those of his fellow liberal critics), while the suppression of his proper name, and those of other contemporary defenders of moral seriousness, undermines the potency of the entrenched liberal position that trades on the gravitas of those names.

Additionally, with regard to the homosexual valences of Sontag's writing from this period, it's worth recalling that the book in which "Camp" was republished, *Against Interpretation*, was dedicated to the bisexual artist Paul Thek. Genette notes that "dedicating a work is a public act that the reader is, as it were, called on to witness. . . . The dedication always is a matter of demonstration, ostentation, exhibition: it proclaims a relationship, whether intellectual or personal, actual or symbolic, and this proclamation is always at the service of the work, as a reason for elevating the work's standing or as a theme for commentary."[53] Though Thek was relatively unknown as an artist and not necessarily known for his queerness, the dedication to him conjoined with the dedication to the famously queer Wilde, may be seen as calling on the reader (even if only the "in-the-know" reader) to witness a relationship of amity and allegiance with the gay artistic community and with the urban gay subculture in which that community thrived.

Attacks and Defenses

Certainly, critics of the time did not need to be convinced of Sontag's largely sympathetic attitude to homosexuals—or of camp's connection to homosexuality. In December 1964 *Time* precipitated the dissemination of camp by publishing a summary of the essay, noting that "Miss Sontag is not one to deny" the homosexual implications of camp.[54] Camp's ascendancy was tracked in an article by Thomas Meehan in the *New York Times Magazine* in March 1965, in which Sontag's "defense of camp" was ranged against "an anti-camp New York psychiatrist," whose attack mobilized the full battery of psychoanalytic castigations of homosexuality: "Camp is a form of regression, a rather sentimental and adolescent way of flying in the face of authority. . . . Camp is a way of running from life and its real responsibilities. . . . It's not only extremely childish but also potentially dangerous to society—it's sick and decadent."[55] Homophobic attack was also the strategy of the critic John Simon's response to the essay, in a letter that appeared in the winter 1965 issue of *Partisan Review*. Simon began by noting Sontag's omission of Eric Partridge's definition of camp in *A Dictionary of Slang* as "effeminate, esp. homosexual mannerisms of speech and gesture." Quoting Sontag's characterizations of the gay subculture, Simon accused Sontag of "accept[ing] without challenge a 'self-elected class, mainly homosexuals' as the 'aristocrats of taste,'" and he cast camp's supposed erosion of standards in gay-baiting terms, charging it with the "purpose" of "making the good undistinguishable from the bad, the purposive submerged in the sterile, backwards as good as forwards. Once the *outré* and the inverted become the quotidian, the aberrant becomes the order of the day."[56] Simon anxiously forecasts the "spread" of camp, whereby "the heterosexual Smiths will be induced, through the mediation of the androgynous 'fashion world' to keep up with the homosexual Joneses," evoking, as James Penner notes, "the spectacle of queer culture dominating the cultural scene."[57] Simon's letter thus fed into the endlessly circulated midcentury account of the unhealthy influence of gay men in the arts, identifying camp as a particularly effective tool of this "imagined conspiracy."[58]

Vivian Gornick subsequently took up the theme in a rabid piece in the *Village Voice* in April 1966, "It's a Queer Hand Stoking the Campfire." Stating flatly that "popular culture is now in the hands of the homosexuals," Gornick went on to enumerate the deleterious effects of camp on the arts and on "middle-class taste." Sontag's essay is dubbed "brilliant" but in the next breath derided as "nonsense." Camp is not "tender," as Sontag writes in the essay, but "arch, sly, hysterical, schizophrenic," a "malicious fairy's joke . . . on the middle classes."[59] It is "the homosexual temperament," Gornick argued, "which is guiding the progress of Pop art . . . making 'underground' movies, selling cast-iron lamps shaped like roses to sophisticated schoolteachers" (1) and producing a modish homosexual literature "frightening in its steely-eyed slickness, its language of surfaces, its heartlessness, its unbearable loathing of humanity" (21). Gornick's example of the latter is Hubert Selby's *Last Exit to Brooklyn* (1964); novels "such as *Giovanni's Room* and *Another Country*," which "merely [deal] with homosexual love" are "quite another matter altogether" (21). No doubt Baldwin's own dislike of camp and of effeminacy was congenial; Baldwin's bracketing "homosexual love" off from subcultural manifestations is compatible with Gornick's offense at "the homosexual culture" (20), which she attempts to keep distinct from anti-homosexual prejudice per se, noting as she does that "the homosexual," like "the Jew and the Negro," is excluded from "the great heterosexual WASP banquet" (1). But this lip service to gay oppression is utterly undermined by the fevered contempt with which Gornick paints "the homosexual" as "a brutal caricature of the femaleness he so violently rejects. . . . He has become the woman he despises, in a form grotesquely frivolous and vicious" (20).

In his book about the midcentury conspiracy theory of gay influence in the arts, Michael Sherry notes that an antigay attitude was widely acceptable, indeed "hip," in leftist circles in the mid-1960s, as Gornick's piece in the eminently hip *Village Voice* demonstrates: "Just when the spirit of liberation was rising—in black protest, a new feminism, antiwar activism, the counterculture—its extension to queers was resisted."[60] If straight New Leftists could (sometimes) recognize the structural oppression of homosexuals, by and large this did not translate to any interest in the transformation of this situation. The common view of homosexuality as "sick and decadent" (to requote Meehan's psychiatrist) underwrote this position. In her piece Gornick deploys against homosexuality the well-worn charge of regression (evident as well in the psychiatrist's comments in Meehan's piece and in Simon's accusation that camp makes "backwards as good as forwards"), singling out pop art as a particularly baleful example of the influence of camp that has "set the course of American art back some hundred years" (20).[61] Homosexuals were a regressive force rather than associated with the forward-oriented energies of liberation and revolution, developments that leftists were beginning to talk about as serious possibilities in the mid-1960s. There were important exceptions to the left disdain for homosexuality, of course, including the influential Grove Press, which published Jean Genet and John Rechy's best-selling *City of Night* (1963), and bohemian artistic and literary movements, such as the Beats and the San Francisco Renaissance, in which straight and homosexual men mingled, albeit not always entirely comfortably. But in general, spokespeople of the New Left tended to iterate and even exceed the homophobia that characterized conservative cultural commentary.[62]

As indicated, Sontag's reaction to this homophobic climate was defensive, though her terms were muted. In a response to Simon's attack, which was printed beneath his letter, Sontag in some ways moved to distance herself from camp, activating the essay's opening caveats in a way not much in evidence in the essay itself. Simon, she charges, is unwilling or unable "to distinguish what he calls 'tribute' from explication and analysis."[63] "What can I say," she asks of Simon's allegation that she "accepts without challenge" the homosexual influence on taste, "but sigh? Is Mr. Simon totally unable to tell approving of something from describing it?" But Sontag also hinted at Simon's homosexual panic, responding to his anxiety that camp will make the good undistinguishable from the bad by stating, "Mr. Simon, no one is trying to contaminate your bodily fluids." And she concluded by accusing Simon of "waving the red herring of homosexuality" with his opening quotation of Partridge; "the connection between homosexuality and camp taste—which I tried to explain in the 'Notes'—is a part of the phenomenon, not an argument against it."[64]

Sherry contends that "Camp" is a defense of "queer creativity" that "deploys an idiom rooted in attacks on it"—that is, on "ideas about queers prone to decorative artifice—as lacking the depth to address 'the moral sense.'"[65] Thus, for all its reticence, Sontag's defense might be understood as counterdiscursive—an assertion of the value of queer culture that revalues the terms of antiqueer condemnation. In a much-cited moment in "Camp," Sontag compares the homosexual affinity for camp with the Jewish "affinity for liberal and reformist causes," an analogy that is "not frivolously chosen," in that "Jews and homosexuals are the outstanding creative minorities in contemporary urban culture. . . . The two pioneering forces of modern sensibility are Jewish moral seriousness and homosexual aestheticism and irony." Both sensibilities, she argues, are in part self-legitimating: "The Jews pinned their hopes for integrating into modern society on promoting the moral sense. Homosexuals have pinned their integration into society on promoting the aesthetic sense" (290). Sherry finds the comparison between the "political sensibility" of Jewish liberalism and the aesthetic sensibility of camp "strained."[66] But, in line with the deliberately provocative stance indicated by Sontag's address of the essay to Trilling, the comparison works slyly and audaciously to align the (liberal, largely Jewish) milieu of the New York intellectuals, with their vaunted "moral sense," and the gay world, positing parity between sanctioned and unsanctioned sensibilities.

Sherry is troubled by what he sees as Sontag's "extravagantly generalized" language about homosexuals and her "strikingly specific" statements about "what they had decided" about integration through promotion of the aesthetic sense. But Sontag qualifies her generalizations by noting that the homosexual (and Jewish) "creative minorities" she describes are phenomena of "contemporary urban culture." Particularizing gay culture in this way, Sontag not only points toward the subcultural embeddedness of camp; she also indicates the limits of the gay culture of which she speaks—that is, that "gay culture," as Mark Finch would put it in 1986, "means something more specific than it pretends: a discursive system developed out of a metropolitan, white, middle-class and male gay community."[67] Sontag does not use the language of race and class, of course. But, in another gesture toward specificity, on the first page of "Camp" she notes that camp is "a private code, a badge of identification even, among small urban cliques" (275): a coded comment on codification that indicates, for those in the know, the role of camp in the solidification of "ethnic" gay identity. The comment is immediately followed by a reference to Christopher Isherwood's "lazy two-page sketch" on camp in *The World in the Evening* (1954), a knowing reference to a gay author's account of the connection between the subculture and camp, albeit made in the form of a dismissal that enables the elaboration of Sontag's contrastively "authoritative and inventive" discussion. Though Sontag stood accused in the 1990s of dehomosexualizing camp, the essay is actually quite clear about its subcultural importance, while refusing, rightly, to simply equate camp taste with gayness. As Leland Poague puts it, Sontag "hardly writes around the topic" of camp and gay culture; "she writes toward it, in the sense that she addresses it in sustained fashion in the last pages of the essay."[68] Even more strongly, we can say that the essay helps positively enforce a sense of gay "ethnicity," thus making a key contribution to what Jeffrey Escoffier, taking up a phrase from C. Wright Mills, identifies as the connection between homosexual visibility and "the sociological imagination." Escoffier traces how the "emergence of a discourse in popular sociology about homosexuality" in books like Jess Stearn's *The Sixth Man* and Martin Hoffman's *The Gay World* (1968) helped disrupt "the hegemony of the psychiatric discourse of individual pathology," refashioning "homosexuality as a social phenomenon" in two ways: "First, [these writers] defined homosexuality as a *social problem*, ambiguously framing it either as an issue of homosexuals' social adjustment or as a matter of eliminating prejudice against homosexuals. Second, [they] publicly recognized the existence of a homosexual social world."[69] The circulation of this popularized sociological discourse, not only in these best-selling books but across a wide range of print (and other) media, is a key factor in the growing sense of homosexual solidarity that in turn gave impetus to ideas about civil rights, emancipation, and liberation. Even as an avowed aesthete, Sontag is affected by and contributes to the sociological understanding of homosexuality.

Sherry's objection to the alignment of the political and the aesthetic notwithstanding, Sontag's analogy between Jews and gays can also be read as pointing to the political potential within the aesthetic, and therefore the erotic—which Sontag, quite as much as her critics, tends to conflate with the aesthetic. Not only did Sontag declare in the title essay of *Against Interpretation* that "in place of a hermeneutics, we need an erotics of art," but in "Camp" she states that "Camp taste draws on a mostly unacknowledged truth of taste: the most refined form of sexual attractiveness (as well as the most refined form of sexual pleasure) consists in going against the grain of one's sex" (279)—a statement singled out by Simon as particularly objectionable. Sherry argues that "Camp" is "a defense *of* [homosexuals]—on their presumed behalf—not *by* them," and while it's true, of course, that Sontag does not self-identify as homosexual (or a camp lover) in this essay, the sentence that so upset Simon comes close to indicating personal experience of the queer feeling of "going against the grain of one's sex."[70] Similarly, in her 1967 interview with Ephron, Sontag is unusually frank about her autobiographical relation to camp, noting that she was introduced to it "in Paris, after graduate school": "I had been terrifically solemn, scholarly. . . . It opened something up for me."[71] She continues, "It wasn't Miss Librarian breaking out, but it opened certain things for me that academic work hadn't."[72] Evoking the Hollywood trope of the sexually awakened librarian even as she rejects it, Sontag hints at the alignment of sexual energy and camp in her experience (albeit through a cliché of heterosexual seduction). In her time in Paris in 1958–59, Sontag was not only introduced to camp taste by Stein; on furlough from her by-then moribund marriage, she also underwent a sexual "reawakening," taking up again with Sohmers, her first lesbian lover, who was then living in the city.[73]

Acknowledging the "mostly unacknowledged truth of taste" of the power of gender nonconformity in regard to both sexual attractiveness and sexual pleasure, Sontag asserts queerness—albeit smuggling in the more daring point about sexual pleasure under cover of parentheses. What, though, is meant by a "mostly unacknowledged truth"? Sontag is perhaps suggesting, along Freudian lines, the largely repressed, universal significance of homosexual libido. But by associating queer sexuality with "truth," the phrase also gestures toward a potentially liberatory view of homosexuality and of camp. Homosexuality is granted the authenticity it was usually denied, an authenticity accessed *through* artifice ("going against the grain"). Admittedly, the point is made in passing. The politics that Sontag explicitly associates with homosexuality (and with Jewishness) is a politics of integration: "Homosexuals have pinned their integration into society on promoting the aesthetic sense" (while Jews have pinned their hopes for integration on "promoting the moral sense"). Thus, Marcie Frank argues that the essay is decidedly preliberatory in its attitudes: "After Stonewall . . . it could no longer be said of a gay movement agitating for legal and political recognition that it advocated a purely aesthetic sense" or "propose[d] integration as [gay men's] goal."[74] But my point is that by equating sexuality here with taste and refinement, Sontag not only casts homosexuality (and gay culture) as aestheticized but gestures toward the political implications of taste. The implications were taken up in Meehan's *New York Times Magazine* piece, where he defined camp as "anarchic, anti-Establishment and often infuriatingly perverse."[75] The buzzword "anti-Establishment" aligns camp with a growing sense that modes of taste and lifeways—including styles of sexuality—are themselves politically charged. I now turn to two other chapters from *Against Interpretation* in which Sontag again touches on the politics of sexuality, her essay on Jack Smith's *Flaming Creatures* (1963) and her response to Norman O. Brown's *Love's Body* (1959). More explicitly utopian in inflection than "Notes on 'Camp,'" these pieces align liberation with "polymorphous" desire rather than ethnic gayness. Utopian conceptions of the polymorphous—which make a comeback in the indeterminacies of queer theory—are, however, not easily historically separated from the project of gay liberation, as these two essays suggest or anticipate. First published "before she was famous" (the review of Brown appeared in the *Columbia Daily Spectator* in 1961, a shorter version of the essay on Smith in the *Nation* in 1964, a few months before "Notes on 'Camp'"), the essays take on new resonance in their republication in *Against Interpretation*, alongside the name-making "Camp," endowing Sontag with a formative role in the conceptualization of what would shortly be called the *counterculture*, in which politics, lifeways, and unorthodox sexual styles were fused.

Making a Counterculture

A key entry in 1960s underground cinema, Jack Smith's *Flaming Creatures* is described by Sontag thus: "A couple of women and a much larger number of men, most of them clad in flamboyant thrift-shop women's clothes, frolic about, pose and posture, dance with one another, [and] enact various scenes of voluptuousness, sexual frenzy, romance, and vampirism." The film also features "close-ups of limp penises and bouncing breasts, . . . shots of masturbation and oral sexuality" and "the group rape of a bosomy young woman, rape happily converting itself into an orgy."[76] Smith's film was seized by the district attorney's office on the grounds of obscenity during its initial New York run in 1963, starting "a long line of legal maneuvers, court appearances, appeals, and counter-appeals, culminating in the ban of the film in the State of New York, and its eventual investigation [in 1968] by a Senate commission."[77] Jonas Mekas, founder of the influential journal *Film Culture* and doyen of New York's underground cinema scene, was the film's great champion, and he continued to arrange showings throughout this period, being arrested for his trouble in 1963 and then again when he showed Jean Genet's *Un chant d'amour* at a benefit for the *Flaming Creatures* trial in early 1964. The original version of Sontag's essay was published in the *Nation* on 13 April 1964, after Mekas's second arrest and while the trials of *Flaming Creatures* and *Chant* were still pending. A headnote to the essay specifies these circumstances and refers the reader to an anticensorship editorial in the 30 March edition of the *Nation* sparked by the controversy.[78]

Sontag begins the essay with a nod to the film's embroilment in the politicized context of censorship debates, stating her urbane regret that the film's sexual content and nudity "make it hard simply to talk about this remarkable film; one has to *defend* it" (226). She then proceeds, somewhat uneasily, to try to keep the realms of politics and aesthetic achievement distinct, identifying the film as a "lovely specimen" of pop art, which, she says, is distinguished by "the way it blasts through the old imperative about taking a *position* toward one's subject matter." In parentheses Sontag concedes that "there are certain events about which it is necessary to take a position. . . . All I'm saying is that there are some elements of life—above all, sexual pleasure—about which it isn't necessary to have a position" (229). Conflating sexuality with the supposedly apolitical realm of the aesthetic, Sontag ends by claiming that "the space in which *Flaming Creatures* moves is not the space of moral ideas, which is where American critics have traditionally located art," but "aesthetic space, the space of pleasure" (231).

In the essay's concluding section, Sontag quotes *Film Culture*, which, awarding *Flaming Creatures* its Independent Film Award in 1963, said "[Smith] has struck us with not the mere pity or curiosity of the perverse, but the glory, the pageantry of Transylvestia and the magic of Fairyland. He has lit up a part of life which most men scorn." Sontag demurs, averring that *Flaming Creatures* "is much more about intersexuality than about homosexuality"; it "[has], for its subject, the poetry of transvestism" (230). The *Film Culture* citation conflates homosexuality and transvestism and, deploying the trope of exposure so much in evidence in early 1960s coverage of homosexuality, credits the film with having "lit up" this part of life. Similarly, but disapprovingly rather than celebratorily, the *Congressional Report* that investigated the film gathered a detailed and somewhat "inflamed" account of the film's polymorphous images under the umbrella term "homosexual content."[79] For Sontag, in contrast, *Flaming Creatures* is to be distinguished from "those serious and stirring films about the beauties and terrors of homoerotic love, Kenneth Anger's *Fireworks* and Genet's *Chant d'Amour*," because, in Smith's film, "one cannot easily tell which are men and which are women." "These are 'creatures,' flaming out in intersexual, polymorphous joy," and the film's "primary image is the confusion of male and female flesh" (230).

Sontag's focus on the liberatingly polymorphous "joy" of the film is in accordance with her favorable view of the arguments of Herbert Marcuse and Norman O. Brown, evident in her review of the latter's *Life against Death* (1959), in which she contends that "the twin subjects of eroticism and liberty are just beginning to be treated in a serious way" in America.[80] Again, contemporary censorship battles are a key context—here the obscenity trials of *Lady Chatterley's Lover* that took place in 1959:

> A country in which the vindication of so sexually reactionary a book as *Lady Chatterley's Lover* is a serious matter is plainly at a very elementary stage of sexual maturity. . . . Yet Lawrence must still be defended, especially when many who reject him have retreated to an even more reactionary position than his: treating sex as a matter-of-fact adjunct to love. The truth is that love is more sexual, more bodily than even Lawrence imagined. And the revolutionary implications of sexuality are far from being fully understood. (257)

In a similar vein, the narrator of *The Benefactor* states: "We may well say of sexuality: what a promise of freedom it is, how astonishing that it is not outlawed."[81] Indeed, *The Benefactor* is preoccupied with affective-erotic liberation, with what Hippolyte calls "a general revolution of feeling—a revolution not yet named, a dislocation of consciousness not yet diagnosed," a preoccupation that Hippolyte pursues through attempts to make his dreams into realities.[82] Like Elliott Stein's room in the note I quoted at the beginning of the chapter, *The Benefactor* in this respect seems uncannily predictive of the countercultural 1960s—a result, I suggest, of Sontag's synthesis of a range of intellectual tendencies within modernism and surrealism (Rimbaud's "disorganization of the senses" and so on), as well as her attraction to Freudian radicalism. While *The Benefactor* ends on a note of skepticism, in which Hippolyte's life-transforming project is cast in doubt (it's suggested that he is mad), in her essay on Brown, Sontag promotes the insights of Freudian radicalism against the "anti-Utopian and anti-political" impetus of socially conformist American psychoanalysis. Brown sees psychoanalysis "as a project for the transformation of human culture, and as a new and higher level in human consciousness. . . . Freud's psychological categories are thus correctly seen, in the terminology of Marcuse, as political categories" (258). Arguing that "mankind is unalterably, in the unconscious, in revolt against sexual differentiation and genital organization" (259), Brown "invites us to accept the androgynous mode of being" as a form of liberation (258).

In her 1960s work, Sontag oscillates between an account of sexual pleasure as political—as in her Brown piece—and as apolitical and quasi-aesthetic. (In her important 1967 essay "The Pornographic Imagination," she also focuses on the "demonic" and self-annihilating potential of sexuality; but this is a stand-alone account that qualifies rather than undoes her position on sexuality's potential for positive transformation.)[83] As I've argued, even in the seemingly apolitical arguments of "Camp" and "*Flaming Creatures*," there are intimations of social and cultural change. The tension evident in her *Flaming Creatures* piece, in which Sontag is obliged to "defend" the film in the politicized context of censorship battles yet attempts to do so on entirely aesthetic grounds, does not merely rehearse the argument that seeks to redeem sexually explicit material in terms of "artistic merit." In its celebration of Smith's queer style, the essay also feeds into the countercultural merging of politics and aesthetics, in which, as Marcuse put it in 1969, "the political protest . . . reaches into" the formerly "apolitical" "aesthetic dimension."[84] Another way of putting this is that Sontag's essays anticipate the way in which "the most revolutionary features of American life" during the 1960s were "in fact cultural," as Dennis Altman stated, summing up the changes of the previous decade in 1971.[85] Sontag herself noted in 1969 "the indispensability of a radical personal culture or life-style" to leftist consciousness; the "failure to revolutionize their personal lives," she speculates, is perhaps what rendered the Old Left vulnerable to "co-option by the liberal establishment in the late 1930's and the 1940's."[86] If the New Left often treated moves toward homosexual emancipation with indifference or hostility, the widely promoted imperative to do one's own thing, culturally and sexually, helped supercharge the gay liberationist impulse.

The Freudian radical emphasis on the polymorphous taken up by Sontag is at odds with received ideas about "authentic" gayness that characterize many contemporary accounts of the postliberation 1970s. Yet the gay liberation movement that emerged around 1969 often embraced the polymorphous, arguing for the abandonment of the "artificial categories" of sexual identity.[87] In a key text of the movement, *Homosexual: Oppression and Liberation* (1971), Dennis Altman drew on Marcuse and Brown to outline the utopian project of gay liberation as the attainment of universal bisexuality: "Gay liberation will have achieved its full potential when it is no longer needed, for we see each other neither as men and women, gay and straight, but purely as people with varied possibilities."[88] Annamarie Jagose and others have anatomized the parallels between the liberationist ideal of polymorphousness and queer theory's emphasis on the indeterminacy of identities (Jagose also gives a succinct account of the differences—notably queer theory's Foucauldian rejection of repression and its antifoundationalist critique of "wholeness" or authentic selfhood).[89] But what particularly interests me about these parallels here is the paradoxical centrality of same-sexuality to both the liberationist and queer projects. If queer theory and liberationist thought project a world without sexual identities as we now know them, the stubborn historical fact of homosexual categorization tends to drag like an undertow on both efforts to imagine an indeterminate empyrean. For Altman, for instance, attainment of the "polymorphous whole" paradoxically depends on emancipated gay identity.[90] "It may be the fate of homosexuals," Altman writes, "to liberate both gays and straight[s],"[91] sacrificing their own hard-won identities and cultures on the altar of derepression (Altman forecasts "the end of the gayworld as we now know it"[92]). And Eve Sedgwick, in her influential discussion of queer, associates the term with "the open mesh of possibilities, gaps, overlaps, dissonances and resonances, lapses and excesses of meaning when the constituent elements of anyone's gender, of anyone's sexuality aren't made (or *can't* be made) to signify monolithically"; yet she also asserts that "given the historical and contemporary force of the prohibitions against *every* same-sex sexual expression, for anyone to disavow those meanings, or to displace them from the term ['queer']'s definitional center, would be to dematerialize any possibility of queerness itself."[93] While in the early 1960s Sontag may have promoted bisexuality and "the androgynous mode of being" as means to sexual liberation, in the general understanding these kinds of derangements of gender and sexuality were, and have continued to be, collected under the rubric of homosexuality.[94]

Michael Moon notes that Sontag "became in a sense more 'famous' for *Flaming Creatures*" than did Smith, due to the film's long history of repression and difficulty of access; "for every person who saw Smith's film, perhaps a hundred know it from Sontag's description of it."[95] Smith resented the censorship controversy and, apparently, Sontag's role in it, voicing in a 1978 interview his displeasure that his "comedy" was "turned into a magazine sex issue. . . . Lesbian writers were finding purple titillations."[96] Here, then, is one more instance of the way in which Sontag's public profile was enhanced by the work of less famous gay men. Sontag's own image took on a "perverse" cast as a result of her close relations to gay culture, but she herself remained unidentified as lesbian—Smith's cryptic comment notwithstanding. Aligned with same-sexuality yet distanced from it, as a celebrity intellectual Sontag helped promote a discourse of sexual liberation, widespread by the late 1960s, in which homosexuality had a central if often underestimated place. In the next chapter, I turn to Gore Vidal's 1968 novel *Myra Breckinridge*, which for many seemed to distill the possibilities and the perils of the sexual revolution—possibilities and perils that, again, were collected by commentators under the rubric of homosexuality, even though the novel has little of what would commonsensically be understood as "gay" content. Understandings of the novel as gay had more than a little to do with the unspoken recognition of Vidal's own same-sexuality; and the ways in which Vidal's celebrity status both enabled and occulted this recognition anchor my discussion in the following two chapters.

5 The Moment of *Myra Breckinridge*

MORE THAN ONE CRITIC has characterized Gore Vidal's best-selling satirical novel *Myra Breckinridge*, with its no-holds-barred assault on orthodox sexuality and gender, as a harbinger of gay liberation. Catharine Stimpson writes that *Myra* and earlier Vidal novels "helped make [Stonewall] possible through the clarity of their confrontations with homophobia," while Dennis Altman states that "in some ways *Myra* foreshadows the radical gay liberation movement, which emerged the following year."[1] Certainly Vidal challenged homophobia throughout his long career as a celebrity writer and pundit, and thus, like Baldwin and Sontag, he helped "co-ordinat[e] the ideas, choices and actions of large numbers of people" about homosexuality.[2] But Vidal was also notorious for his rejection of the gay identity that formed over the post–World War II period. From the late 1950s, Vidal began to state in his writings that humans are inherently bisexual and potentially capable of any sexual act. The corollary, as he frequently put it, is that "there is no such thing as a homosexual or a heterosexual person. There are only homo- or heterosexual acts."[3]

For Vidal, the rejection of a homosexual identity that both friends and foes frequently attempted to apply to him went hand in hand with a sense of his own specialness. In a 1993 interview, he stated, "All my life there was a category to which I was assigned. Well, I don't feel like I belong in any category."[4] Vidal's felt sense of singularity was informed by the patrician origins that he claimed to have repudiated but on which he continually focused his nostalgic attention.[5] The grandson of a senator and the son of a famous aviator, Vidal several times quipped that he was "a third-generation celebrity."[6] The figure of heritable celebrity aptly sums up the combination of entitlement and ambition that characterized Vidal's relation to fame. At the same time, the idea of celebrity repeating across the generations implies the seriality and replaceability of celebrity status—the way in which the apparent specialness of celebrity is perhaps not so special after all. As Sharon Marcus puts it, "Even as celebrity confects a fantasy about peerless, inimitable presence, it turns individuality into a tissue of citations, since not only are stars widely copied, they often present themselves as copies: Lady Gaga echoes Madonna echoing Marilyn echoing Jean Harlow; Wilde echoed Byron echoing Brummel."[7]

As we've seen, critics of celebrity have often distinguished celebrity from fame, with fame being seen as the consequence of distinctive achievement, for instance, on the battlefield or on the page, while celebrity is viewed as a debased version of fame, characteristically modern or postmodern, which can attach to anyone regardless of achievement.[8] While much recent scholarship on celebrity has rightly challenged this distinction for its value-laden and gendered implications, in the context of this chapter's argument I want to bracket this debate in order to take up the way in which celebrity can be thought of as a "common" category rather than as an outgrowth of unique personhood.[9] In proclaiming his own celebrity, then, Vidal inadvertently points to his own inhabitation of a category rather than to his uniqueness. Similarly, in proclaiming his rejection of the category of gay identity in the interview just quoted, Vidal testifies to the way in which his felt singularity was constantly compromised by the "assignations" of the twentieth-century system of sexual identity. In what follows, developing the account of sexual liberation and the counterculture of the previous chapter, I draw out some of the implications of these parallels between celebrity and homosexuality as they are played out in *Myra Breckinridge* and in its publicity and reception.

This chapter and the next are organized by an assumption of the significance of the year 1968 for the interrelated histories of gay liberation and of sexual "permissiveness" in American culture. Building on the discussion of previous chapters, I move away from the common account of gay and lesbian liberation that connects it to other new social movements such as Black Power and second-wave feminism, emphasizing instead its embeddedness within the highly mediatized "sexual revolution" of the 1960s.[10] *Myra* was a *succès de scandale* that was celebrated for its insolent wit and derided as pornography; reviewers and commentators often adopted these positions simultaneously. The ambivalent response to the novel indicates the way in which *Myra*, along with a number of other late 1960s media texts, became flashpoints for shifting understandings of sexuality—what should or shouldn't be represented and what should or shouldn't be accepted.

That the sexual revolution that *Myra* indicated or embodied was in essence a media revolution is persuasively argued by Eric Schaefer in the introduction to a recent collection of essays on sexually permissive representation in the late 1960s and early 1970s.[11] Schaefer draws on the historian Alan Petigny's argument, based on statistical evidence particularly about the rate of illegitimate births, that there was a "quiet revolution" in "attitudes toward sex and sexual behavior that was well underway in the 1940s and 1950s." Rather than dramatic changes in sexual behavior or attitudes, it was "a rapidly and radically sexualized media," Schaefer suggests, that "accounts for what we now think of as the sexual revolution of the late 1960s and early 1970s."[12] It was the *making public* of the previously usually private matter of sex in the media formats of print, film, TV, radio, and recorded sound that was variously appalling, thrilling, or bewildering for Americans. Prior to the late 1960s there had of course been public displays of sexuality—for instance, in burlesque, pulp fiction, and exploitation films—but these disreputable forms of popular culture "trafficked in titillation; they suggested rather than showed."[13] The relaxation of censorship laws and of self-censorship across all media formats during the 1960s saw a sudden and widespread rise in explicitness about sex. "Before the 1960s sex had been largely something that was known only through personal experience," Schaefer writes, while during the decade "sex was no longer something that was concealed; it was on display in a way that was unprecedented in American history."[14] Schaefer identifies 1968 as the year of the "eruption of public sex," citing *Myra* along with such milestones as the onstage nudity of *Hair*, Mart Crowley's unambiguously gay play *The Boys in the Band*, and the Rolling Stones' "Let's Spend the Night Together."[15] If 1968 marks the beginning in earnest of the sexual revolution, then 1973, the year of *Deep Throat* and porno chic, can be taken as the end point of this period in which the possibilities of explicit sexual representation were vigorously explored.[16] This time frame roughly corresponds to the era in which *Myra* also had its most significant impact.

In this chapter, I build on the comments of Stimpson and Altman about the way the novel prefigured or helped usher in gay liberation. At the same time, my argument responds to Michael Trask's recent contrary contention that *Myra* may be read as an antiliberationist critique.[17] I propose that while the novel's wide-ranging satirical vision of late 1960s America certainly includes among its targets the aspirations toward social transformation that energized the moment of 1968, it is nonetheless enfolded within and a manifestation of that liberationist moment. As John Weightman wrote in a contemporary review, the novel is "both part of the phenomenon it describes and a marvellously spirited commentary on it."[18] Retrospectively, Vidal concurred, stating in a 1988 interview that in *Myra* he was "sort of sending everybody up, including the sexual revolution, and I'm sending up the '60s types' too, because I'm not taking them too seriously," but also that Myra, the character, "in a way has the spirit of '68. She is wild, she breaks all the rules."[19] The novel's ambivalent perspective toward the emergent discourse of gay liberation is, I suggest, inextricably related to the category of celebrity with which Vidal also had a complicated relationship. While Vidal reveled in his fame, he was also critical of celebrity culture, and *Myra Breckinridge* is one of his most trenchant and extended critiques, even as it is animated by his own fannish relation to 1940s Hollywood and its stars. Yet *Myra* became a media event, and Myra, the narrator-heroine, like Vidal, became a kind of celebrity, albeit a virtual one. *Myra* the novel and Myra the virtual celebrity, I argue, enabled Vidal both to acknowledge his investment in same-sexuality and to deflect his connection to a rapidly consolidating and ever-more-visible gay identity.

Myra, Meta-Camp Diva

Before the novel's action begins, Myron, a gay film critic, has been surgically transformed into the narrator-protagonist Myra—in her own view, a fearsome embodiment of female godhead. Myra seeks to destroy male heterosexuality, in order, as she puts it, "to realign the sexes, thus reducing population while increasing human happiness and preparing humanity for its next stage."[20] An early and idiosyncratic second-wave feminist, Myra wants to bring humanity back to the future through a restoration of the "primacy" of "the feminine principle" (6). The mission is informed by Myra's cinephilic view of American history. An obsessive student of Hollywood, Myra holds the italicized view that "*in the decade between* 1935 *and* 1945, *no irrelevant film was made in the United States*" (13). For her, this high point of cultural achievement is intertwined with the apogee of American political and sexual vigor. In the 1940s, she writes, "American boys created a world empire" because of their emulation of the ideals of masculinity embodied in male movie stars (34). Since the end of World War II, Myra finds, American manhood has gone into sad decline—hence the need for the creative destruction of heterosexual masculinity that Myra seeks to bring about, a project that will also avert the "population explosion" that Myra, like many concerned citizens of the late 1960s, expects. The mission becomes centered on

Rusty Godowski, a macho young acting student, whom Myra rapes with a dildo in the book's most outrageous scene. Myra next turns her libidinous attention to Rusty's girlfriend, Mary-Ann, though her plans to further derange orthodox heterosexuality are unexpectedly complicated by feelings of love for her prey. Myra's mission is brought to an abrupt halt when a hit-and-run incident results not only in Myra's retransformation into the male bodily form of Myron but in a complete personality change: Myron Mark II is a suburban square who renounces his former lives and settles down with Mary-Ann in the San Fernando Valley in a sardonic happy ending.[21] Though Myra's revelation that she used to be Myron is a climactic point in the narrative, there are hints of Myra's original gender before this moment, and contemporary reviewers invariably gave away her "secret," just as invariably stating that any intelligent reader would guess it. Myra's gendered identity was thus positioned by reviewers as an open secret that could be broached without compunction.

As this very partial summary of the novel's riotous plot indicates, *Myra*'s satire of heteronormativity is bound up with a satire of stardom and celebrity worship. Mixed in with these satirical interests are send-ups of a host of modish late-1960s cultural phenomena, including the French new novel, Marshall McLuhan, pop art, youth culture, orgies, and camp. The novel's relation to the last of these is complicated, crystallizing the way it points in both proto- and antiliberationist directions. As Altman notes, *Myra* is "part of a major cultural assault on the assumed norms of gender and sexuality which swept the western world in the late 1960s and early 1970s, cousin at least to *Hair*, *The Rocky Horror Picture Show*, David Bowie's *Ziggy Stardust*, and Mick Jagger's character in the film *Performance*"—to which list we might add Bowie and Jagger's cross-dressing propensities and professions of bisexual taste.[22] *Myra* is an important link between the "underground" gender confusions of artists like Jack Smith and Warhol and the mainstreaming of counternormativity that Altman describes. As in the nascent countercultural expressions examined in the previous chapter, homosexuality, or at least the perception of homosexuality, is central to *Myra*'s impact. Although what is commonsensically understood to be gay sex is actually quite tangential in the novel, *Myra*, like *Flaming Creatures*, was regularly identified by reviewers as being "about" homosexuality. In making this assertion, reviewers picked up on the novel's engagement with camp—the way in which, as one reviewer put it, *Myra*'s concern with "falsity and artifice" stresses "the homosexual view of life: we do not make it; we are made."[23]

However, the novel is in important respects distanced from rather than immersed in camp perception. For Myra, "the films of the 1940's are superior to all the works of the so-called Renaissance, including Shakespeare and Michelangelo" (18); but while this excessive celebration of dated Hollywood product reads like an example of the knowing inversion of camp taste, Myra is not being ironic. Indeed, Myra is never ironic. She is positioned as camp object rather than camp subject. Her humorlessness and grandiosity render her an example of what Sontag labeled "pure" or "naïve camp," the result of "failed seriousness."[24] Though this distanced view of Myra is certainly not the only way in which she can be read, what I want to stress for now is the way in which an audience effect of camp appreciation is built into the novel whereby the presumptive reader—and Vidal himself—are distanced from Myra in a knowing appreciation of the silliness of which she remains unaware.

The novel might thus be understood as elaborating a kind of meta-camp that repurposes camp for its satirical project. As Philip Core, insightfully if somewhat obscurely, puts it, "[Vidal] *uses* camp, knowingly and for a detached purpose."[25] Michael Trask argues that the novel's detached use of camp renders it an example of what he calls "mean camp," "the goal of which is to appropriate camp for decidedly impolitic ends."[26] Trask contends that practitioners of mean camp, among whom he also numbers the filmmakers Paul Morrissey and John Waters, use camp against itself, negating the connection between camp and "a politics of social transformation" that was contentiously claimed in the postliberation period by some gay activists and theorists and that is anticipated in Sontag's 1960s writing.[27] For Trask, the ending of *Myra* with its "default to the status quo ante" indicates Vidal's "cynical view" of the new social movements of the 1960s, which, like Myra, sought "renewal or metamorphosis."[28] While this reading lines up with Vidal's occasionally voiced skepticism about the efficacy of 1960s radicalism, I think it overemphasizes the novel's ending at the expense of full consideration of its satire on gendered and sexual norms; as the English novelist Brigid Brophy noted in a contemporary review that takes that satire fully into account, the ending can also be understood as a "nightmare consist[ing] in the triumph of conformism."[29] However, I think the arguments of Trask and others about the novel's detached use of camp helpfully gesture toward Vidal's characteristic disavowal of his own investment in camp, a disavowal bound up with his resistance to gay identity—a point to which I will return.

One of the novel's main examples of meta-camp is Myra's relation to her intellectual touchstone, Parker Tyler, the gay surrealist writer and pioneering myth-critic of Hollywood, to whose study *Magic and Myth of the Movies* (1947) Myra alludes many times, but to the playful tone of which she is deaf. Myra takes literally Tyler's equation of Hollywood stars with divinity, and her perception of her own goddesshood is in part manifested in an aspiration to stardom—though with so many other projects in the offing, Myra's ambition to get into the movies does not get much attention. In a way, Myra's obsession with old Hollywood is very "now" (for 1968). In his 1988 essay "Uses of Camp," Andrew Ross identifies the debasing reduction of old Hollywood films to TV fodder that took place from the late 1950s on as a key element in the formation of 1960s camp culture.[30] What Myra calls the "gray cloudy miniatures on the Late Show" (53) that became a familiar part of the TV viewing experience engendered a wave of ironic nostalgia, democratizing the cultic investment in obsolescent film-star celebrity that was an important strand of underground cinema culture—for instance, in the veneration of Maria Montez by Jack Smith and in the necrophiliac extravaganza of Kenneth Anger's *Hollywood Babylon* (1959). But Myra's irony deficiency entails a yawning gap between her attitude toward old Hollywood and these more self-aware versions of celebrity cathexis.

Myra's delusiveness is also conveyed though her conception of 1940s Hollywood as a design for living. Her behavior and appearance, she frequently tells us in meticulously detailed references, recall those of her idols. Thus, she describes herself as resembling "the beauteous Fay Wray . . . left three-quarter profile if the key light is no more than five feet high during the close shot" (3); the "careful, low-pitched" tone of her voice in one scene is "modeled on that of the late Ann Sheridan (fifth reel of *Doughgirls*)" (13); elsewhere, "I whispered like Phyllis Thaxter in *Thirty Seconds over Tokyo*" (120); and so on. Myra's incessant quotation of old Hollywood comically undermines her own claims to singular status. "My own uniqueness is simply the result of self-knowledge," she proclaims, drawing attention of course to her lack of both these qualities (118).

But the crazy overkill of Myra's imitative investment in Hollywood also throws into satirical relief normative celebrity and the normative audience relation to it: the ways in which celebrity "turns individuality into a tissue of citations," even as it "confects a fantasy of peerless, inimitable presence," to requote Sharon Marcus. Myra sees not only herself but others through the scrim of 1940s film: "He gave me a level gaze reminiscent of James Craig in the fourth reel of

Marriage is a Private Affair" (122); Mary-Ann's "breasts are *better* than Lana Turner's in *They Won't Forget*" (179); and so on. And while Myra's vision of life as imitation of 1940s Hollywood is eccentric, the novel indicates that "mimesis is normal," with the students of the academy where Myra teaches appropriating the appearance and mannerisms of "stars of television series" in a "fitful, mindless shuffling of roles" (34). Myra's only "demur" from this phenomenon is that "today's models" are a debased contrast with those of the 1940s, when "American boys created a world empire because they chose to be James Stewart, Clark Gable and William Eythe" (34–35). The bathos of the uniconic Eythe in this lineup is a joke on Myra's indiscriminateness, but Myra's cluelessly humorous observation is also a serious, critical point about the inflection of everyday life by celebrity culture.

Similarly, Myra's reverent view of the star system as a configuration of mythic *types* gestures toward the way in which the celebrity system is driven by the imperatives of seriality and replaceability, recalling Marcus's point that "not only are stars widely copied, they often present themselves as copies." Myra declares to the Hollywood agent Letitia Van Allen, "We deal in *myths*. At any given moment the world requires one full-bodied Aphrodite (Jean Harlow), one dark siren of flawless beauty (Hedy Lamarr), one powerful inarticulate brute of a man (John Wayne)," and so on (105). The search for stars, she continues, "means carefully analyzing Olympus to find out which archetypal roles are temporarily vacant and who are the contenders": "as in any other business, we must begin with market research" (106). Myra's perception of Hollywood as simultaneously Olympus and a business points up the standardization of the celebrity image.

There is thus a sharpness to many of Myra's observations, even if it is inadvertent or hedged around with humor. The text offsets disidentification from Myra with certain elements that encourage engagement. Myra is not simply delusional but a compelling mix of delusion and formidableness. Her lunatic voice is seductive, and she succeeds in most of her plans right up to the hit-and-run accident. Her rape of Rusty is, as Catharine Stimpson writes, "ugly," but it is also a persuasive demonstration of her power.[31] The text impels the reader to be carried along by Myra's obsessions even as it mocks them.

The mix of disengagement from and identification with Myra that the book promotes also structures Vidal's relation to his creation. As Margot Hentoff noted in the *New York Review of Books*, the presentation of Myra as "super-ridiculous" is compromised by her role as "a sort of wistful spokesman for [Vidal's] own best hopes."[32] Myra iterates Vidal's theory of human bisexuality, stating in an extreme though representative version of Vidal's position, "Between a beautiful girl and an unattractive man . . . I shall always be drawn, like any healthy-minded woman, to the girl" (91). And while Vidal in interviews initially distanced himself from Myra's vision of a pansexual future as a solution to the supposed crisis of human overpopulation, the crisis itself was by the late 1960s one of Vidal's firmest convictions and a major theme of his public statements. Myra also mouths other frequently stated views of Vidal's, if often in comically exaggerated or garbled form, such as his disdain for psychoanalysis and his belief that human relations are primarily a competition for power.

After the book's publication, we often find Vidal iterating Myra's views rather than the other way around. Eventually, in the post-Stonewall period, Vidal was to explicitly endorse the position that homosexuality was a means of averting the population explosion.[33] Additionally, as Marcie Frank observes in her book on Vidal and TV, Vidal in a 1974 interview even endorsed Myra's view of the cultural influence of TV commercials—Myra's nostalgic cathexis onto Golden Age Hollywood is combined with an avant-garde appreciation of TV that out-McLuhans McLuhan and that, as Frank further argues, is in line with Vidal's own appreciation of the medium's centrality in what he characterizes as an "amnesiac" age. Frank states, "The tantalizing possibility that Myra really speaks for Vidal, or Vidal for Myra, like many questions of literary voice, remains undecidable," and "Vidal's signal contribution is to brilliantly illuminate the conditions" of that undecidability: "the current cultural matrix that determines that we can't distinguish among history, memory, what we have seen on the big or small screens or on the page."[34] Celebrity, with its uncertain relations to agency and to voice, I suggest, is a crucial component of this cultural matrix, this mélange of representation and reality. In the case of *Myra*, the complexities of celebrity were evident not only in the text's satire but also paratextually in the novel's marketing and publicity, which again simultaneously suggested and disavowed the connections between Vidal and his heroine.

For if Vidal was well established as a celebrity writer by 1968, the content of the book and the publicity that surrounded the book's launch constructed Myra herself as a kind of celebrity. With regard to the content of book, the crucial factor here is Myra's distinctive, compelling voice. The published commentary on the novel reveals that Myra has her fans, critics who largely eschew the option of distanced assessment in favor of a delirious-yet-serious diva worship—a "kinky for Myra" approach that, by surrendering to her worldview, affords the heuristic dividend of seeing where Myra's radical unsettling of the conventions of gender and sexuality might take us.[35] Outside the book, Myra's celebrity status was reinforced by the interplay of her voice with her creator's, making her, as Frank suggests, a kind of alter ego for Vidal. From almost the moment of the novel's publication, Myra frequently provides a supplementary perspective in Vidal's interviews, sometimes complementary, sometimes dissenting, an opportunity for humorous play (asked for his view on the upcoming Democratic nomination for president by the *Los Angeles Times* in April 1968, for instance, Vidal replied, "I'm for McCarthy at the moment. . . . Myra is for Hubert Humphrey").[36]

If Myra quickly became a familiar public figure, however, her debut was carefully contrived to be mysterious. *Myra Breckinridge* was released in February 1968 without any publicity and without advance copies being supplied to reviewers—ostensibly because Vidal did not want reviewers giving away the "secret" of Myra's sex change but also quite probably because Vidal and his publisher, Little, Brown, feared negative reactions. The decision to supply no buzz created effective buzz, with the book going into a third printing before even reaching the stores, so intense was the interest in this unheralded book from a famous author. It was only with the release of the paperback edition in July 1968 that the book was officially marketed, with the paperback publisher, Bantam, mounting a print ad campaign that declared, in part, "Everything you've heard about MYRA BRECKINRIDGE is true! . . . The book that has become the year's #1 topic of conversation" (Figure 4).

Presenting *Myra*'s scandalous concerns as the subject of gossip and rumor, the campaign appeals to the operations of celebrity in order to sell the book, conflating the book with its protagonist and transforming Myra into a virtual scandalous celebrity, a process licensed and encouraged, of course, by the novel's eponymous title.[37] Myra's talked-about notoriety persisted as a central selling point in subsequent print ads, with the "year's #1 topic of conversation" tag reused in later ads that capitalized on the attributes of the giant statue of the showgirl that formed the campaign's sole image, with one ad announcing, in an allusion to the statue's stance, that Myra was "strutting her way to the top of the bestseller lists."[38]

This showgirl statue, which featured in the narrative and appeared on the cover of both hardback and paperback editions, was, in a further promotional campaign by Bantam in September 1968, driven on a two-week tour around

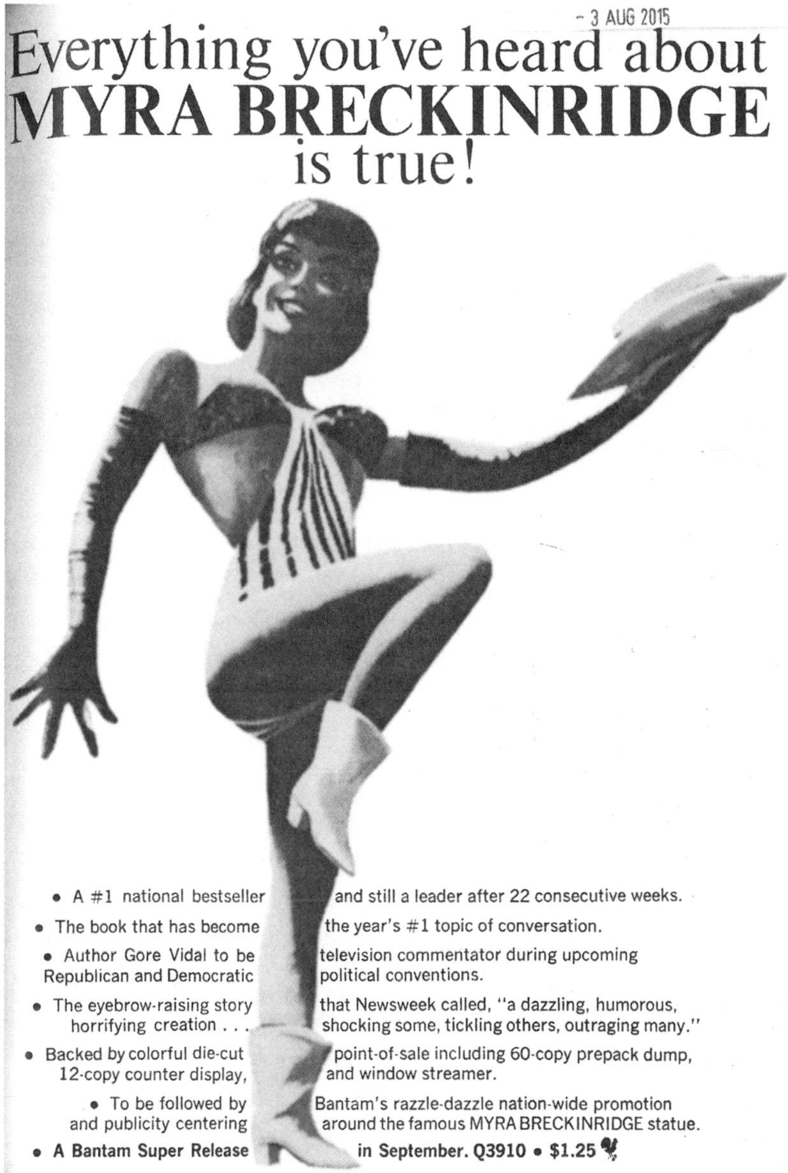

Figure 4. Original print ad for the Bantam edition of *Myra Breckinridge* (*Publishers Weekly*, 29 July 1968).

major American cities in a float emblazoned with the slogan, "Here Comes Myra Breckinridge" (Figures 5 and 6). The showgirl was, Vidal claims in his 2006 memoir *Point to Point Navigation*, presented to "a dozen governors, who each saw fit not to accept."[39] Print coverage of the tour indicates that the statue was presented to city officials rather than to governors; but the lack of willing takers was certainly played up in the publicity.

The eighteen-foot-high statue had originally revolved high above the part of Sunset Boulevard known as Sunset Strip between 1957 and 1966, advertising, along with a billboard, the show and lounge room attractions at Las Vegas's Sahara Hotel. In the novel Myra can see the statue from the window of the rented apartment in which she writes her journal. "For me she is Hollywood and mesmerizing," she tells us (77). A gargantuan embodiment of glamorous femininity, the showgirl is an apt focus both for Myra's obsession with Hollywood and her gynocentric philosophy. Myra rhapsodizes that the showgirl is "beautiful and omnipotent, the very image of deity!" (169). Both in the novel and in the promotional material the showgirl becomes a fetish, a stand-in for Myra herself. Her oversize and artifice indicate the delusional ambitions and inauthenticity that mark Myra as a character, while her rictus grin, to borrow Jonathan Beckman's observation on painted smiles, makes us wonder "what sinister machinations lie behind it."[40] Totemic yet tawdry, the showgirl embodies *Myra Breckinridge*'s satirical view of the false promise of celebrity. In her combination of fame and anonymity, she also points up the emptiness of celebrity as a category. In an ambiguous superlative, Jim Moran, the veteran publicist responsible for the showgirl's tour, described her as "the most well-known piece of sculpture California ever produced," echoing Daniel Boorstin's famous 1961 definition of the celebrity as "a person who is known for his well-knownness."[41]

In newspaper coverage of the tour, Moran revealed that the showgirl had been found in "a San Fernando Valley dump."[42] "A 500-pound, laminated fiberglass confection" created by commercial sculptor Rudy Vargas, the statue was, Moran informed reporters, bought by Bantam for "a mere $1500" but was now "priceless." Proclaiming the showgirl to be "the first piece of pop art in America," Moran issued laments to the press that no city would take her, declaring himself "appalled by the bad taste of . . . civic officials." He decried, for instance, the uninterested attitude of Los Angeles, "a city of rootless, apathetic people who are letting their cultural artifacts slip out from under them while they sit with their smug, bleary eyes glued to TV sets."[43] Moran's tongue-in-cheek assessments of

Figure 5. Cover of original hardback edition of *Myra Breckinridge* (Boston: Little, Brown, 1968).

Figure 6. Gore Vidal with publicist Jim Moran, *Myra Breckinridge* promotional tour, 1968. "Photographs" from *Point to Point Navigation: A Memoir by Gore Vidal*, copyright © 2006 by Gore Vidal. Used by permission of Doubleday, an imprint of the Knopf Doubleday Publishing Group, a division of Penguin Random House LLC. All rights reserved.

the showgirl's worth are textbook cases of camp taste as Andrew Ross formulates it: "the re-creation of surplus value from forgotten forms of labor." The repurposing of the showgirl, who was literally found in a dump, fulfills Ross's definition of camp as "a rediscovery of history's waste"—the way that camp "irreverently retrieves . . . unsalvageable material that has been picked over and found wanting by the purveyors of the 'antique.' "[44] Additionally, the showgirl, as a stand-in for Myra, embodies and literalizes what camp's hostile critic Vivian Gornick bemoaned as "camp's current celebrity" in 1966.

But if Moran's publicity tour mobilizes a camp appreciation of the showgirl, more conventional middle-class taste condemns her as kitsch. In her original incarnation, the showgirl statue was positioned opposite the Chateau Marmont Hotel, and in a history of that establishment, Raymond Sarlot and Fred Basten title their chapter on the showgirl "A Dark Day," identifying her as a harbinger of the garish clutter of spectacular advertisements that has made the present-day Strip a byword for the worst excesses of consumerism and celebrity culture.[45] This view of the showgirl was endorsed by Vidal, implicitly in the novel and explicitly in a 1977 interview. Asked then, "Did you write *Myra Breckinridge* at the Chateau Marmont with that awful, revolving figure outside?," Vidal answers: "No, I didn't write it there, but when I was at Metro, I lived at the Chateau Marmont. Oh, God, to wake up in the morning with a hangover and look out and see that figure turning, turning, holding the sombrero—you knew what death would be like."[46] Associating the showgirl with his stint as a scriptwriter in the late 1950s and early 1960s, Vidal, like Myra, identifies the showgirl with Hollywood, but in the mode of disdain rather than celebration, resisting the camp reading elaborated in the publicity tour and in Moran's deadpan comments to the press.

Gay Vidal

Vidal's reluctance, here at any rate, to enter into such a reading of the showgirl is symptomatic of his tendency to dissociate himself from camp, with its codings of homosexuality and effeminacy. Camp may have been democratized and mainstreamed in the wake of Sontag's essay, but I suggest that for Vidal, who wished to avoid categorization as gay, the homosexual and effeminate legacy of camp remained unsettling. Throughout his career, Vidal stressed the "naturalness" of homoeroticism, that is, its compatibility with normative masculinity; the flip side of this position was disdain for effeminate or "faggy" homosexuality, a matter I return to in the next chapter. Yet Vidal was also a master of the "game of bitchy putdowns" that is a key component of the camp sensibility.[47] For instance, in his long-running feud with Truman Capote, the prime target of his effeminopobia, Vidal's main rhetorical strategy was the camp insult, something that brought him rather too close in the public eye to the very effeminacy he sought to attack.[48] Similarly, the availability of the showgirl for a camp reading that was evident in the publicity tour indicates the closeness of Vidal's meta-camp or mean camp representation to the kind of gay-coded camp perspective that Vidal officially resisted. The book's other cover art also hints at Vidal's closeness to camp and to gayness. The back cover dust jacket features two metal casts of Vidal's face (Figure 7). Substituting for a conventional author photo, the image of the sculpted faces suggests relations of equivalence between Vidal, the sculpted showgirl, and the character for which she is a stand-in.

If 1968 was still the era of the open secret, an era during which celebrities were rarely *explicitly* identified as homosexual, many celebrities, both gay and straight, were subjected during this period to gay innuendo in the media and, unsurprisingly, given the outrageousness of *Myra Breckinridge*, such innuendo was a not uncommon feature of the novel's reviews. In his review in *Look*, for instance, Peter Prescott averred that Myra's "detailed and highly vocal appreciation of the male physique" was rendered "in terms to which only a homosexual can respond."[49] The takes-one-to-write-like-one charge leveled against Vidal here is fairly clear. In a review for the *New York Times*, James MacBride sounded a still more insistent note of insinuation. Styling *Myra* as "the underground novel to end all underground novels," MacBride speculated that the withholding of copies from reviewers is a means of "permitting the author to find his readers unassisted," with the novel's "teasing blurb echo[ing] this promise." This blurb was the only description carried on the book's inside cover flap: "A new and very different novel from the author of *Julian* and *Washington D.C.*" MacBride continues: "The poker-faced jacket art manages to be both sexy and epicene; even the dedication will be a tip-off to the In-group."[50] The dedication—to Christopher Isherwood, a novelist widely assumed or known to be gay—clinches MacBride's list of veiled references to a sexual underground, a list that, through its summary of teasing promises and tip-offs, itself constitutes one big tease, with the giveaway of Isherwood's name withheld and the precise nature of the "In-group" solicited by the book unspecified. The idea that the novel was an appeal to an in-group was also the theme of a review by Sidney Thomas in the *Atlanta Constitution and Journal* titled "Vidal's 'In' Joke Leaves Reader Out." Thomas wrote that the dedication to

Figure 7. Back cover of original hardback edition of *Myra Breckinridge* (Boston: Little, Brown, 1968).

Isherwood was perhaps meant to be "amusing" but that the novel as a whole was a "travesty" (pun presumably intended).[51] Identifying Vidal with an in-group of which Isherwood is also a member, MacBride and Thomas implicitly relegate Vidal to the category of gay identity, and indeed to the gay subculture. As with Myra, whose profession of uniqueness is belied by her imitation of Hollywood stars, Vidal's conviction of his evasion of the category of gayness is undermined by these reviewers' insinuations. As I've mentioned, the open secret of Myra's original gender was routinely revealed by reviewers; Vidal's own secret, however, remained, officially at least, under wraps. But the force of the innuendo in some reviews indicates just how paper-thin the open secret of Vidal's sexuality had become with the publication of *Myra*.

Myra to the rescue: if *Myra* the novel was in part a vehicle for Vidal's preoccupation with sexual nonnormativity, Myra the distinctive voice and celebrity character helped direct attention away from her author's own sexual orientation. Constructed as virtual celebrities for the purposes of marketing, Myra and the showgirl to a certain extent displaced Vidal's own celebrity, with the showgirl's tour of America, for instance, substituting for a book tour by Vidal himself (although Vidal did undertake an "intensive schedule" of TV appearances to promote the novel).[52] As a scandalous celebrity, Myra also deflected rumors about Vidal's own potentially scandalous sexuality that might have been given fresh impetus by such an audacious book. In her discussion of Byron's prototypical scandalous celebrity, Clara Tuite argues that "scandalous celebrity renders the distinction between fame and notoriety redundant, because the new economy of celebrity is about translating bad fame—infamy and notoriety—into good fame" so that "any publicity is good publicity." Nearly 150 years after Byron's death, Vidal reaped the monetary and publicity benefits of the way celebrity "reconfigure[s] the value of notoriety, converting it from negative to positive"; but scandal was displaced from Vidal's "private" life onto Myra.[53] Despite reviewer innuendo, the outrageousness of Myra's gender and sexuality provided a point of public focus, or, to use the language of the ad campaign, a "topic of conversation" that overrode potential conversation about Vidal at a moment in which liberated, open gay identity was in the process of emerging.

In an analysis of eighteenth-century stage celebrity Julia Fawcett notes that "scholars of celebrity studies have tended to read the celebrity as symbol around which a culture demarcates permissible identities, less a subject than a 'something.'" But this understanding of celebrity is continually in tension, as Fawcett writes, with the efforts of celebrities themselves to "create their self-images, to define the meaning and the limits of their identities instead of being defined by them."[54] Focusing on the career of the actor Coller Cibber, Fawcett develops the idea of "over-expression," a defensive tactic in which the celebrity "exaggerate[es] into illegibility" certain defining features of his persona, thereby stymying audience attempts "to divine a celebrity's character."[55] While the cultural setting examined by Fawcett is very different from the moment of *Myra Breckinridge*, I suggest that her argument is apt for an understanding of Vidal's relation to his creation. Like the eighteenth-century celebrities discussed by Fawcett, Vidal "depended on the scopophilia of his audience" yet felt in some ways helpless to guard against "the identities his spectators might assign him"—the identity of homosexuality above all.[56] The production of the "overexpressive" Myra Breckinridge, I am arguing, served in part to protect Vidal from gay identification. Like the overexpressive personae of the eighteenth century, Myra is bewitchingly and bewilderingly "excessive" and "spectacular"—"impossible for the spectator to categorize or make conventional."[57] While Myra has a history as a gay man, she is excessively and spectacularly multigendered and polymorphous. She and the novel that bears her name refer to homosexuality, but they are irreducible to it. Moreover, the public could not easily identify Vidal with Myra, even as his and her voices mingled.

As I will explore in the next chapter, however, Vidal's immunity from explicit identification came to a dramatic end, even as Bantam's promotion for *Myra* was under way, when the right-wing pundit William Buckley called Vidal a "queer" during a live TV debate. I will suggest that, although it was a spontaneous and intemperate moment, Buckley's name-calling needs to be set in the context of the climate of openness about homosexuality that had been growing apace throughout the 1960s and that was an important precondition of gay liberation. Indeed, as we've noted, the idea of liberation was explicitly and insistently raised as part of the discussion of homosexuality throughout the pre-Stonewall decade; it is *Myra*'s relation to this discussion that I now turn.

Myra, Liberator from the Underground

As we've seen, along with increasingly frank fictional treatments of homosexuality in literature and cinema, the 1960s saw an exponential rise in the number of nonfictional reports on the gay world in the press, in books, and even, eventually and tentatively, on TV.[58] Running the tonal gamut from sober to salacious, these reports had in common the tendency to take the form of the exposé, revealing a notionally secret homosexual "underworld" or "underground" to curious readers. In their investigations of the homosexual "problem," they also commonly, however grudgingly, held out the possibility of a reconfiguration of current sexual orthodoxy. The mediatization and narrativization of the gay world almost necessarily raised the possibility of liberation, given that world's subordinated situation. As noted in the Introduction, an early example of this position is the March 1959 *Village Voice* article by Seymour Krim, "Revolt of the Homosexual," which calls for a homosexual rights movement. The imagery of rebellion and overturning continued throughout the 1960s, with the publication of books bearing titles such as *The Homosexual Revolution* (1962), *The Homosexual Explosion!* (1968), and *The Homosexual Uprising* (1967). While no doubt meant to be attention grabbing, these titles also indicate the common perception of the socially disruptive effect that openness about homosexuality was making or could make.[59]

In its centralization of sexual unorthodoxy, *Myra*, like the 1960s reports on homosexuality, was associated by many critics with "the underground"—as we saw in MacBride's innuendos in his *New York Times* review. The term was widely used in the 1960s to refer to dissident forms of cultural production that often made sexual queerness central—for instance, the underground cinema of Jack Smith and Andy Warhol. Myra's connection to the cultural underground is also reflexively indicated in the narrative, as Myra has appeared in a number of "underground movies" while living in New York, an experience that "gave [her] a sense of what it must be like to be a star" (25). Janet Staiger notes that, in tandem with this idea of a cultural underground, the print media applied the term "underground" in a political sense throughout the 1960s to refer to "the association of minorities [including homosexual minorities] not just in resistance against the dominant but also in a common cause unified by a political agenda for change."[60] Krim's call in the *Village Voice* for a homosexual rights movement was answered the next week with an article titled "The Gay Underground," which discounted the possibility of such a movement but made clear the association of the term with political resistance. Thus, as Staiger writes, by the early 1960s, "the term underground had connotations not of the hidden but of alternative communities and political activism."[61]

While many critics deplored *Myra* for its allegedly pornographic excesses, others understood it, in its frankness, as a plea for the kind of liberatory politics associated with the underground. *Playboy*, for instance, noted in a brief review that Vidal "suggests a freer view toward all sexuality—a more permissive attitude in regard to homosexuality, for openers," while *Newsweek* more obscurely opined that the novel is "a kind of erotic propaganda."[62] Margot Hentoff referred to what she saw as the novel's sincere hope for a "utopian pan-sexual future"; Eliot Fremont-Smith in the *New York Times*, with a nod to Marcuse, made mention of the novel's vision of "a truly polymorphous society."[63] The Freudian radical perspective was taken up with gusto in Brigid Brophy's laudatory review, perhaps the most trenchant and prescient account of the novel's proto-liberationist stance. Her language recalling the images of conflagration and revolution in the titles of the books mentioned previously, Brophy states that the "trans-sex fantasy" of *Myra Breckinridge* "explodes . . . at a level even deeper than the one from which it liberates the homosexual imprisoned in every heterosexual—and also, of course, the heterosexual in every homosexual," disorientatingly and thrillingly taking the reader back to the pre-Oedipal stage "when we were in genuine intellectual doubt about which sex *was* which." Brophy concludes her review by railing against the censorship of the British text of *Myra* agreed to by Vidal, stating that the "images lodged in its citizens' imaginations are part of the socio-political character of a country. To find pornography more exciting than patriotic exhortations, middlebrow family sagas or economics textbooks is a political decision. Sex-censorship *is* political censorship."[64]

As a best-selling elaboration of the revolutionary energies of the gay world, *Myra*, for many critics, seemed to undermine the idea of a specifiable underground. As Hentoff wrote, the novel is "selling with such rapidity as to make the book's publication itself a parody of things underground. A parody so successful that one begins to wonder if the underground still exists, and where."[65] Critics like Hentoff were responding to the greater sexual permissiveness that marked virtually the whole spectrum of cultural production in the late 1960s. Similarly in his review, published before the book's official publication date, Eliot Fremont-Smith, after expatiating on the book's underground credentials, states that the book "can justly be called a *succès de scandale*" and predicts that "once the word gets round, it will sell like popcorn at a double feature."[66]

While Janet Staiger relates the term "underground" to alternative communities and political resistance, Loren Glass in his examination of the groundbreaking countercultural publisher Grove Press has shown that it also had commercial application in relation to erotically explicit material. He notes that Grove "almost single-handedly transformed the term 'underground' into a legitimate market niche for adults in the second half of the 1960s, starting with a campaign inviting readers to 'Join the Underground'" by subscribing to Grove's *Evergreen Review* and by joining the Evergreen Club, "a conduit for distributing Grove's rapidly expanding catalog of 'adult' literature and film."[67] The best-selling status of *Myra* ("like popcorn at a double feature") confirmed the commercial possibilities of the underground—not just for the leading-edge Grove but for a mainstream house like Little, Brown as well. The perception of a collision or conflation between the overground and the underground that featured in many of *Myra*'s reviews resembled and indeed was intertwined with accounts of the way in which the putatively hidden or private matter of homosexuality, and sexuality more generally, was coming into public view.

I have suggested that the overexpressive capacity of Myra as a virtual celebrity enabled Vidal the celebrity novelist to voice his intense interest in same-sexuality but also to displace clear identifications of himself as a homosexual. But as a key example of the sexually audacious media texts of the late 1960s, *Myra* also made a compelling early contribution to the defiant and prideful discourse of gay liberation—a discourse in which Vidal was, however reluctantly, caught up. As the moment of *Myra Breckinridge* morphed into the 1970s, Vidal became more firmly and openly assigned to the sexual category he officially refused.[68] But if this situation seems reductive or disrespectful of Vidal's own views on sexuality, it is also worth noting that, for all his frequent and fearless challenges to homophobia in the pre-Stonewall period, it was only after 1969 that Vidal publicly professed his own experiences of same-sexuality, indicating an unacknowledged indebtedness to the liberation movement that had made such professions "safe." If Vidal rejected the role of gay celebrity, his celebrity status both before and after Stonewall was entangled with the discourse of gay liberation that he both distanced himself from and helped advance.[69]

Coda: Myra's Afterlives

If Myra's capacity to deflect attention from Vidal's sexuality fell away after Stonewall, her charismatic persona nonetheless ensured for her a respectable career into the 1970s and beyond. In 1991, for instance, responding to Camille Paglia's *Sexual Personae*, Vidal stated that Paglia "sounds like Myra Breckenridge on a roll. . . . I have no higher praise."[70] But the period of the sexual revolution was Myra's heyday. After constantly referring to Myra in interviews of the late 1960s and early 1970s, Vidal eventually gave her a sequel, *Myron* (1974), in which she goes back in time to 1948, battles Myron for control of their shared body, and eventually switches bodies with the camp film cultist's favorite, Maria Montez, realizing at last her ambition to become a star. Rather than develop an analysis of this sequel, however, I close by noting two cultural artifacts, both from 1970, that further indicate Myra's dominance of a moment that had not yet fully absorbed the idea of the sexual revolution and that was still excitedly elaborating the cultural and commercial possibilities that the idea implied.

First, the film of *Myra Breckinridge*, directed by Michael Sarne. Plagued by major scripting, casting, and shooting difficulties, the X-rated *Myra* was released to a chorus of critical vituperation, with *Time* describing it as "about as funny as a child molester," *New York* calling it the "creation of an infant smearing about in its own excrement," and *Life* editorializing that it was "unforgivable" in its vulgarity.[71] This mainstream media reaction, however, contrasted with its reception in the city of the Stonewall riots. J. Hoberman notes that the crowd outside the Criterion cinema on the day of the film's opening was "filled with brazen drag queens." "Indeed," he continues, "*Myra*'s opening preview[ed] the [first] Christopher Street Liberation Day March held later that week." The *East Village Other* reported that the screenings had a "festive, often violent atmosphere" reminiscent of student unrest at Columbia, and the *New York Times* that "between two and ten thousand 'screaming' citizens blocked Times Square, 'crashing through barricades and breaking store windows.' "[72] In her cinematic guise, Myra spectacularly failed to win over the arbiters of middle-class taste—a contrast to the reception of the novel, for even critics who disliked it tended to credit Vidal's skill as a writer. But, presiding over riotous expressions of unorthodox sexual identity, the film version of *Myra* also fulfilled the novel's prefiguration of liberatory queer politics. Myra's role as a kind of patron saint of gay liberation was subsequently attested to in the Boston gay activist John Mitzel's freewheeling celebration of her in "Patriarchy vs. 'Pornography,' " his contribution to the offbeat pamphlet *Myra and Gore*, and in the testimony of sex-radical writer Boyd McDonald that Myra's appearance to him in a dream inspired him to found the pioneering gay porn zine *Straight to Hell*.[73]

The second, less well-known artifact is the result of Myra, like many another celebrity before and after her, extending her brand by publishing a cookbook. Authored by Vidal's longtime companion Howard Austen and the Rome-based American sculptor Beverly Pepper, *The Myra Breckinridge Cookbook* names and thematizes its generally straightforward recipes according to twinned preoccupations of Hollywood and sex (Figure 8). It features sections such as "The Immortals,"

Figure 8. The cover of *The Myra Breckinridge Cookbook* (Boston: Little, Brown, 1970) features a still of Joan Collins in *Island in the Sun* (1957), a film unlikely to have been an object of Myra's veneration but an apt choice of image given the book's smirking conceit.

and "W. C. Fields Memorial" (cocktails, of course), and recipes such as "Cod Pieces," "Bearded Oysters," and "Cumin Covered Cock." The book plays on and exploits the appeal of the celebrity cookbook genre, whereby the public figure of the celebrity is phantasmically brought into the private domain of the fan's home. The fact that Myra is a virtual rather than an actual celebrity, however, works to undermine the fantasy of personal access to celebrity provided by the genre, and in this way the *Cookbook* might be thought of as continuous with its precursor text's critique of celebrity. Less advertently, perhaps, the book also shows up the contrivance of the celebrity cookbook through its "ghostwritten" status.

Ostensibly delivered in Myra's voice, the introductions to each section lack the sophistication of Vidal's writing, instead soliciting laughter through smirking double entendres, though some choice lines from the novel are recycled. A large-format paperback of 344 pages, lavishly illustrated with black-and-white stills from Golden Age Hollywood cinema, the *Cookbook* in its heft and design recalls Kenneth Anger's dark-camp masterpiece *Hollywood Babylon*, but its affect is contrastively bland. Bathetic though it is, the *Cookbook*, by juxtaposing classic film stills with sexually suggestive prose, nonetheless participates in the derepression that also marked its precursor text, attesting to the continuing mutual inflection of media and sexuality that was a hallmark of the sexual revolution in general and the gay liberation that was a particular permutation of that revolution.

6 Gore Vidal's Sexuality in the Public Sphere

ON 28 AUGUST 1968, at a heated moment in a live TV debate, the right-wing pundit William F. Buckley Jr. called Gore Vidal a "queer." The debate was one of a series featuring Buckley and Vidal covering that year's Republican and Democratic Conventions. Both were seasoned TV personalities: Buckley had been appearing on TV since the early 1960s and hosting his own talk show, *Firing Line*, since 1966; Vidal was by the late 1960s much in demand for small-screen appearances in which he held forth on political and cultural matters. The two men had sparred in the past on TV, and they were brought together by the ABC network to cover the conventions because of the potential entertainment they offered as politically polarized commentators. The night in question was at the height of the now-infamous police violence against students protesting the Democratic Convention's pro–Vietnam War platform. Buckley was roused to his use of the offending epithet by Vidal's identification of him as a "pro- or crypto-Nazi" because of his support for the police. In response, Buckley raised his voice: "Now, listen, you queer! Stop calling me a crypto-Nazi or I'll sock you in your goddamn face and you'll stay plastered" (Figure 9).[1] After the broadcast concluded, Buckley, by his own account trembling with indignation, was confronted in his trailer by Vidal's friend Paul Newman. In Buckley's words (from a 1969 *Esquire* article): " 'I want you to know,' [Newman] said . . . , 'I think that was the foulest blow I ever saw.' I approached him feverishly: 'Have you ever been called a Nazi?' I spat the words out at him. His voice mellowed. 'That,' he explained, opening his hands wide as one does in expressing the obvious, 'was purely *political*. What you called *him* was personal!' "[2]

Newman's "obvious" point relied on the distinction made by both sympathetic and unsympathetic commentators during the postwar, pre–gay liberation period between the *personal*, *individual*, or *private* matter of homosexuality and the public realm of politics, a distinction tracked throughout the preceding chapters. The distinction was upheld in ABC's decisions to cancel the time-delayed West Coast version of the Chicago broadcast and to use static to cover the word "queer" in its archival tape.[3] Vidal's biographer Fred Kaplan makes clear the unprecedented nature of the incident: "The ten million people watching had heard a first, something almost unbelievable in those censored and sensitive days. . . . [Buckley] had used a homophobic epithet at a time when the general understanding was that such epithets were only for private use. . . . It was a deeply embarrassing, even shameful moment" (601). Kaplan goes on to note that many newspapers reporting on the Vidal/Buckley broadcast were forbidden to print the offending epithet (603).

Kaplan's characterization of this moment as "deeply embarrassing, even shameful" picks up on the question put to Buckley by Harold Hayes, the editor of *Esquire*, after Buckley approached him in November 1968 with the suggestion that he write for that magazine an account of the incident: "Sure . . . but in light of the embarrassment to everyone concerned, including 10 million viewers—why?" (604). Part of what I want to do in this chapter is to explore the implications of the affect of embarrassment that collected around this early instance of celebrity "outing" in particular and around the mention of homosexuality more

Figure 9. Buckley in mid-outburst, reacting to Vidal's "pro- or crypto-Nazi" taunt. Democratic Convention coverage, ABC News, 28 August 1968.

generally at this time. For Hayes's comment was not the only one to use "embarrassment" or "shame" to talk about the Buckley/Vidal encounter or to gesture toward the matter of homosexuality in 1968. Referring specifically to Buckley's name-calling, Neil Compton in *Commentary* wrote of "the shameful pleasure" of watching Buckley and Vidal "match wits."[4] The *Chicago Sun-Times* wrote up the 28 August broadcast as an "embarrassing, near-brawl scene, viewed by millions."[5] A TV review from 25 August in the *Oxnard Press-Courier* hinted at the homosexual inflection of the Buckley/Vidal dialogues by noting their tendency to degenerate into "bitchy, feline and snaky" back-and-forths and pronounced the nightly encounter "a face-spitting exchange that was irresistible as well as embarrassing."[6] And reviewing the Republican Convention debates, Stephanie Harrington in the *Village Voice* wrote: "What political analysis ABC did try for turned out to be the most embarrassing ingredient in its grand innovation" of providing a recap of and discussion about the convention rather than, as was the established procedure, broadcasting it in its entirety. ABC's potentially explosive pairing of Buckley and Vidal was, Harrington writes, "clearly a sequel to that painful moment some years back when Buckley, during a televised debate with Vidal, descended to his unique level of argument and in a typically Buckleyesque display of dirty debater's tricks, destroyed his opponent not by logic but by using his personal life against him."[7] Harrington does not give the details of this earlier incident, but her account makes the same, implicit association between embarrassment and homosexuality that Hayes's did.

Embarrassment was also the term invoked to talk about homosexuality in 1968 by the liberal journal the *New Republic*. Commenting on the increasingly vocal homophile groups of the period, the journal stated, "History indicates that politicians generally prefer to leave such embarrassments in obscurity . . . but the homosexuals profess determination to make an issue of this serious problem for society."[8] My sample of quotations from 1968 associating homosexuality with embarrassment (or shame) is admittedly small. But the fact that this association is independently repeated across diverse contexts helps us understand how homosexuality was widely construed on the cusp of the gay liberation period.

There is a substantial body of queer theoretical writing that argues for the ineradicable but potentially productive relationship of queerness to shame, and I argue in Chapter 1 that this work offers a productive perspective on the interrelations of homosexuality and celebrity in Baldwin's career.[9] This chapter proposes that embarrassment may be equally and differently helpful in understanding how 1960s American culture positioned homosexuality. Kaplan's statement that Buckley's outburst was "deeply embarrassing, even shameful" suggests a kind of affective sliding scale, whereby embarrassment is merely a minor variant of shame, or shame a more profound version of embarrassment. By contrast, a wealth of critical literature informed by diverse disciplinary perspectives seeks to distinguish embarrassment from shame, arguing that shame is a profoundly individual experience, while embarrassment is markedly social. For instance, in an essay on embarrassment in Jane Austen, Thomas Edwards distinguishes between the two affects by using embarrassment to describe "unpleasant states of mind caused by someone or something else and shame for unpleasant states of mind caused by self-assessment."[10] Similarly, in a philosophical discussion of embarrassment, Luke Purshouse states that "shame involves a negative evaluation of an aspect of one's own character," while embarrassment "seems only to occur in situations where a subject views himself as actually coming into contact with other human beings."[11]

In what follows I call into question the hard-and-fast distinction between embarrassment and shame that so many critics make. As my citation of the *Commentary* writer's description of the "shameful pleasure" of watching Buckley insult Vidal indicates, shame has a role to play in the argument I develop about embarrassment, but, in a reversal of the commonsensical ranking of the two emotions, it is the minor one. I suggest that the opposition of shame and embarrassment represses the similarity between the two affects. It is the real or imagined presence of others that seems to define the kinds of psychic disturbance denoted by both embarrassment and shame. Critics emphasize the key role that the audience plays in producing embarrassment, but the idea of the audience is no less important for recent work in the humanities on shame, which tends to argue that the affect is characterized by a paradoxical combination of isolation and theatricality. As Jacqueline Rose puts it, "Shame requires an audience. . . . Shame relies on the art of exposure, even if exposure is what it hates most and what it struggles against."[12] Rose's interest in shame includes, among other things, its role in celebrity culture. Developing my point that there is a structural similarity between shame and embarrassment, I adapt Rose's contentions about shame to embarrassment, arguing for the culturally and politically productive part that embarrassment may play, both in the media performance of the individual celebrity and in the reception of that performance by the audience.

One way of understanding the structural similarity between shame and embarrassment is as an indication of the intersubjective basis of *all* emotions. This point, it seems to me, raises a pressing issue about the deployment of affect theory in literary and cultural analysis: the danger of positivism. While the precise accounts of affects and emotions delineated in recent humanities work have enabled some salutary arguments, there is also a risk of reductiveness courted by discussions that sharply differentiate emotion *x* from affect *y*.[13] In this chapter, I try to strike a balance between respecting the useful calibrations of shame and embarrassment developed by other critics and alertness to what Fredric Jameson has recently termed the "chromaticism" of the affects, whereby "proteiform, metamorphic" affects can ultimately be understood as indeed arranged on a "sliding scale."[14] For me, then, the common conflation of embarrassment and shame, both in some of the critical literature and in everyday speech, does not constitute terminological sloppiness but indicates the chromaticism of the affects and explains why even so careful an arguer as Erving Goffman, in his classic essay on embarrassment, tends unembarrassedly to use "shame" as a placeholder for "embarrassment."[15] The potential fungibility of the two affects underpins what may look like a contradictory shift from the previous chapter, in which homosexuality was conceived in terms of *scandal*, to the present emphasis on the surely less dramatic phenomenon of embarrassment. In Chapter 5 I argue that Myra's scandalous celebrity deflected attention from the potentially scandalous nature of the unambiguous revelation of Vidal's same-sexuality. But the scandal was only potential; and celebrity "scandals" are not necessarily career-destroying, shame-laden debacles but may turn out to be embarrassing ruffles of transgression that are soon forgiven and forgotten.[16]

If shame and embarrassment are close to each other, then, this does not mean that the terms are always interchangeable, and important for my argument in this chapter is the relatively weak emotional impact and relatively strong social implication of the experience we tend to name embarrassment. I pick up on what Nick Salvato identifies as the affect's "collectivizing tendency or communitarian force . . . constituted by its embeddedness in relationality."[17] The collectivizing tendency or communitarian force of embarrassment, I argue, means that it can potentially be figured as transindividual, a symptom of particular stresses in the ideological fabric of a given sociocultural moment—in this case, stresses concerning homosexuality and heteronormativity in 1968. My account of the transindividual embarrassment produced by the 1968 broadcast also resonates with some of the less usual uses of the verb "to embarrass" disclosed by the *Oxford English Dictionary*: "to encumber or impede" and "to perplex, to throw into doubt or difficulty." To raise homosexuality from the "obscurity" in which it conventionally lay buried was, in 1968, in certain discursive contexts, to obstruct and to perplex the social fiction of universal heterosexuality.

The emphasis I am putting on the year in which Buckley's televised utterance took place extends the significance accorded in the previous chapter to 1968 as the year sex went public, focusing particularly here on open statements about homosexuality. I argue that the identification of Vidal as "queer" on TV is a staging post in both the development of open media talk about the homosexuality of celebrities and in the unfolding of gay liberation. To fix on 1968 in this way is of course to risk buying into the teleological narrative of the inevitable emergence of liberation that much careful scholarship about the past of same-sexuality has warned us against. Throughout this book, I have relied on the arguments made by historians of American sexuality, which have demonstrated that the process of gay and lesbian liberation was in fact a gradual and uneven one, taking place over the several decades between the end of World War II and the 1970s and influenced by a host of factors—most important, for my argument, the growing media representation of homosexual identity and community. Yet it is incontestable that there was an explosion of radicalized gay and lesbian discourse, as well as a marked increase in the growth and vibrancy of urban gay and lesbian subcultures after 1969, and in this chapter I assume, hopefully productively, that "around 1969" there was an epistemic break with regard to the cultural position of homosexuality—much as David Harvey states that "around 1972" capitalism shifted from Fordism to post-Fordism.[18] I heuristically take up or turn back to this popular version of homosexual history because I am interested in the difference that liberatory or proto-liberatory openness about homosexuality can make. I want to extrapolate an account of the political force of openness from my specific interest in the difference it makes to embarrassingly identify Gore Vidal as queer on TV in 1968. Buckley's naming Vidal as a queer on national TV, I suggest, was a paradigmatic instance of the transformation of proto-visibility into visibility that also fed into the move toward liberation. Although queer criticism is itself a distant consequence of the liberatory openness I am describing, and although it relies on that openness for its current institutional currency, it is more likely to parse the limitations, and even the oppressiveness, of open statements about homosexuality than it is to stress their value. In many queer theoretical arguments, the political desirability of openness or visibility is acknowledged, but only as a prelude to an account of its pitfalls. While, as elsewhere in this book, my argument is in accord with queer theory's foundational assumption about the contingency of sexual identity, I want here to think about the value of saying things aloud and of bringing things to light.

Embarrassing Exchanges

To elaborate these various claims, I need first to turn to the fallout of the Vidal/Buckley broadcast. Kaplan's account of the immediate aftermath of the broadcast presents Vidal as magnanimously putting Buckley's intemperance aside. When Vidal's father "expressed concern that Buckley's condemnation of him as a 'queer' before millions of listeners might harm his public image," Vidal responded, as noted by Kaplan, "Forget it, Buckley's considered a far greater creep than I am. This is the way the world goes" (603). Although Vidal did not pursue legal action against Buckley, as the network had apparently feared might be the case, he characteristically did not let go of the matter without a parting shot. The morning after the broadcast, Vidal told the *Chicago Sun-Times*, "I've always tried to treat Buckley like the great lady that he is. He's given to neurotic tantrums and I feel sorry for him" (604). While Kaplan sees Vidal's comment as pointing up the "ironic implication" of "someone who considered it the height of condemnation to call someone a 'queer' himself seeming somewhat suspect" (604), less charitably, I see it as a sortie in the exchange of homophobic slurs that characterized the aftermath of the broadcast and indeed its prehistory.

However, it is true that after this statement to the press, Vidal seems to have put the incident behind him. By contrast, Buckley brooded on it, eventually approaching Harold Hayes with his request that *Esquire* print his account. In an unpublished manuscript, Hayes recorded the reply already quoted: "Sure . . . but in light of the embarrassment to everyone concerned, including 10 million viewers—why?" Buckley's response, according to Hayes and quoted by Kaplan: "I have been hounded at every turn about my part in it. I think if I were to try and write about it I might be able to work out why I said what I did. I will need some length, and I must be assured that your lawyers will allow me to call Vidal a homosexual in print. Otherwise there is no point in my undertaking it" (604). As Kaplan notes, it must have been clear to Hayes that Buckley "was interested in justifying himself and punishing Vidal," as "otherwise private opportunities to 'work out why' would have sufficed" (604).

Enraged at being labeled a pro- or crypto-Nazi, Buckley had reached for the epithet "queer" to publicly shame Vidal. For, as Judith Butler notes, "the term 'queer' has operated as one linguistic practice whose purpose has been the shaming of the subject it names or, rather, the producing of a subject *through* that shaming interpellation."[19] Butler is surely right that the invocation of *queer* helps form "a social bond among homophobic communities . . . through time," but the inadmissibility of this term in the mass-mediatized public sphere of 1968 spurred Buckley into a compensatory act of public self-justification.[20] One way of reading this self-justification might be as a particularly peculiar example of the "peculiarly contagious" nature of shame explored by Eve Kosofsky Sedgwick: seeking to shame Vidal, it was Buckley who was himself shamed, his epithet ricocheting back on him.[21] Such a reading of Buckley's determination to justify himself would be in accord with the psychological literature on shame that sees the affect as potentially causing "momentary losses of self-esteem" that may prompt "aggressive, self-serving behavior."[22] However, if we consider that the event took place on TV, then I think "embarrassment" works better to explain not only Buckley's behavior but also the disruptive difference to public discourse his outburst made.

Goffman argues that embarrassment often arises "when the self projected is somehow confronted with another self which, though valid in other contexts, cannot be sustained in harmony with the first. Embarrassment, then, leads us to the matter of 'role segregation.' Each individual has more than one role, but he is saved from role dilemma by 'audience segregation.' "[23] The embarrassment caused Buckley by his outburst can be understood, then, as a failure of the self being projected into the situation of public sphere commentary—an embarrassment unlikely to have been generated by his utterance of the epithet away from TV cameras before an audience of intimates. As Kaplan notes, Buckley "had used a homophobic epithet at a time when the general understanding was that such epithets were only for private use" (601). Blurting out an insulting interpellation deemed improper for a television audience, Buckley demonstrated Goffman's point that "embarrassment has to do with unfulfilled expectations."[24] But the embarrassment prompted by this occasion extended beyond Buckley himself to the collective context of the audience, as the reviews and comments quoted previously indicate. Echoing Sedgwick's characterization of shame, Goffman notes that embarrassment "seems to be contagious, spreading, once started, in ever widening circles of discomfiture." The effect of Buckley's outburst, which spread, in its embarrassing ramification from Buckley to the audience, indicates how, as Goffman puts it, embarrassment is "located not in the individual but in the social system wherein he has his several selves."[25] Embarrassment, then, potentially at least, is transindividual: less a failure of self-esteem than a failure of the social compact.[26] Contrasting with this generalized embarrassment, however, Vidal himself seemed unfazed by the epithet, meeting Buckley's outburst with a smile, apparently triumphant that he had goaded his opponent into a face-losing moment (Figure 10). Although he was reticent about publicly attesting to his same-sexual interests, the moment does not seem to have presented any kind of emotional crisis for Vidal, perhaps bearing out his frequent boast about his self-assured, "aristocratic" distance from bourgeois morality.[27]

Despite his doubts about Buckley's motivations, Hayes was keen to publish the suggested piece, feeling, as Kaplan puts it, "the attraction of famous names and lively controversy" (604). But he needed to establish two things. First, he asked Buckley if he would accept that *Esquire* needed to allow Vidal to respond. To this, Buckley agreed. Second, Hayes needed to check with *Esquire*'s lawyer about whether Buckley's insistence that he be allowed to call Vidal a homosexual in his article would leave the magazine open to a charge of libel. The lawyer advised that the magazine would be well protected if it could demonstrate that whatever

Figure 10. Vidal reacts to being called a "queer." Democratic Convention coverage, ABC News, 28 August 1968.

it printed was "true in fact and fair in comment." Hayes had two *Esquire* staff members search for corroborating information, and although the result indicated that Vidal had never admitted to being homosexual, there seemed to be enough support for the claim to protect *Esquire*, should Vidal sue (605).

Although uninterested in responding to Buckley when Hayes first approached him, Vidal changed his mind after Hayes sent him a first draft of Buckley's article. Once Vidal had agreed to write, *Esquire*, to protect itself from libel suits from either party, sent the two men successive drafts of each other's articles, with both Vidal and Buckley demanding changes, a process that took several months. Finally, Buckley's "On Experiencing Gore Vidal" and Vidal's "A Distasteful Encounter with William F. Buckley Jr." appeared, respectively, in the August and September 1969 issues. Despite all the magazine's precautions, Buckley promptly sued both *Esquire* and Vidal for libel. The legal conflict played out over the next three years, Buckley eventually agreeing to drop charges in return for *Esquire* paying his costs. His motivation appears to have been legal advice that there was enough evidence from his published writings for a jury to find him to be racist and anti-Semitic—a pro- or crypto-Nazi, in other words. However, Buckley subsequently misrepresented the outcome of these machinations as a win for him and a legal finding that Vidal had indeed libeled him (603–19).

Buckley's rambling and incoherent article takes some time to work itself up into anything resembling an argument, but when it does, in its final pages, Buckley attempts to justify his outburst by troubling the personal/political distinction to which Paul Newman had appealed in their encounter after the broadcast. Buckley turns Newman's criticism on its head, suggesting that to be branded a crypto-Nazi is not "merely a *political* charge"—that is, that Vidal's identification of Buckley as some kind of Nazi was an attack on his character.[28] Additionally, while Buckley, unsurprisingly, does not define homosexuality as a politicized identity, he does seek to show that through publicizing homosexuality in his writing, Vidal has forfeited his right to privacy: "The man who in his essays proclaims the normalcy of his affliction, and in his art the desirability of it, is not to be confused with the man who bears his sorrows quietly. The addict is to be pitied and even respected, not the pusher." Attributing the "affliction" of homosexuality to Vidal, Buckley doubles down on the direct identification of Vidal made in his outburst. If, ideally, the homosexual is a "man who bears his sorrows quietly," Buckley also recognizes that the time of discreet silence is coming to an end—indeed, he has contributed to the increasing talk about homosexuality by tagging Vidal and then writing a justification of it. Vidal's outspokenness represents a culture war, in which the battles will be—already are—between collective forces rather than individuals: "Evangelists for bisexuality must endure evangelists for heterosexuality."[29]

Vidal's article, a model of crispness and clarity in contrast with Buckley's, culminates with an account of an incident that took place in 1944, in which three of Buckley's sisters had vandalized an Episcopalian church in the family's hometown of Sharon, Connecticut, apparently in retaliation for the minister's wife, a real estate agent, having sold a property in the town to a Jewish family. (Vidal had raised the incident during the TV debate after Buckley's insult—"What happened at Sharon?"—but amid the brouhaha didn't get to pursue the issue.)[30] Though Buckley was not involved in this incident, Vidal tars him by association, arguing that Buckley's sisters were roused to their act of vandalism by their father's anti-Semitic views, and that the members of the Buckley family are "devoted to one another . . . and on the important issues, they think alike."[31] The story of the incident at Sharon clinches the evidence of anti-Semitism and racism from Buckley's writing and public statements that Vidal adduces elsewhere in the article in support of his claim that Buckley is a pro- or crypto-Nazi. But if the argument of Vidal's article pivots on a demonstration of the veracity of this claim, much of its rhetorical force derives from Vidal projecting onto Buckley the same charge of queerness that Buckley leveled against Vidal.

Early in his article Vidal accuses Buckley of commonly making "sniggering sexual innuendos about a range of public figures" and implies that Buckley's intemperate use of "queer" on TV was simply the logical conclusion of his "morbid obsession" with homosexuality. Rather than reject Buckley's practice of homophobic slurring, Vidal turns on Buckley the same line of argument-by-innuendo that Buckley turned on Vidal, when, reviewing the frequency of homosexual representation in Vidal's work, he charged him with "obsession."[32] Vidal proceeds by further smearing Buckley. He points out that Norman Mailer "even shouted the word 'fag' at Buckley during a Les Crane taping: it was cut from the show. . . . How innocent television was before Chicago last summer!" (949). He writes that a gay publication, *The Homosexual Handbook*, claimed Buckley was a homosexual who conducts his TV show "with such brilliant gestures and hand movement, that Gore Vidal is reputed to have called him 'the Marie Antoinette of American politics.'" Vidal notes that "to include Buckley in a list of homosexuals is doubtless slanderous" but that "every public figure is vulnerable to this sort of rumor, which is why it seems to me odd that someone like Buckley, himself suspect, should be so quick to smear others as 'queers'" (950). Some pages later, after having supposedly dispensed with the issue of homosexual slander, Vidal states that when he first encountered Buckley in the early 1960s he dismissed him as a "Right Wing Liberace" (956). By associating Buckley with another celebrity figure rumored to be gay, Vidal reinforces the innuendo established by the charge of morbid obsession and by his repetition of Mailer and *The Homosexual Handbook*'s statements. Indeed, Vidal knowingly draws attention to his own disingenuousness on the matter of slander by quoting the *Handbook* quoting his own "reputed" likening of Buckley to Marie Antoinette, a characterization that chimes with Vidal's identification of Buckley to the *Chicago Sun-Times* as a "great lady." Similarly, at a point in the 28 August broadcast before Buckley lost his cool, Vidal associated Buckley with Myra Breckinridge herself, saying to his adversary that he "based her entire style polemically upon on you, passionate and irrelevant."[33] Vidal's argumentative tactics, then, quite as much as Buckley's, bespeak a historical and cultural context in which public identifications of others as homosexual can only be slanderous. Like Buckley in the broadcast, Vidal seeks to shame through an association with homosexuality. Moreover, Vidal relies on stereotypical, damning associations of homosexuality with effeminacy and flamboyance. I will come back to Vidal's effeminophobia, but it's worth noting at this point that during the convention broadcasts, before his infamous outburst, Buckley also unsurprisingly resorted to innuendos of (effeminate) homosexuality, stating snidely of Vidal, "We know you'd like nothing to sully your lips" and characterizing him as "feline."[34]

What, then, of Vidal's own sexuality? How did he respond in his article to Buckley's identification of him as queer? In line with the findings of Hayes's researchers that Vidal had never publicly admitted to homosexuality, Vidal sidesteps the issue. Referring to digs about *Myra Breckinridge* that Buckley had made in the debates, Vidal writes:

> [H]is motive was plain. *Myra Breckinridge* is about a homosexual who becomes a woman, falls in love with a girl and then becomes, more or less, a man again. To connect me with the book would mean to certain souls that the author was a homosexual who had become a woman who had become a woman who had then become a man, etc. . . . This is pretty simple-minded reasoning but Buckley himself has a simple mind. . . . Needless to say, identifying authors by their books is a feckless game. (951)

To indict Buckley with such absurdly "simple-minded" author-character identification, is of course itself absurd; but it also does the serious work of exempting Vidal from discussing his sexuality. Here we have a particularly clear example of Vidal using the "overexpression" of Myra's persona to deflect attention from his own sexual unorthodoxy, which was, as Buckley correctly assumed, connected to the preoccupations of *Myra* and other Vidal novels. Indeed, if Vidal chose to smear Buckley by identifying him as Myra, Buckley returned the compliment in the moments following the exchange of name-calling in the 28 August broadcast: "Let Myra Breckinridge go back to his pornography and stop making any allusions of Nazism."[35]

While happy to use the homosexual smear against his opponent, Vidal also elaborates in his article the left-liberal tolerance of homosexuality as a matter for the private individual. In response to Buckley's accusation that he is an "evangelist for bisexuality," Vidal states, "I am not an evangelist of anything in sexual matters except a decent withdrawal of the state from the bedroom" (960). This was a position that Vidal had elaborated in his essay "Sex and the Law," published in 1965 in *Partisan Review*. Deploying the notion of the victimless crime, Vidal asked there, "Why should homosexual acts between consenting adults be considered inimical to the public good?"[36] Vidal's 1960s defenses of homosexuality ostensibly do not emerge out of any personal experience but are based on the abstract ideal of individual freedom. Like Vidal's smearing of Buckley as a "great lady" or as "Myra Breckinridge," and like the overexpression of Myra herself, these arguments have the effect of distancing Vidal from homosexuality and reinforcing his position as a liberal intellectual, for whom there is no contradiction between tolerance of homosexuality and condescension to it. As noted previously, despite his notorious rejection of gay liberation politics, it was not until the 1960s morphed into the 1970s and the cultural impact of gay liberation was felt that Vidal began to talk publicly about his own erotic liaisons with men, openly indicating that his impulse to defend sexual nonnormativity may have involved something other than disinterested liberalism.

From Identity to Acts

However, it seems likely that many observers in the 1960s would have assumed that Vidal was a homosexual. Vidal had after all at the age of twenty-three published the gay protest novel *The City and the Pillar* (1948), which provided a frank and sympathetic account of homosexuality. And subsequently Vidal was, as

Buckley intimated, a frequent public apologist for homosexuality, or bisexuality, whose apologies moreover moved beyond the liberal argument about the victimless crime to proclamations of the "naturalness" of same-sexual desire. From the late 1950s Vidal began to state in his writings that humans are inherently bisexual and that *homosexuality* described behavior rather than identity. His position is close to the Foucauldian precept of queer theory, and Dennis Altman has noted the curious lack of serious attention to Vidal's work in that field.[37] As Altman also observes, however, the critique of sexual identity categories is not Foucault's (or Vidal's) innovation but common to "most western students of sexuality from Freud through to Kinsey"; indeed, both Baldwin and Sontag also assumed that sexual identities are culturally fashioned.[38] I am interested not in claiming Vidal as a queer theorist *avant la lettre* but in complicating his claim to see, and to be, beyond the homo/hetero binary. It is the way this binary *informs* his thinking (as, we have seen, it informs the utopian, anticategorical thinking of queer theory and gay liberation) that is my concern.

Altman rightly characterizes Vidal's position on universal bisexuality as "Platonic rather than Freudian"—informed by his reading of Aristophanes's famous myth in the *Symposium*, and, more generally, by his deep, sympathetic engagement with the classical world.[39] Vidal first set out this position in an essay responding to Robert Graves's translation of the Roman historian Suetonius's book *The Twelve Caesars*, where he wrote that the "underlying assumption" of pre-Christian antiquity was that "man is bisexual" and that "one suspects that despite the stern moral legislation of own time [we] are no different. If nothing else, Dr. Kinsey revealed in his dogged, arithmetical way that we are all a good deal less predictable and bland than anyone had suspected."[40] In his "Author's Note" to the collection *United States* (1993), Vidal claims "The Twelve Caesars" was written in 1952 and that "it took a long time before anyone would publish so 'outrageous' a commentary."[41] As Graves's translation was published in 1957, there is good reason to doubt Vidal's claim; there is, I suppose, a possibility that Vidal had written an early version of an essay on Suetonius before the translation appeared, though his extensive archive shows no trace of it. The earliest version of the essay in Vidal's archive is a draft typescript dated 1959; and it was first published in the 1962 collection of essays *Rocking the Boat*.[42] But I am not as much interested here in sorting out whether Vidal has engaged in a deliberate mistruth or experienced a failure of memory as I am in demonstrating that what appears to be a backdating of the Suetonius essay helps (either intentionally or unconsciously) establish a consistency to Vidal's position on human bisexuality that he wished to convey but that the record does not support.

In contrast with Vidal's later insistence on innate bisexuality, the original version of *The City and the Pillar* establishes an essentialist account of homosexual identity. Vidal extensively revised the novel for reissue in 1965 and appended an afterword, in which he wrote that in writing the novel, "I wanted to take risks, to try something no American had done before. I decided to examine the homosexual underworld (which I knew less well than I pretended), and in the process show the 'naturalness' of homosexual relations, as well as making the point that there is of course no such thing as a homosexual."[43] Vidal talks up his daring and misrepresents the singularity of his book. Without denying the riskiness of his endeavor in terms of his own career, *City* was actually part of a wave of gay protest novels that appeared in the five years or so following the end of the war, including Richard Brooks's *The Brick Foxhole* (1945), Charles Jackson's *The Lost Weekend* (1946), and John Horne Burns's *The Gallery* (1947); like *City*, these novels "exposed middle-class readers to sensational, decadent, and ultimately tragic images from a hidden, exotic underworld," while "also encourag[ing] readerly sympathy through the suffering of the main characters."[44] More important, in his 1965 afterword, Vidal misrepresents the original version "as making the point that there is of course no such thing as a homosexual." As Claude Summers has convincingly argued, "the novel does not illustrate [this] point but rather its opposite, for despite the author's well-known belief in the natural bisexuality of the species and his frequent insistence that *homosexual* is an adjective rather than a noun (a position also held by Alfred Kinsey), the novel succeeds primarily as a bildungsroman tracing its protagonist's gradual acceptance of a homosexual identity."[45] Even in its revised version, the "all-American" protagonist Jim is exclusively homosexual and Bob, the lifelong object of his passion with whom he had an adolescent affair, leaves same-sex desire behind him to become exclusively heterosexual. Moreover, despite the novel's promotion in both the 1948 and 1965 versions of normatively masculine homosexuality in the figure of Jim, it also "rather contradictorily conceives of homosexuality as an abnormal state demanding psychological explanation. For all its reformist zeal, it is nevertheless clearly a document reflective of its era."[46] This reflectiveness is evident in the book's preoccupation with etiologies of homosexuality: there are long discussions between the gay characters about whether their sexuality is the result of smothering mothers, a fear of women, or the effeminization of American society. Jim's staunch masculinity aside, the 1948 version especially tends to conceive of homosexual identity in terms of the still widely accepted terms of gender inversion. In one passage, Jim characterizes butch-femme lesbianism as a kind of "defiance." Butch-femme lesbians, he says, are "so hunted that they have, at last, become totally perverse as a defense." Such perverse homosexuality is contrasted with the "thousands" of "perfectly normal men and women, except for this overdevelopment of the other sex in them. They live in hiding now all over the country; I think that only a few ever practice what they feel. Most of them marry and have children and try to destroy the other sex in them; they never succeed, of course. Those are the ones who should make themselves known, who should be allowed to grow outwardly, to search for love, as all humans should."[47] In the scheme of the book, the contrast between "perverse" butch-femme and "perfectly normal" homosexuals is more a matter of degree than kind, because the latter also are characterized by an "overdevelopment of the other sex in them." Unsurprisingly, this passage with its elaboration of the idea of fundamental, if secreted, homosexual identities involving gender inversion was cut from the 1965 version, as Vidal sought to bring the novel into line with his endlessly iterated position on the illusiveness of the gay/straight divide.

If Vidal's representation of homosexuality in the original version of *The City and the Pillar* cleaves to orthodox midcentury understandings of fixed homosexual identity, what explains his shift in position on this topic? Probably there are multiple determinations, including his reading of classical literature. I suspect, however, that an important, unacknowledged factor is Kinsey, who, as Summers reminds us, also held the position "that *homosexual* is an adjective rather than a noun." Vidal was in fact interviewed by Kinsey for *Sexual Behavior in the Human Male* (1948). Many years later, in his memoir *Palimpsest* (1995), Vidal reported that "Kinsey told me that I was not 'homosexual'—doubtless because I never sucked cock or got fucked. . . . I would not have had it otherwise, since, even then, I did not believe in fixed sexual categories; and finally Kinsey appears not to have believed in them either."[48] Here Kinsey's belief in the artificiality of categories "finally" succeeds Vidal's own putatively intuitive one—Vidal tells us that when he met Kinsey, "I had not read Plato; I had no theory."[49] But it seems that if Kinsey did not bring about Vidal's conviction about sexual identity categories, he certainly bolstered it. We have already seen Vidal appeal to Kinsey's "dogged, arithmetical" demonstration of the artificiality of categories in "The Twelve Caesars." In Vidal's breezily comic 1952 novel *The Judgment of Paris*, too, in a passage about the postwar growth of "tolerance," the narrator states the sanguine view that "sexual behavior," the "last cherished area for intolerance was suddenly declared out of bounds by a celebrated statistical report which revealed that one third of the nation's men had, at one time or another, committed a homosexual act."[50]

Although this passage from *Judgment* refers explicitly to homosexual behavior rather than identity, the narrator draws an analogy with intolerance of groups defined by ethnic and racial identity (African Americans, Jews, and Italians), claiming (again overly sanguinely and no doubt partly jokingly) that these groups had benefited from the growing postwar "intolerance of intolerance," a reaction to the war's "pogroms and experiments with genocide."[51] Vidal's work actually evinces a tension between universalizing and minoritizing models of homosexuality that, in Eve Sedgwick's influential argument, is a central contradiction of "modern sexual definition."[52] Vidal's mixed feelings about minoritization are expressed in a fascinating letter from 1954. Responding to an invitation from the gay writer James Fugaté to contribute to the homophile *ONE* magazine, which had produced its first issue in 1953, Vidal attests to being conflicted about the idea of the publication. While the magazine, he can see, does "give comfort to the isolated. . . . Homosexuality is not a flag, a nation, a religion. . . . It is a form of sexual activity common to all in some way, claiming a few exclusively, many partially, and some only by indirection." Rather than appeal exclusively to the minority group of "homosexuals (see? strongly as I feel I still use it as a noun!)," Vidal proposes that *ONE* disseminate "propaganda of Kinsey's sort" that will convince the general population that all sexual feeling is "essentially mysterious and irrelevant" and that consenting adult behavior is not the business of the state: "Americans love statistics. . . . Well, give them graphs." In the letter Vidal firmly rejects the idea of gender inversion, which only five years earlier had informed *The City and the Pillar*, even as that novel had strenuously insisted on the compatibility of masculinity and homosexual behavior. Homosexuals "most definitely are not" a "third sex," he states, adding that "the ones who wish to dress up like mother and play house are not in quality much different from those, who, sane in other matters, regard themselves secretly as Joan of Arc or Napoleon." Appealing again to Kinsey, Vidal sets out what would become his official position on sexual identity categories. But the torsions of his prose tellingly and self-consciously indicate the impossibility of completely setting identity aside ("strongly as I feel I still use it as a noun!").[53]

The mixed position on minoritization is evident eleven years later in his essay "Pornography" (1965), Vidal's contribution to the anticensorship arguments of the mid-1960s. Touching on his conviction that "we are bisexual," Vidal writes:

> Certainly to maintain that a homosexual act in itself is antisocial or neurotic is dangerous nonsense, of the sort the astonishing Dr. Edmund Bergler used to purvey when he claimed that he would "cure" homosexuals, as if this was somehow desirable, like changing Jewish noses or straightening Negro hair in order to make it possible for those who have been so altered to pass more easily through a world of white Christians with snub noses.[54]

The slide from "homosexual act" to "homosexuals" in this passage is indicative. It is an exercise in Deconstruction 101 to show how often Vidal's insistence on the adjectival rather than the nominal status of "homosexuality" is undermined by his resort to the notion of sexual identity.[55] Thus, if the passage from *Judgment* quoted earlier defines homosexuality as a behavior rather than an identity, elsewhere the book's resolutely heterosexual protagonist encounters, and is lusted after by, several decidedly gay-identified men as he makes his picaresque way through postwar Europe. Or we could point to Vidal's frequent bestowal upon others of the epithet "faggot" throughout his career. "Faggot," as Vidal uses it, names a particular type of homosexual identity—the effeminate gay man; Vidal resembles many men of his era, both gay and straight, in his effeminophobia (in his letter to Fugaté he identifies effeminacy with mental illness). Aware of the tension between his anti-identitarian stance and his recourse to identity categories, Vidal often makes the case that homosexual (and heterosexual) identities are cultural distortions of authentic human sexuality. In "Pornography," for instance, he concedes that "opportunity and habit incline us toward this or that sexual object";[56] and in the letter to Fugaté, he acknowledges that homosexual taste "claim[s] a few exclusively." But if homosexual identification is a "mysterious" matter—as he puts it on more than one occasion, including in his letter to Fugaté—that does not make it any less culturally forceful and liable to impress itself on Vidal's writing.

In contrast to those who assume Vidal's "consistent" opposition to sexual identities, then, my close, historically situated reading of his published and unpublished statements on the matter suggests that he actually moved from a standard belief in or at least strong orientation toward the veracity of sexual identity categories to his more familiar contrarian dismissal of them. Or, more precisely, we could say that Vidal's position—like that of Baldwin—mixes an anticategorical understanding of homosexuality with an acknowledgment, made with varying degrees of explicitness, of the inescapability of identity categories. The backstory of Vidal's relations to gay identity I've outlined shows that, despite his best efforts, he was unable to resist the force of the midcentury shift to minoritization.

The Embarrassment of Identification

Vidal was approached in 1954 by Fugaté to contribute to *ONE* on the basis of being well known for having written about homosexuality. A letter from Fugaté to Tennessee Williams held in the *ONE* archive that also solicits a contribution is likely to have been largely identical to the one sent to Vidal. Fugaté records there that the idea to appeal for support from a number of "top writers in this country who have written on homosexuality" came out of a conversation with Christopher Isherwood. Stressing the parlous but "intrepid" nature of the *ONE* enterprise, Fugaté states that the magazine "need[s] to reflect the prestige of important writers in the field of sexual deviation, writers whose names are so well known and respected that to publish them is to automatically increase circulation and acceptance among homosexual and heterosexual groups alike."[57] An early effort to apply the sheen of literary celebrity to the homosexual rights cause, Fugaté's appeal appears to have succeeded solely, and perhaps unexpectedly, with Norman Mailer, who published his essay "The Homosexual Villain" in *ONE* in 1955 (later collected in his book *Advertisements for Myself* [1959]). As for Vidal, almost buried among the hectic musings of his letter to Fugaté is a commitment to supply a contribution, though he warns that he means to "irritate your parishioners."[58] In a reply to Vidal, Fugaté states that this willingness to contribute "has made me very happy, and I must admit, done much to renew my waning faith in celebrities." In a handwritten message to Dorr Legg, an editor and founder of *ONE*, appended to Legg's copy of this reply, Fugaté records his excitement at a prospect that was never fulfilled: "Look what we've got! Gosh, this is wonderful! . . . This is a great stride forward! Don't ever let me down with this fellow. I'd feature him on the cover. . . . He's big and his good opinion will do you much good."[59] In the years following this correspondence, Vidal never again came close to association with the homophile movement, with its, to him, troubling emphasis on homosexuals as a minority. However, if Vidal never literally became a cover boy for homosexual identity, as Fugaté hoped, his celebrity status overlapped with his same-sexuality in ways that proved outside his control.

When Buckley named Vidal as a queer—and when Vidal intimated that Buckley was a "faggot"—each man positioned the other at that charged intersection of celebrity and sexuality in which, as Vidal put it in his *Esquire* article, "every public figure is vulnerable to this sort of rumor." If celebrity, as Jacqueline Rose writes, "depends for its existence on hearsay, innuendo and gossip," then in a culture in which it is marked as a kind of secret knowledge, homosexuality is one of the primary manifestations of the hearsay, innuendo, and gossip that defines celebrity.[60] Buckley's calling Vidal a queer on national TV disrupted Vidal's official stance of the liberal public intellectual. His personal attack depended for its force on the personal dimension of celebrity—the interest taken in a public figure's private life, not only in what he does or says as an entertainer or as an entertaining intellectual. However, Buckley's attack was importantly *not* innuendo but a direct identification. It was the *naming* of Vidal as queer on TV that was deeply embarrassing—that was, as Kaplan states, "a first." Some rare well-known figures, such as Allen Ginsberg, were professedly homosexual in the 1960s; Ginsberg was in fact interviewed by Buckley on *Firing Line* in May 1968, with Buckley introducing the poet as homosexual, among other indications of his "unconventional" persona.[61] Was it then Buckley's exposure of someone as homosexual who had not consented to being so named that gave his outburst its particularly embarrassing flavor?

To an extent, this is surely the case. Yet, as the comment quoted earlier from the 1968 edition of the *New Republic* indicates, homosexuality was in *general* in 1968 widely held to be embarrassing—a matter best not mentioned in public. The imperative to keep this embarrassing matter under wraps was, however, increasingly displaced by the growing focus on the gay subculture in print, in cinema, and even on TV: the groundbreaking CBS documentary *The Homosexuals* (1967) featured Vidal prominently, speaking up once more for the "naturalness" of homosexuality but not, needless to say, being identified as homosexual himself.[62] Exemplifying those less familiar denotations of embarrassment—"to encumber or impede" and "to perplex, to throw into doubt or difficulty"—this growing talk about homosexuality impeded and perplexed the heteronormative settlement. While exposés such as *The Homosexuals* were homophobic in tenor, they also created an embarrassing confrontation with matter that disrupted heteronormative ideology.

Queer Theory's Knowingness

There is another way in which the Buckley-Vidal contretemps, as well as the 1960s exposures of the gay subculture, might be interpreted—as manifestations of the "knowingness" that structures a homophobic society's relation to homosexuality. This is the knowingness manifested in *the open secret*, a vernacular phrase for the social registration of homosexuality (among other indiscretions) that was originally elaborated in a theoretical register by D. A. Miller and that has proved to be a highly durable tool for analysis of the reticulation of power and knowledge around queer identity.

If a queer theorist were to turn her attention to Buckley's outburst, I suspect she would parse it in terms of the logic of knowingness about homosexuality that structures homophobic culture, whereby, as Sedgwick puts it, "a suppositionally virginal" discursive surface is "pornographically . . . violated and violated yet again each time anew, by always the same information in fact possessed and exploited from the start."[63] For my hypothetical queer theoretical reading of the 1968 broadcast, with Vidal (and maybe Buckley as well) presumed to be homosexual, the combined thrill and discipline of naming homosexuality inevitably waited in the wings.[64]

I do not suggest that knowingness played no part in the interactions between Buckley and Vidal. I alluded previously to the way in which Vidal knowingly draws attention to his own knowingness about Buckley's putative effeminacy, a move that Marcie Frank, in a discussion of the fallout of the 1968 broadcast, describes as a " 'takes one to know one' retort."[65] So if, as I have argued, Vidal's effeminophobic slurs worked to distance him from the contamination of gayness, there is a ghostly sense in which in his camp acts of slurring Vidal might be understood as copping to his own intimate knowledge of homosexuality. Vidal's camp wit—his mastery of the arch putdown, displayed in his written and spoken response to Buckley—might be understood as obliquely signaling his own nonnormative sexual orientation, for if camp wit is not the sole preserve of gay men, it comes to be widely understood as a distinctive feature of urban gay subcultures in the postwar period.[66] But Vidal's camp insults do not have the capacity to expose or to reveal that embarrassment does; they are instead examples of the kind of innuendo that Vidal accused Buckley of wielding against others.

It is the revelatory force of embarrassment, I suggest, that queer theory, with its knowing emphasis on knowingness, forecloses. If we adopt the queer theoretical account of the open secret, the eruption of the private into the public can never surprise—it can never have a political effect. But if private and public are inextricably intertwined in postwar American culture—as many cultural theorists have argued—this is not to say that distinctions are meaningless or that the emergence of private material into the public domain (or vice versa) may not be experienced as disjunctive, scandalous, or depredatory.

Writing about embarrassment in his germinal discussion of the open secret, D. A. Miller declares:

> Nothing . . . is more striking than the disproportion between the embarrassed subject and the occasion of his embarrassment: while the former imagines his subjectivity on conspicuous and defenseless display, the latter has usually been rendered all but invisible by its sheer mundaneness, its cultural or physiological predictability. Rarely does anyone even think to watch the spectacle we assumed we were making of ourselves. We say truly "I could have died of embarrassment," but nearer than one's fantasized murder at the hands (the eyes, the tongues) of the others is the danger lest such worldly homicide prove embarrassingly unnecessary, the subject who fears extinction having already died out on his own.[67]

In Miller's account, our sense of embarrassment, premised on our notion of ourselves as unique subjects, is displaced by the embarrassing sense in which we are, like everyone else, predictable subjects of Foucauldian disciplinary modernity. But again, this too-knowing analysis misses the way in which embarrassment might disrupt the social surface rather than exemplify its smooth functioning. Moreover, Miller's comment ignores the way in which embarrassment might be a collective rather than a politically null individual experience; it is the political implications of the collective sense of embarrassment induced by Buckley's utterance that I have attempted to draw out.

Let me conclude by picking up on the relation of those political implications to Vidal's celebrity status. For naming an unfamous individual as a queer on TV in 1968 would surely not have had the resonance that this particular act of naming had and continues to have. The outburst is one of the best-remembered facts about both men, as its frequent citation in their respective obituaries attests; and 2015 saw the release of *Best of Enemies*, a documentary film about the Vidal-Buckley relationship, in which the infamous broadcast was the inevitable climax.[68] In order to think about the relation of Vidal's celebrity to embarrassment, I draw on Rose's speculation that "there might be an intimate, even passionate, connection between the cult of celebrity and shame."[69] In line with my comments about the sliding scale between shame and embarrassment, I modify Rose's speculation, proposing a connection between celebrity and embarrassment.[70] As I note in relation to Baldwin in Chapter 1, Rose moves from the observation that "celebrity is often a ritual of public humiliation" to ask if celebrity is "our guilty secret, a veiled way of putting into public circulation certain things which do not easily admit to public acknowledgment."[71]

Despite his sidestepping of the issue of his sexuality in the preliberation era and his repudiation of gay identity in the postliberation era, Vidal as a celebrity became one particular, public, if usually "veiled," embodiment of the embarrassing matter of male homosexuality. Through his celebrity presence Vidal contributed, however inadvertently, to the making public of homosexuality that fed into gay liberation. Buckley's furious unveiling of Vidal as a "queer" represents one of the less glorious moments in this process of making public. But the response of the writer with whom I began this book, John Cheever, to an appearance by Vidal on TV in the early 1960s indicates the more liberatory possibilities inscribed within Vidal's status as celebrity homosexual. Writing about Vidal's "personable and intelligent" public performance, Cheever noted in his journal that "perhaps we have reached a point where men of this persuasion are not forced into attitudes of bitterness, rancor and despair."[72] Cheever anticipates the liberated homosexuality that he did not live out himself, instead becoming posthumously a byword for unhappy closetedness. Vidal's public performance, by contrast, formed part of the prehistory of the politics of gay pride, even if that prototypical pride was sometimes shot through with embarrassment.

AFTERWORD

Visibility, Revisited; or, Delete the Closet?

TOWARD THE END OF 2017, Newnownext, an online offshoot of the digital channel Logo, like many other LGBT-focused websites, featured a listicle tallying celebrities who had come out that year.[1] The celebrities had variously come out as bisexual, gay, lesbian, queer, trans, and intersex—even, in the case of actor Haaz Sleiman, as a gay bottom. The eagerness of these public figures to identify themselves was somewhat tempered by the resistance of a couple to "labels." Actress Natalie Morales ("best known for playing Tom Haverford's girlfriend Lucy on *Parks and Recreation*") explained, "I don't like labeling myself, or anyone else. . . . But if it's easier for you to understand me, what I'm saying is that I'm queer. What queer means to me is just simply that I'm not straight. That's all." And Steve Lacy, a member of the band The Internet, we are informed, had replied to a question whether he was gay or straight on Tumblr by replying, " 'I'm human.' . . . On Twitter, he suggested 'let's delete the whole closet concept and just let kids be themselves without having to announce what/who they're into sexually.' " The statements of Morales and Lacy invoke an anti-identitarianism that is only seemingly in tension with the premise of the listicle—coming out. The listicle is headed with a pull quote, "Now it's time to become a whole person," from Gavin Russom ("LCD Soundsystem's resident electronics whiz"), who "came out as trans in July." In the article, faith in authentic selfhood intersects with refusal of sexual identities. Whether the celebrities listed associate themselves with specific categories or reject them, the announcement of sexuality is always an announcement of the truth of personhood ("just let kids be themselves"). Self-actualization is freighted with utopian implications, as testified to by a commenter on the article, who writes: "Imagine a world where announcements don't need to be made. You are what you are. It's coming. And that is fantastic." But the pansexual utopia forecast by the commenter is subject to the logic of self-transparent identity in which sexuality is central ("you are what you are"). Thus, defining oneself as "fluid" in terms of gender or sexuality also requires announcement (another listicle: "5 Young Celebs who Won't Be Defined by Strict Notions of Sexuality").[2]

For scholars of sexuality, of course, the assumptions informing these announcements are easily critiqued. The Foucauldian argument more or less writes itself. It has more or less "written" my preceding paragraph. However utopian in spirit, these celebrity comings out attest not to the "different economy of bodies and pleasures" that Foucault, in 1976, espied on some distant historical horizon but simply further exemplify "the austere monarchy of sex"—our dedication to "the endless task of forcing its secret, of exacting the truest of confessions from a shadow."[3] Throughout this book, though, I have wanted in large part to "forget Foucault," turning away from the automatized Foucauldian argument about the deployment of sexuality by power.[4] I have sought to highlight the ways in which the work of Baldwin, Sontag, and Vidal responded to the ways in which sex, particularly homosexuality, has been "prohibited or barred or masked or misapprehended."[5] While I find Foucault's long-view account generally persuasive, zeroing in on a particular moment, the 1960s, illuminates the power of liberation for historical subjects rather than its status as simply a continuation of "the ruses of sexuality."[6] I have argued that the work of Baldwin, Sontag, and Vidal attests, wittingly or not, to a liberationist desire that, however inflected by utopia, was also realized in a set of concrete historical developments that transformed the lives of sex- and gender-diverse people as well as transformed understandings of sexual orientation and gender identity in American society more generally—which is not to say that such transformations have been uniformly positive or that they have been evenly distributed across the axes of class, race, and region. The celebrity of my three writers, I've contended, was essential to their dissemination of liberationist ideas. If celebrity, as I've argued, helps define the norms of sexual identity and the permissibility of varieties of sexual expressions and attitudes at a given historical moment, how might we regard the current relations of celebrity to unorthodox sexuality, keeping in play Foucault's undoubted insights about the connection of sex to personhood but eschewing the automatism of my opening remarks?

The celebrityscape of today presents quite differently than that of the 1960s, while also exhibiting clear continuities. In terms of what is different, most immediately apparent of course is the impact of the Internet, particularly the heightened interactivity between fans and stars that social media has made possible.[7] Less noticed, or at least less theorized by scholars of celebrity, is the impact of gay and lesbian liberation. The speech act of coming out, the foundational political strategy of gay and lesbian liberation, has become an increasingly noticeable feature of modern-day celebrity culture, with social media enhancing opportunities for its solicitation and expanding the opportunities to carry it out (as in Steve Lacy's response to his fans on Tumblr). While the 1960s was the era of proto-visibility for some queer celebrities, exemplified in the careers of Vidal, Baldwin, and Sontag, present-day celebrity culture is importantly informed—though not, I would say, dominated—by the imperative of visibility. The hypervisibility of celebrities has become an important arena for the exercise of sexual visibility; the open secret has, to a large extent, been displaced by the injunction to decloset oneself. If Lacy, like many queer theorists, would like to "delete the whole closet concept," the closet remains a defining feature of postliberation sexuality.[8] Invented in the 1960s as a means of organizing knowledge about unorthodox sexuality, it shows no signs as yet of dissipating. Indeed, its purchase has expanded beyond same-sexuality to include a panoply of diverse identifications (trans, intersex, genderqueer, etc.). The "world where announcements don't need to be made," imagined by the commenter on Newnownext may be "coming," but we might say it has been a long time coming, given that Freudian radicals intimated it in the 1950s and 1960s, that gay and lesbian liberationists were looking forward to it in the early 1970s, and that queer theory has been imagining it since the early 1990s. My point here is not to dismiss such utopian aspirations but to indicate the seemingly hard-to-shake logic of sexual identity and, beyond that, to suggest that celebrity affirmations of identity make a difference to the usual functioning of the culture industries and to heteronormative culture in general. A strong tendency within queer theory summons fears of surveillance, voyeurism, fetishism, and colonization whenever visibility is mentioned.[9] Invisibility, indeterminacy, and opacity are consequently valorized. In contradistinction to this position, I contend that being talked about and being seen are indispensable preconditions for the equitable treatment of sexual minorities. Sedgwick notes that "the deadly elasticity of heterosexist presumption" means that there "can be few gay people . . . in whose lives the closet is not still a shaping presence."[10] The closet shapes the lives of queer celebrities uniquely in that, for them, coming out means coming out in the media rather than the announcement of one's orientation to friends, families, and workmates that constitutes coming out for the "ordinary individual." The high degree of publicity accorded to famous people coming out renders celebrity culture an important vector of liberatory affect.[11]

Does this mean that I endorse the politics of visibility that queer theory, and critical theory more generally, has staunchly argued against? Yes and no. Obviously, representation is "not enough" in terms of political power. As Peggy Phelan quipped in an important early critique of visibility politics, "If representational visibility equals power, then almost-naked young women should be running Western culture."[12] Phelan notes some of the questionable presumptions of visibility, including that "the relationship between representation and identity is linear and smoothly mimetic. What one sees is what one is"; and that "if one's mimetic likeness is not represented, one is not addressed." I don't disagree that these presumptions deserve continued scrutiny. Where I depart from Phelan's analysis is her emphasis on the "real power in remaining unmarked." Phelan acknowledges the political value of representation, but in a move typical of 1990s critical theory, she wants (ironically) to bring to light "the power of the unmarked, unspoken and unseen" that visibility politics "erases."[13] Phelan's move parallels Judith Butler's in "Imitation and Gender Insubordination," in which Butler offhandedly acknowledges that "the discourse of 'coming out' has clearly served its purposes" but then rhetorically asks whether the "new opacity" produced by out gayness is "*to be valued*, a site for the production of values, precisely because the term ["gayness"] now takes on a life that cannot be, can never be, permanently controlled?" Clarity about sexuality has all too "clearly"—by which Butler also seems to mean "merely"—"served its purposes." The value of gay and lesbian identities is instead to be found in the lack of clarity they engender, the ways in which they can become "rallying points for a certain resistance to classification and to identity as such."[14]

However, in a world in which "resistance to classification and to identity as such" can itself become an identity ("5 Young Celebs Who Won't Be Defined by Strict Notions of Sexuality"), does "a life that cannot be, can never be, permanently controlled" look feasible, let alone politically meaningful? One way of reading contemporary celebrity culture's articulation of gendered and sexual diversity, or of gendered and sexual fluidity, is as incorporation, a ruse of power, an extension of the inexorable colonizing force of commodification. Yet, as I hope this book has attested, sexuality cannot meaningfully be said to *precede* mediatization. Media helps make sexual identities public, meaningful, and political rather than simply appropriating them, distorting them, marketizing them. The "controlling" force of the media also enables possibilities. Liberation is tightly intricated with media formations, such as celebrity, rather than lying outside them, as a utopian "beyond."

Of course, the kind of sexual liberation manifested in an online listicle can look rather one-dimensional (to humanities scholars, at least). One of the other key differences between the world of celebrity discussed in this book and the celebrity coming out familiar to us today is the difference between literary and culture industry celebrity. If there was a close fit between literary celebrity and nascent liberation discourse in the decade before Stonewall, manifested in the proto-visibility of a number of famous writers, the culture industries (paradigmatically Hollywood) were infamously closeted. Today the situation is effectively reversed. It is hard to think of a present-day writer whose coming out has caused much of a stir. (Chuck Palahniuk is maybe an exception, but his "cult" status arguably distinguishes him from your standard writer of literary fiction, making him closer to a pop celebrity.) It's not only the case that, in the literary world, there is doubtless less felt need to mask unorthodox sexual identification in the interests of career. The changed situation also indicates the decline of literature's status as an object of cultural prestige and barometer of cultural change. I have assumed in *Categorically Famous*, however, that the exercise of individual creativity has lent a richness and complexity to the particular texts I have examined. If the texts of literary celebrity emphasize what Glass calls individual authorial consciousness in ways that culture industry celebrity does not, does that mean that valuable nuance and subtlety have been lost in the new focus on culture industry celebrities as the most prominent exemplars of sexual and gender diversity? Perhaps. But mass-mediatized queer celebrity is obviously meaningful for many, helping to organize both public understanding and individuals' lived experience of LGBT identities. And the continuing articulation of queer sexuality across a range of media—literature as well as more popular formats—and across a range of celebrity personas suggests the ongoing urgency and vibrancy of the project of liberation.

Notes

Introduction

1. *Seinfeld*, "The Cheever Letters," directed by Tom Cherones, written by Larry David, Elaine Pope, and Tom Leopold, episode 8, season 4, NBC, 28 October 1992.

2. Susan Cheever, *Home before Dark: A Biographical Memoir of John Cheever by His Daughter* (1984; repr., New York: Simon and Schuster, 1999); John Cheever, *The Journals of John Cheever*, ed. Robert Gottlieb (1991; repr., New York: Vintage, 2008); John Cheever, *The Letters of John Cheever*, ed. Benjamin Cheever (New York: Simon and Schuster, 1988).

3. *Seinfeld*, "The Smelly Car," directed by Tom Cherones, written by Larry David and Peter Mehlman, episode 21, season 4, NBC, 15 April 1993. It is revealed that Susan's lesbianism "didn't take" in "The Engagement," directed by Andy Ackerman, written by Larry David, episode 1, season 7, NBC, 21 September 1995.

4. Geoff Dyer, review of *The Journals of John Cheever*, by John Cheever, *The Guardian*, 21 October 2009, https://www.theguardian.com/books/2009/oct/31/journals-biography-john-cheever-dyer. The quoted phrases appear in Cheever, *Journals*, 344, 349–50.

5. Barry Reay, *New York Hustlers: Masculinity and Sex in Modern America* (Manchester, UK: Manchester University Press, 2010), 178.

6. My use of the terms "queer studies" and "queer theory" in this book is informed by but also differs slightly from that of Robyn Wiegman in *Object Lessons* (Durham, NC: Duke University Press, 2012). While I find useful her account of "queer studies" as "the interdisciplinary frame for work that shares no specific theoretical preference or priority but is defined more generally as a critical project shaped by antinormative critical intentions" (305n7), I also assume that "queer theory," a body of work generally informed by or elaborated as literary and critical theory, has been the forcing house of many or most of those antinormative intentions. For this reason, I find it less important than Wiegman, in her account of the institutionalization and "normalization" of queer studies, to differentiate between the two entities.

7. For scholarship that decisively indicates the meaningfulness of homosexual identity for many men and women with same-sex orientations by midcentury, see, e.g., Craig M. Loftin, *Masked Voices: Gay Men and Lesbians in Cold War America* (New York: State University of New York Press, 2012); Martin Meeker, *Contacts Desired: Gay and Lesbian Communications and Community, 1940s–1970s* (Chicago: University of Chicago Press,

2006). It's true that effeminacy was a vexed issue for many midcentury gay men who endorsed a gender-conformist image of homosexuality—as was butchness for some lesbians. But the preliberation debates over effeminacy—charted, for instance, by Loftin in his analysis of letters to the homophile *ONE* magazine—indicate precisely the narrowing of the gap between normative masculinity and homosexual identity that in Reay's argument is put off until the 1970s. That Cheever's two statements come from 1978, by which time the liberationist tropes of pride and social oppression had considerable cultural traction, actually supports one of the points I make in this book about the impact of liberation discourse on those who officially reject it. Voicing sentiments entirely compatible with liberation discourse, Cheever indicates the interpellative force of that discourse for many who experienced what Reay calls "same-sex cravings" (*New York Hustlers*, 178).

8. Graeme Turner, *Understanding Celebrity*, 2nd ed. (London: Sage, 2014), 8.

9. The appropriateness of "the closet" as a rubric for the investigation of same-sexuality during the preliberation period has, however, been challenged on the grounds of anachronism; see, e.g., Loftin, *Masked*, 10–11; Michael Sherry, *Gay Artists in Modern American Culture: An Imagined Conspiracy* (Chapel Hill: University of North Carolina Press, 2007), 105–9. I discuss this challenge in Chapter 3.

10. In her underappreciated study *Entertaining Lesbians: Celebrity, Sexuality, and Self-Invention* (New York: Routledge, 2003), Martha Gever argues that the category of the lesbian celebrity is "oxymoronic, nonsensical" (7) before the 1990s when figures such as Martina Navratilova and Ellen DeGeneres publicly came out; it is no doubt significant that talk about Sontag's lesbianism became noisier during this decade, when there was a media appetite for such stories. For Gever, famous figures such as Gertrude Stein or Radclyffe Hall do not qualify as "lesbian celebrities" because there was no public coming out involved; the very idea of "coming out of the closet" is anachronistic in the preliberation period. I agree with the broad terms of Gever's analysis but would argue that Stein and Hall might indeed be read as *proto*-lesbian celebrities; for a reading of Stein in precisely these terms, see Jeff Solomon, *So Famous and So Gay: The Fabulous Potency of Truman Capote and Gertrude Stein* (Minneapolis: University of Minnesota Press, 2017). That famous queer female writers (apart from Sontag) are conspicuously missing from the midcentury period is an interesting issue that doubtless has multiple determinations, including the general exclusion of women from literary celebrity in an era that privileged stridently masculinist writers (John Updike, Norman Mailer, Philip Roth).

11. P. David Marshall, *Celebrity and Power: Fame in Contemporary Culture* (Minneapolis: University of Minnesota Press, 1997), 65; Robert van Krieken, *Celebrity Society* (London: Routledge), 56.

12. Following some key early contributions on film stars—e.g., Edgar Morin, *The Stars*, trans. Richard Howard (1957; repr., Minneapolis: University of Minnesota Press, 2005); Richard Dyer, *Stars* (London: BFI, 1979), and *Heavenly Bodies: Film Stars and Society* (London: Macmillan, 1987)—the field of celebrity studies gained momentum in the late 1990s. The field's current vitality is indicated by the foundation of the journal *Celebrity Studies* in 2010.

13. On literary celebrity, the eighteenth century, and Romanticism, see, e.g., *Romanticism and Celebrity Culture, 1750–1850*, ed. Tom Mole (Cambridge: Cambridge University Press, 2009). On the nineteenth century, see, e.g., Eric Eisner, *Nineteenth-Century Poetry and Literary Celebrity* (Houndmills, UK: Palgrave Macmillan, 2009); Brenda Weber, *Women and Literary Celebrity in the Nineteenth Century: The Transatlantic Production of Fame and Gender* (Burlington, VT: Ashgate, 2012). Along with the studies I mention elsewhere, an important contribution on the modern and contemporary situation is James F. English and John Frow, "Literary Authorship and Celebrity Culture," in *A Concise Companion to Contemporary British Fiction*, ed. James F. English (Oxford: Blackwell, 2006), 39–57. The consolidation of celebrity as a focus of study for literary critics is indicated in "Celebrity, Fame, Notoriety," ed. Joseph A. Boone and Nancy J. Vickers, special issue, *PMLA* 126, no. 4 (2011).

14. Sharon Marcus, "Salomé!! Sarah Bernhardt, Oscar Wilde, and the Drama of Celebrity," *PMLA* 126, no. 4 (2011): 1001.

15. Loren Glass, *Authors, Inc.: Literary Celebrity in the Modern United States, 1880–1980* (New York: New York University Press, 2004), 4.

16. Ibid.

17. Ibid., 3.

18. Eisner, *Nineteenth-Century Poetry*, 15, quoted in Clara Tuite, *Lord Byron and Scandalous Celebrity* (Cambridge: Cambridge University Press, 2015), xix.

19. I am thinking here particularly of Aaron Jaffe's identification of the unique style of the modernist author as the *imprimatur* and Jonathan Goldman's identification of the same as the *trademark*. See Aaron Jaffe, *Modernism and the Culture of Celebrity* (Cambridge: Cambridge University Press, 2005); Jonathan Goldman, *Modernism Is the Literature of Celebrity* (Austin: University of Texas Press, 2011). While Baldwin, Sontag, and Vidal miss the boat historically as far as the usual definition of modernism goes, they enact the modernist imperative of the distinctive individual style, as I demonstrate in this book. In this respect they fit the profile of what David Genter defines as "late modernism." See David Genter, *Late Modernism: Art, Culture, and Politics in Cold War America* (Philadelphia: University of Pennsylvania Press, 2010); Genter in fact devotes a chapter to Baldwin.

20. Edward W. Said, *Beginnings: Intention and Method* (Baltimore: Johns Hopkins University Press, 1975), 226, 227. See also Guy Davidson and Nicola Evans, "Introduction: Brilliant Careers?," in *Literary Careers in the Modern Era*, ed. Guy Davidson and Nicola Evans (Houndmills, UK: Palgrave Macmillan, 2015), 1–16.

21. Said, *Beginnings*, 234. Though Said admits that his exemplars of the modern literary career (including Joseph Conrad, Marcel Proust, and Stéphane Mallarmé) are "exaggerated" in their obsessive, even self-destructive relations to the writing life, his choice of authors, in their extremity, helpfully brings into relief the common experience of the overlap between the personal life and literary output experienced by the twentieth-century author.

22. It's notable that Baldwin, Sontag, and Vidal were all, to their chagrin, commonly thought of as better essayists than novelists, and throughout *Categorically Famous* I attend

closely to each author's essayistic output, even when my focus is a work of fiction. The 1960s was a period of significant innovation in what has come to be known as creative nonfiction, most notably in the New Journalism, which highlighted the authorial response to the real-life situation being described. While the essays of Baldwin, Sontag, and Vidal are at some distance in their materials and methods from this work, their indirect references to personal, particularly sexual, experience, nevertheless bear some affinity with the openness regarding authorial affect for which New Journalism is noted.

23. Solomon, *So Famous*, 21. Henry Abelove, in *Deep Gossip* (Minneapolis: University of Minnesota Press, 2003), argues specifically that a group of writers including Baldwin, Elizabeth Bishop, Allen Ginsberg, and Jane and Paul Bowles were "enormously productive" for the New York Gay Liberation Front (GLF) and "significantly contributed to the development of its outlook and values" (73) by providing a "rhetoric for connecting queerness to decolonization and its struggles" (80). I follow Solomon in expanding Abelove's argument about "writing as a productive force" (72) past the GLF to the gay and lesbian liberation movement more generally. Abelove identifies awareness of decolonization as a common feature of the writers he examines, all of whom lived outside the United States for considerable periods of time; and while such awareness does not figure as a concern in *Categorically Famous*, it is worth noting that, like Baldwin, Vidal and Sontag were cosmopolitan in outlook and lived abroad at various times (Vidal lived in Italy for many years, Sontag in France in the late 1950s, Baldwin in Turkey and France for much of the postwar period). In each case these experiences of and orientations toward non-American contexts were importantly related to these writers' attitudes toward same-sexuality, with each testifying to the liberatory aspect of their European experiences.

24. On Hollywood, see David Ehrenstein, *Open Secret: Gay Hollywood, 1928–1998* (New York: William Morrow, 1998); and on lesbian Hollywood specifically, see Gever, *Entertaining Lesbians*, chap. 5.

25. See, however, Gavin Butt's excellent discussion of midcentury visual art, gossip, and queer identity, *Between You and Me: Queer Disclosures in the New York Art World, 1948–1963* (Durham, NC: Duke University Press, 2005). The now extensive body of scholarly work on Warhol as queer or gay was initiated by Jennifer Doyle, Jonathan Flatley, and José Esteban Muñoz, eds., *Pop Out: Queer Warhol* (Durham, NC: Duke University Press, 1996). For an important reassessment of Warhol in terms of celibacy rather than same-sexuality, see Benjamin Kahan, *Celibacies: American Modernism and Sexual Life* (Durham, NC: Duke University Press, 2013), chap. 5.

26. In *Authors, Inc.*, Glass argues that the "cultural authority" of masculinist literary celebrity, arising out of the dialectic of mass culture and modernism, is "greatly diminished in scale and scope" in the era after second-wave feminism and postmodernism (197), and he makes a case that Norman Mailer is "the last celebrity author," who "ballasted his mass cultural fame in a model of masculine modernist genius that was, by the post-World War II era, clearly residual" (177). While conceding that today celebrity "remains a crucial ingredient in the marketing of books" (199), Glass contends that literary celebrity has lost its capacity for cultural cut-through. Although the outline of Glass's argument

is compelling, it can be nuanced at the level of historical detail and with regard to its gender emphasis. Indeed, in a later essay on the present-day celebrity of Philip Roth, Glass himself states that his earlier position on Mailer's status was "premature"; in this essay, Glass also notes the gendered bias of much of literary celebrity studies, including his earlier book. See Loren Glass, "Zuckerman/Roth: Literary Celebrity between Two Deaths," *PMLA* 129, no. 2 (2014): 224. Cited by Glass, Faye Hammill, *Women, Celebrity, and Literary Culture between the Wars* (Austin: University of Texas Press, 2007), and Weber, *Women and Literary Celebrity*, usefully complicate the emphasis on male literary celebrity in their attention to middlebrow and popular women writers who attained great fame during their lifetimes but who have been neglected by scholarship.

On the decline of literature's cultural authority, see also Marcie Frank, *How to Be an Intellectual in the Age of TV: The Lessons of Gore Vidal* (Durham, NC: Duke University Press, 2005). Noting that Vidal once explained to an interviewer that in 1990s America "one can be famous and a novelist but not famous as a novelist" (2), Frank situates Vidal as the author who most "ably negotiated" (18) the shift in cultural dominance from print to TV during the postwar era. In "'Just a Couple of Fags: Truman Capote, Gore Vidal and Celebrity Feud," *Celebrity Studies* 7 (2016): 299–308, I argue that media coverage of the decades-long rivalry between Capote and Vidal demonstrates the continuing, but decreasing, importance of individual authorial consciousness from the 1940s to the 1970s, as matters of literary style and merit were displaced as objects of public attention by the two authors' entertaining media personalities.

27. For an illuminating account of these battles, see Loren Glass, *Counterculture Colophon: Grove Press, the* Evergreen Review, *and the Incorporation of the Avant-Garde* (Stanford, CA: Stanford University Press, 2013), chap. 3. Glass notes that "censorship of the printed word in the United States essentially ended in the 1960s" (101).

28. Whitney Strub, "Historicizing Pulp: Gay Male Pulp and the Narrativization of Queer Cultural History," in *1960s Gay Pulp Fiction: The Misplaced Heritage*, ed. Drewey Wayne Gunn and Jaime Harker (Amherst: University of Massachusetts Press, 2013), 55.

29. Richard Bernstein, "Susan Sontag, as Image and Herself," *New York Times*, 26 January 1989, movies2.nytimes.com/books/00/03/12/specials/sontag-herself.html.

30. That celebrity image is unmanageable by the celebritized person is a foundational point of celebrity studies: see, e.g., Chris Rojek, *Celebrity* (London: Reaktion), 10–11; and, in the literary context, Loren Glass's discussion of Gertrude Stein, *Authors, Inc.*, 1. *Categorically Famous* builds on this well-established point by factoring the ineluctability of sexual identity categories into the discussion of celebrity.

31. Joe Moran, *Star Authors: Literary Celebrity in America* (London: Pluto, 2000), 19.

32. On Williams, see, e.g., David Savran, *Communists, Cowboys and Queers: The Politics of Masculinity in the Work of Arthur Miller and Tennessee Williams* (Minneapolis: University of Minnesota Press, 1992); Michael Paller, *Gentlemen Callers: Tennessee Williams, Homosexuality, and Mid-Twentieth-Century Broadway Drama* (New York: Palgrave Macmillan, 2005). On Capote, see, e.g., Michael Bibler, "How to Love Your Local Homophobe: Southern Hospitality and the Unremarkable Queerness of Truman

Capote's 'The Thanksgiving Visitor,'" *Modern Fiction Studies* 58, no. 2 (2012): 284–307; Solomon, *So Famous*. While I agree with Solomon about the influence of Capote on a gay audience, I would argue that his work and his somewhat clownish persona present a more oblique relation to ideas of liberation than do the writers I examine here. Williams once proclaimed that he was the "founding father of the uncloseted gay world" (quoted in Paller, *Gentlemen*, 11), but if his work helped promote cultural awareness of homosexuality and homosexual self-awareness, he overstated here both his own openness (he announced his sexuality only after Stonewall) and the connection of his pre-1970s work to the subcultural expression of gayness; the latter is a key factor in the work of Baldwin, Sontag, and Vidal that I examine.

33. For an astute reading of Ginsberg's distance, even after 1969, from the "liberationist's demand to assert self-identity," see Michael Trask, *Camp Sites: Sex, Politics, and Academic Style in Postwar America* (Stanford, CA: Stanford University Press, 2013), 92–93; quote at 93. For a more positive assessment of Ginsberg's relation to liberationist ideas, see John D'Emilio, *Sexual Politics, Sexual Communities: The Making of a Homosexual Minority in the United States*, 1940–1970, 2nd ed. (Chicago: University of Chicago Press, 1998), 177–81.

34. R. E. L. Masters, *The Homosexual Revolution* (New York: Belmont, 1964), vii.

35. Meeker, *Contacts*, 110.

36. For a discussion of these texts and their influence, see ibid., 115–50. Aldrich, a pseudonym of Marijane Meaker, published five nonfiction books about the lesbian subculture between 1955 and 1972.

37. D'Emilio, *Sexual Politics*, 148.

38. Jeffrey Escoffier applies this term from C. Wright Mills to his discussion of the period in "Homosexuality and the Sociological Imagination: Hegemonic Discourses, the Circulation of Ideas, and the Process of Reading in the 1950s and 1960s," in *American Homo: Community and Perversity*, by Escoffier (Berkeley: University of California Press, 1998), 70–98.

39. Masters, *Homosexual Revolution*, 37; Meeker, *Contacts*, 111.

40. Seymour Krim, "Revolt of the Homosexual," *Village Voice*, 18 March 1959, 12, 16. This piece is reprinted in Jeffrey Escoffier, ed., *Sexual Revolution* (New York: Thunder's Mouth, 2003), 468–75; quotes at 473, 472, 475.

41. D'Emilio, *Sexual Politics*, 147.

42. As is well documented, the Mattachine Society, founded in 1951, had radical beginnings. Its original members included communists and other leftists, and at its formation it stressed "the uniqueness of gay identity, projected a vision of a homosexual culture with its own positive values, and attempted to transform the shame of being gay into a pride in belonging to a minority with its own contributions to the human community" (D'Emilio, *Sexual Politics*, 58). However, changes in the group's structure and leadership saw it retreat from militancy, and throughout most of the preliberation era the group sought to convince American society that homosexuals were "respectable" citizens who could be safely assimilated, an approach duplicated in the Daughters of Bilitis, the

most prominent female homophile group. Militant actions and radical analysis by some homophiles did not go into complete abeyance in the 1950s, however, and increased throughout the 1960s. See D'Emilio, *Sexual Politics*, chap. 3; Donn Teal, *The Gay Militants* (New York: Stein and Day, 1971), 38–50. The tension in the early liberation years between radicalism and rights-based reformism is often illustrated by the 1969 schism in the New York chapter of the GLF that engendered the rights-focused Gay Activists Alliance (though the GAA's activism, which included "zaps," sit-ins, and other forms of theatricalized protest, was very "High Sixties" in style). See, e.g., Teal, *Gay Militants*, chap. 7; Lillian Faderman, *The Gay Revolution: The Story of the Struggle* (New York: Simon and Schuster, 2015), 214–26.

43. Wilhelm Reich, *The Sexual Revolution: Toward a Self-Governing Character Structure*, trans. Therese Pol (New York: Farrar, Straus and Giroux, 1986).

44. "The Second Sexual Revolution," *Time*, 24 January 1964; reprinted in Escoffier, *Sexual Revolution*, 4–19, quotes at 5.

45. As Terence Kissack notes in his important essay "Freaking Fag Revolutionaries: New York's Gay Liberation Front, 1969–1971," *Radical History Review* 62 (1995): 104–34, the gay movement is ignored or only cursorily treated in many major studies of 1960s radicalism, including James Miller, *Democracy Is in the Streets: From Port Huron to the Siege of Chicago* (New York: Simon and Schuster, 1987); Todd Gitlin, *The Sixties: Years of Hope, Days of Rage* (New York: Bantam, 1987); Sohnya Sayres, Anders Stephanson, Stanley Aronowitz, and Fredric Jameson, eds., *The 60s without Apology* (Minneapolis: University of Minnesota Press, 1984). For other notable efforts to reinstate homosexual liberation within the historiography of the 1960s, see Richard Meyer, "Gay Power circa 1970: Visual Strategies for Sexual Revolution," *GLQ* 12, no. 3 (2006): 441–64; Justin David Suran, "Coming Out against the War: Antimilitarism and the Politicization of Homosexuality in the Era of Vietnam," *American Quarterly* 53, no. 3 (2001): 452–88.

46. Theodore Roszak, *The Making of a Counter Culture: Reflections on the Technocratic Society and Its Youthful Opposition* (Berkeley: University of California Press, 1969).

47. The idea that the personal or the private is political is, of course, primarily associated with second-wave feminism. I don't in any way mean to underplay feminism's dissemination of this precept by pointing out its congruence with the countercultural assumption that unorthodox lifeways constitute forms of political resistance.

48. Foucault does mention Reich a couple of times. See *The History of Sexuality*, vol. 1, *An Introduction*, trans. Robert Hurley (Harmondsworth, UK: Penguin, 1990), 5, 131.

49. Ibid., 12.

50. Ibid., 48.

51. Eve Kosofsky Sedgwick, *Epistemology of the Closet* (Berkeley: University of California Press, 1990), 83.

52. Foucault, *History*, 101.

53. Judith Butler, "Imitation and Gender Insubordination," in *Inside Out: Lesbian Theories, Gay Theories*, ed. Diana Fuss (New York: Routledge, 1991), 16. For a recent elaboration of this position, which finds sites "for the production of values" in the resistance to

"coming out" by twentieth-century cultural celebrities, see Nicholas de Villiers, *Opacity and the Closet: Queer Tactics in Foucault, Barthes, and Warhol* (Minneapolis: University of Minnesota Press, 2012). De Villiers does not actually mention Butler's essay, which I'd suggest proves my point that her argument has been osmotically assimilated into queer theoretical discussion.

54. Thanks to Benjamin Kahan for helping me formulate this point.

55. Lee Edelman, *Homographesis: Essays in Gay Literary and Cultural Theory* (New York: Routledge, 1994), 10.

56. Leo Bersani, *Homos* (Cambridge, MA: Harvard University Press, 1995), 11–12.

57. Rita Felski, *The Limits of Critique* (Chicago: University of Chicago Press, 2015), 78, 79.

58. Ibid., 79.

59. Ibid., 80.

60. Michael Snediker, "Queer Optimism," *Postmodern Culture* 16, no. 3 (2006): para. 6. See also Solomon, *So Famous*, 18. Solomon notes that Snediker rewrites the quoted sentence slightly in *Queer Optimism: Lyric Personhood and Other Felicitous Persuasions* (Minneapolis: University of Minnesota Press, 2009); like Solomon, I prefer the original wording.

61. Solomon, *So Famous*, 18.

62. Christopher Castiglia and Christopher Reed, *If Memory Serves: Gay Men, AIDS, and the Promise of the Queer Past* (Minneapolis: University of Minnesota Press, 2012), 5.

63. Ibid., 162, quoting Simon Watney, *Imagine Hope: AIDS and Gay Identity* (London: Routledge, 2000), 17.

64. Christopher Looby, "The Gay Novel in the United States 1900–1950," in *A Companion to the Modern American Novel*, ed. John T. Matthews (Chichester, UK: Wiley-Blackwell, 2009), 433.

65. In attending to literary expression of the meaningfulness of sexual categories in the midcentury context, I join and am instructed by a handful of other recent works of literary scholarship, including Jaime Harker, *Middlebrow Queer: Christopher Isherwood in America* (Minneapolis: University of Minnesota Press, 2013); Solomon, *So Famous*; and Trask, *Camp Sites*. See also Ernesto Javier Martínez, *Making Sense: Queer Race Narratives of Intelligibility* (Stanford, CA: Stanford University Press, 2012), which argues for the value of racial and sexual identity categories in counternormative literary and cultural work (including Baldwin's writing).

66. See, e.g., Arthur Marwick, *The Sixties: Cultural Revolution in Britain, France, Italy, and the United States, c. 1958–c. 1974* (New York: Oxford University Press, 1998).

Chapter 1

1. James Baldwin, "The Northern Protestant," in *Collected Essays*, ed. Toni Morrison (New York: Library of America, 1998), 246.

2. James Baldwin, "Notes for *The Amen Corner*," in *The Amen Corner* (Harmondsworth, UK: Penguin, 1991), 11.

3. James Baldwin, *No Name in the Street*, in *Collected Essays*, 459.

4. Peter Kerry Powers, "The Treacherous Body: Isolation, Confession, and Community in James Baldwin," *American Literature* 77, no. 4 (2005): 806; W. J. Weatherby, *James Baldwin: Artist on Fire* (London: Michael Joseph, 1989), 96.

5. Baldwin, "Notes," 11.

6. Possibly the first reference by Baldwin to Strauss's suggestion that he burn *Giovanni's Room*, along with her denial, can be found in the journalist Fern Marja Eckman's 1966 portrait, *The Furious Passage of James Baldwin* (Philadelphia: Lippincott, 1966), 139.

7. James Baldwin, "Go the Way Your Blood Beats: An Interview with James Baldwin," by Richard Goldstein, in *James Baldwin: The Legacy*, ed. Quincy Troupe (New York: Touchstone–Simon and Schuster, 1989), 176.

8. On Baldwin's partially defensive adoption of Black Power's macho rhetoric, see Douglas Field, "Looking for Jimmy Baldwin: Sex, Privacy, and Black Nationalist Fervor," *Callaloo* 27, no. 2 (2004): 466–69; Michele Wallace, *Black Macho and the Myth of the Superwoman*, rev. ed. (London: Verso, 1990), 61–62.

9. Glass writes that the "stubborn audience fascination with the possibility that [the proper name of the author], in the end, must mandate a referential relation between the private consciousness and the public sphere in which it circulates undergirds the culture of authorial celebrity" (*Authors, Inc.*, 8).

10. Jacqueline Rose, *On Not Being Able to Sleep: Psychoanalysis and the Modern World* (London: Chatto and Windus, 2003), 1. Subsequent page references are cited parenthetically in the text.

11. Ruth Leys, *From Guilt to Shame: Auschwitz and After* (Princeton, NJ: Princeton University Press, 2007), 126.

12. Eve Kosofsky Sedgwick, *Touching Feeling: Affect, Pedagogy, Performativity* (Durham, NC: Duke University Press, 2003), 38. Subsequent page references are cited parenthetically in the text.

13. Marshall, *Celebrity and Power*, 65.

14. Baldwin, "Freaks and the American Ideal of Manhood," in *Collected Essays*, 817.

15. Baldwin, "Everybody's Protest Novel," in *Collected Essays*, 15.

16. Ibid., 18.

17. Baldwin, "Preservation of Innocence," in *Collected Essays*, 594.

18. Ibid., 600. For a discussion of the Cold War gay protest novels, see Harker, *Middlebrow*, 12–24. I consider these novels in my discussion of *The City and the Pillar* in Chapter 6.

19. Baldwin, "Preservation," 600.

20. See, e.g., Jerome de Romanet, "Revisiting *Madeleine* and 'The Outing': James Baldwin's Revision of Gide's Sexual Politics," *MELUS* 22, no. 1 (1997): 8; Field, "Looking," 459. There are only three essays in which Baldwin treats homosexuality at any length, all discussed in this chapter: "Preservation of Innocence" (1949), 594–600; "The Male Prison" (1954), 231–35; and "Freaks" (1985), 814–29, all in *Collected Essays*.

21. On Baldwin and liberalism, see, e.g., Michael Nowlin, "Ralph Ellison, James Baldwin, and the Liberal Imagination," *Arizona Quarterly* 60, no. 2 (2004): 117–40.

22. The quoted phrase is from St. Clair Drake and Horace Cayton's landmark sociological study of urban African American culture, *Black Metropolis: A Study of Life in a Northern City* (1945; repr., Chicago: University of Chicago Press, 1993), 1:392. Drake and Cayton further define the race man as "any person who has a reputation as an uncompromising fighter against attempts to subordinate Negros" (394) and as "aggressive, vocal, uncompromising" (395)—both apt descriptions of Baldwin, of course.

23. Hazel V. Carby, *Race Men* (Cambridge, MA: Harvard University Press, 1998), 4. Carby points out that the notion of the race man affirms inequities of gender and sexuality even as it indicates some of the complex effects of racialization. Her book convincingly demonstrates that the figures of the black gay man and the black woman trouble the twentieth-century history of the race man.

24. "Nation: The Root of the Negro Problem," *Time*, 17 May 1963, 26.

25. James Baldwin, *Conversations with James Baldwin*, ed. Fred L. Standley and Louis H. Pratt (Jackson: University Press of Mississippi, 1989), 52, 101, 123; James Baldwin, *The Cross of Redemption: Uncollected Writings*, ed. Randall Kenan (New York: Pantheon, 2010), 95.

26. Justin A. Joyce and Dwight A. McBride, "James Baldwin and Sexuality: *Lieux de Memoire* within a Usable Past," in *A Historical Guide to James Baldwin*, ed. Douglas Field (Oxford: Oxford University Press, 2009), 124.

27. Eckman, *Furious*, 12.

28. "Root," 26.

29. Lee Edelman, "The Part for the (W)hole: Baldwin, Homophobia, and the Fantasmatics of 'Race,'" in Edelman, *Homographesis*, 43.

30. "Root," 26.

31. *Baldwin's Nigger*, directed by Horace Ové (1969; London: BFI, 2005), DVD.

32. Baldwin, *Conversations*, 54.

33. Ibid., 55.

34. Ibid.

35. James Baldwin, *Giovanni's Room* (London: Corgi, 1963), 24.

36. Ibid.

37. Baldwin, "The Male Prison," 234.

38. James Baldwin, *Another Country* (London: Michael Joseph, 1963), 203.

39. Baldwin, *Giovanni's Room*, 33.

40. The explosion of recent scholarship on Baldwin, most of which centralizes his treatment of sexual and racial identity, makes a comprehensive summary of such work impracticable. For important early discussions of Baldwin in terms of intersectionality and/or fluidity, see, however, David Bergman, *Gaiety Transfigured: Gay Self-Representation in American Literature* (Madison: University of Wisconsin Press, 1991), chap. 9; Robert J. Corber, *Homosexuality in Cold War America: Resistance and the Crisis of Masculinity* (Durham, NC: Duke University Press, 1997), chap. 6, and "Everybody Knew His Name:

Reassessing James Baldwin," *Contemporary Literature* 42, no. 1 (2001): 166–75; Cora Kaplan, "'A Cavern Opened in My Mind': The Poetics of Homosexuality and the Politics of Masculinity in James Baldwin," in *Representing Black Men*, ed. Marcellus Blount and George P. Cunningham (New York: Routledge, 1996), 27–54; and the collections Dwight A. McBride, ed., *James Baldwin Now* (New York: New York University Press, 1999), and D. Quentin Miller, ed., *Re-viewing James Baldwin: Things Not Seen* (Philadelphia: Temple University Press, 2000).

41. For instance, in an argument that ignores Baldwin's consistently unfavorable contrasting of subcultural sexual practice with romantic love, Mikko Tukhanen insists that we should not "dismiss as 'homophobic'" Baldwin's representations of the queer underworld because their "affirmation of unclean complexity and hybridity" promotes "ethical openness," much like those of "more recent cartographers of queer spaces" like Samuel Delany and Michael Warner—who, as trenchant defenders and celebrants of subcultural sexual practices, make strange company with Baldwin. See Tukhanen, "James Baldwin on the American Express and the Queer Underground," *English Language Notes* 45, no. 2 (2007): 129. Writing of the "very negative language" with which Baldwin treats the subculture, Douglas Field states that he "resist[s] the adjective 'homophobic,'" instead proposing the "complexity" of Baldwin's views on sexuality; in a later version of the same passage, however, Field suggests that such language "suggest[s] a level of internalized homophobia." See Field, "Looking," 458, and *All Those Strangers: The Art and Lives of James Baldwin* (Oxford: Oxford University Press, 2015), 64. For an assessment of Baldwin's hostility to the gay subculture in autobiographical terms, see James A. Dievler, "Sexual Exiles: James Baldwin and *Another Country*," in McBride, *James Baldwin Now*, 161–83. For a discussion of *Giovanni's Room* in relation to transphobia, see Matt Brim, *James Baldwin and the Queer Imagination* (Ann Arbor: University of Michigan Press, 2014), chap. 2.

42. Baldwin, *Conversations*, 79.

43. Ibid., 80.

44. James Baldwin, *The Devil Finds Work*, in *Collected Essays*, 529.

45. Baldwin, "The Male Prison," 234.

46. James Baldwin, *Just above My Head* (New York: Delta–Random House, 1979), 325.

47. Ibid., 213.

48. Baldwin, *Giovanni's Room*, 46.

49. Ibid., 79.

50. Quoted in David Leeming, *James Baldwin: A Biography* (New York: Henry Holt, 1995), 127.

51. Baldwin, *Another Country*, 251.

52. Ibid.

53. Ibid., 253.

54. James Baldwin, "Preface to the 1984 Edition," in *Notes of a Native Son* (Boston: Beacon, 1990), xxxi.

55. Ibid., xxx.

56. In discussing this essay, my focus is on Baldwin's account of his career ambition

rather than his relationship with Mailer. For discussions of the essay in terms of the latter concern, see Kathryn Bond Stockton, *Beautiful Bottom, Beautiful Shame: Where "Black" Meets "Queer"* (Durham, NC: Duke University Press, 2006), 154–58; Douglas Taylor, "Three Lean Cats in a Hall of Mirrors: James Baldwin, Norman Mailer, and Eldridge Cleaver on Race and Masculinity," *Texas Studies in Literature and Language* 52, no. 1 (2010): 70–101.

57. James Baldwin, "The Black Boy Looks at the White Boy," in *Collected Essays*, 274. Subsequent page references are cited parenthetically in the text.

58. Baldwin's biographers confirm that he began writing what would become *Another Country* in 1956; see, e.g., James Campbell, *Talking at the Gates: A Life of Jimmy Baldwin* (Berkeley: University of California Press, 1991), 111.

59. Said, *Beginnings*, 226–27.

60. Ibid., 234.

61. See, in this respect, Baldwin's recollection in the title essay of *Notes of a Native Son* of the rage induced in him by the de facto segregation he encountered as a young man living in New Jersey. Repeated refusals of service in restaurants culminate in a traumatic incident in which he hurls a water mug at a waitress, then manages to escape the pursuing angered white patrons. See Baldwin, *Notes*, 93–98.

62. Baldwin, *Collected Essays*, 363.

63. Campbell, *Talking*, 7.

64. James Baldwin, "Freaks," 819.

65. Ibid., 823.

66. My reading of Baldwin's freak persona is in some ways close to Marlon B. Ross's account of his "sissy heroics," but I differ from Ross in stressing the relatedness of the freak/sissy persona to gay identity rather than its distance from it. See Marlon B. Ross, "Baldwin's Sissy Heroics," *African American Review* 46, no. 4 (2013): 633–51.

67. Baldwin, "Freaks," 819.

68. James Baldwin, *The Last Interview and Other Conversations* (New York: Melville House, 2014), 92.

69. Presenting popular culture images of brutal virility—his example is the heroes of Mickey Spillane—as extreme, but telling, examples of "the male prison," Baldwin picks up on his critique in the earlier essay "Preservation of Innocence" of the "tough guy" heroes of James M. Cain and Raymond Chandler, "whose masculinity is found in the most infantile and elementary externals and whose attitude towards women is the wedding of the most abysmal romanticism and the most implacable mistrust." See Baldwin, "Preservation," 597.

70. James Baldwin, "Male Prison," 231. Subsequent page references are cited parenthetically in the text.

71. James Baldwin, *The Fire Next Time*, in *Collected Essays*, 296; see also Weatherby, *James Baldwin*, 20.

72. Baldwin's insistence on the life-enhancing role of human connection across barriers of, for instance, race, gender, and sexual orientation is consistent throughout his career, though qualified by the deepening of his political radicalism during the 1960s. I dub

Baldwin's emphasis on connection "Forsterian" to indicate Baldwin's engagement with the mid-twentieth-century American liberal culture iconically represented by Lionel Trilling, for whom Forster was a touchstone, rather than to suggest that Baldwin had a strong interest in Forster himself. In fact, in *No Name in the Street*, Baldwin approvingly cites Forster's famous tag "Only connect" but misattributes it to Henry James (385).

73. Joyce and McBride, "Baldwin and Sexuality," 123.

74. The usefulness of Baldwin for the political project of homosexual liberation during the 1960s is signaled by the use of epigraphs from his work in two books arguing for acceptance of homosexuals and changes in the law: H. Kimball Jones, *Toward a Christian Understanding of the Homosexual* (New York: Association Press, 1966); and Martin Hoffman, *The Gay World: Male Homosexuality and the Social Creation of Evil* (New York: Basic, 1968), which use epigraphs from *Another Country* and *Giovanni's Room*, respectively.

75. Marlon B. Ross, "White Fantasies of Desire: Baldwin and the Racial Identities of Sexuality," in McBride, *James Baldwin Now*, 16.

76. Glass, *Authors, Inc.*, 8.

Chapter 2

1. Lionel Trilling, "On James Baldwin's *Another Country*," in *A Company of Readers: Uncollected Writings of W. H. Auden, Jacques Barzun and Lionel Trilling from the Readers' Subscription and Mid-century Book Clubs*, ed. Arthur Krystal (New York: Free Press, 2001), 153.

2. *Another Country* provides a particularly rich fund of moments in which private and public are oxymoronically or paradoxically brought together. Listening to Ida sing, Vivaldo "knew that she often sang . . . in order to flaunt before him privacies which he could never hope to penetrate" (302). Of New York pedestrians, the narrator notes, "their private lives screamed from their hot and discontented faces" (260). Of New York again (from Eric's point of view): "It was so familiar and so public that it became, at last, the most despairingly private of cities. One was continually being jostled, yet longed at the same time, for the sense of others, for a human touch" (223); the young jeans-clad male pedestrians seem to Eric, as a corollary of their alienation from "human affection" (224), "to be shrinking away from any contact with their flamboyantly and paradoxically outlined private parts" (223). As I argue later, Baldwin's preoccupation with these indicatively sexualized overlaps of public and private allegorically elaborates what he sees as the mission of the novel.

3. Joseph Roach, *It* (Ann Arbor: University of Michigan Press, 2007), 1.

4. Leo Braudy, "Knowing the Performer from the Performance: Fame, Celebrity, and Literary Studies," *PMLA* 126, no. 4 (2011): 1073.

5. Ross, "White Fantasies," 19. Ross's proposal, made in passing in an essay concentrating on *Giovanni's Room*, forms the starting point of Matt Bell's argument that *Another Country* fashions a scenario in which black masculinity is the ground of homosexual emancipation, thus anticipating the way in which late 1960s gay liberation was "modeled after the politics and aesthetics of the black power movement." See Bell, "Black Ground,

Gay Figure: Working through *Another Country*, Black Power, and Gay Liberation," *American Literature* 79, no. 3 (2007): 577.

6. Braudy, "Knowing the Performer," 1070.

7. Quoted in Leeming, *James Baldwin*, 278.

8. On this subgenre, see Moran, *Star Authors*, 68–79.

9. James Baldwin, *Tell Me How Long the Train's Been Gone* (Harmondsworth, UK: Penguin, 1994), 235.

10. Ibid., 291, 316, 325.

11. Field, "Looking," 471; Emmanuel S. Nelson, "The Novels of James Baldwin: Struggles of Self-Acceptance," *Journal of American Culture* 8, no. 4 (1985): 15.

12. Baldwin, *Tell Me*, 379.

13. Emmanuel Nelson suggests that by making homosexuality in the novel "primarily intraracial" and by making the briefly appearing white homosexuals "masochistic in their attraction to black men," Baldwin sought to placate black militants. Positive representations of homosexuality, in other words, are confined to the black community, and any connection to transracial subcultural contexts is disavowed. See "Novels of James Baldwin," 15.

14. See, e.g., James Campbell's assertion that 1963 was "the year [Baldwin's] voice broke," marking a deliberate turning away by Baldwin from his signature "lyrical cadence" to a more urgent, careless style informed by the imperatives of race politics. See *Talking at the Gates*, 181.

15. For recent scholarship arguing for the validity and innovativeness of Baldwin's mid- and late-career compositional choices, see, e.g., on the once near universally reviled *Tell Me*, Jacqueline Goldsby, "'Closer to Something Unnameable': Baldwin's Novel Form," in *The Cambridge Companion to James Baldwin*, ed. Michele Elam (Cambridge: Cambridge University Press, 2015), 25–40; David Kurnick, *Empty Houses: Theatrical Failure and the Novel* (Princeton, NJ: Princeton University Press, 2012), 192–206, on what he argues is the self-awareness and experimentalism of *Another Country* and *Tell Me*.

16. James Baldwin, *Tell Me*, 34.

17. Walter Benjamin, "The Work of Art in the Age of Mechanical Reproduction," in *Illuminations*, ed. Hannah Arendt, trans. Harry Zohn (London: Fontana, 1973), 233; Theodor Adorno and Max Horkheimer, *Dialectic of Enlightenment*, trans. John Cumming (London: Verso, 1979), 154.

18. Morin, *The Stars*, 113. On the midcentury critique of celebrity, see also John Potts, *A History of Charisma* (London: Palgrave Macmillan), 160, 168–69.

19. Cheever's and Roth's comments are respectively cited in Moran, *Star Authors*, 25, 101.

20. Baldwin, *Conversations*, 229.

21. Baldwin, *Tell Me*, 270. Similar to the mention of "gay" in this novel, the reference to a closeted authentic self perhaps indicates the currency of this metaphor by the late 1960s, though, as I've indicated, the novel has little interest in the mode of liberation suggested by the metaphor and does not locate Leo's bisexuality as something he needs to bring into the open. I return to the emergence of the closet metaphor during the 1960s in Chapter 3.

22. Baldwin, *The Devil Finds Work*, 482.

23. Ibid., 483.

24. Baldwin, *Conversations*, 231.

25. Ibid., 482.

26. On the complexities of Baldwin's identification with Davis, see also Cassandra M. Ellis, "The Black Boy Looks at the Silver Screen," in Miller, *Re-viewing James Baldwin*, 191–214; José Esteban Muñoz, *Disidentifications: Queers of Color and the Performance of Politics* (Minneapolis: University of Minnesota Press, 1999), 17–18. On Baldwin's camp performativity, see Danielle C. Heard, "Baldwin's Humor," in Elam, *Cambridge Companion to Baldwin*, 100–117. As Heard notes, the subversiveness of Baldwin's camp style has in part to do with its "whiteness," particularly "the affected accent of [his] speaking voice" (106).

27. For a detailed discussion of the relations between celebrity and the notion of charisma, see Potts, *A History of Charisma*. Potts notes that the increasingly transparent manufacture of celebrity evident, for instance, in reality TV, has led media commentators to "make a clear distinction between celebrity—which is constructed within the apparatus of the mass media—and charisma, which does not depend on such an apparatus" (178). However, such media commentary also notes the coincidence between celebrity and charisma for a minority of stars. I think Baldwin adopts a similar position, in that he marks out particular celebrities as possessing charisma, with fame the reward for their compelling abilities.

28. Baldwin, "The Black Boy Looks at the White Boy," 279.

29. Ibid., 273.

30. As noted in Chapter 1, n. 72, Baldwin does not appear to have had much interest in Forster, and his approving use of the term "connection" perhaps indicates his absorption of mid-twentieth-century American liberal culture, particularly the work of Lionel Trilling, for whom Forster was a touchstone.

31. Baldwin, *Conversations*, 26.

32. James Baldwin, "From *What's the Reason Why? A Symposium by Best-Selling Authors*: James Baldwin on *Another Country*," in Baldwin, *Cross of Redemption*, 39.

33. Ibid., 40.

34. Ibid.; Leeming, *James Baldwin*, 205–6.

35. Baldwin, *Conversations*, 20.

36. Roach, *It*, 183; Rose, *On Not Being Able to Sleep*, 203.

37. Quoted in Leeming, *James Baldwin*, 201.

38. Baldwin, *Another Country*, 128. Subsequent page references are cited parenthetically in the text.

39. Baldwin's initial claim about the peculiarly American pathologization of homosexuality in his comments to Eckman is, however, muddled by a series of qualifications: "The only people who *talk* about homosexuality, you know . . . in this terrible way—are Americans. And Englishmen and French and Germans"—so that (as in *Giovanni's Room*) it is finally only Italy that seems to constitute the exception. See Eckman, *Furious*, 32.

40. See, e.g., William A. Cohen, "Liberalism, Libido, Liberation: Baldwin's *Another Country*," *Genders* 12 (1991): 1–21; Roger Rosenblatt, "Out of Control: *Go Tell It on the Mountain* and *Another Country*," in *Modern Critical Views: James Baldwin*, ed. Harold Bloom (New York: Chelsea House, 1986), 77–96; Terry Rowden, "A Play of Abstractions: Race, Sexuality, and Community in James Baldwin's *Another Country*," *Southern Review* 29, no. 1 (1993): 41–50.

41. Trilling, "*Another Country*," 158.

42. Daylanne English, "Another Country, Another Time: James Baldwin's Social Science Fiction" (2016), unpublished paper.

43. Reed Woodhouse, *Unlimited Embrace: A Canon of Gay Fiction, 1945–1995* (Amherst: University of Massachusetts Press, 1998), 18, 22.

44. Though see Nelson, who states of *Another Country* that "whenever [Baldwin] describes homosexual acts, he becomes eloquently sentimental" ("Novels of James Baldwin," 14).

45. Woodhouse, *Unlimited Embrace*, 35.

46. Ibid., 25.

47. I echo Baldwin's own rhetorical question in this passage, "And what were these terrors?" (191), but supply the answer the passage scrupulously avoids.

48. Kevin Ohi, "I'm Not the Boy You Want: Sexuality, 'Race,' and Thwarted Revelation in Baldwin's *Another Country*," *African American Review* 33, no. 2 (1999): 261–81.

49. The passage also reflexively speaks to Baldwin's view of the novelist's mission, echoing an earlier passage, in which Cass reflects on why Richard's novel-writing efforts have disappointed her. Her reflection is prompted by Vivaldo's confession of a queer-bashing incident in his youth:

> Perhaps such secrets, the secrets of everyone, were only expressed when the person laboriously dragged them into the light of the world, imposed them on the world, and made them a part of the world's experience. Without this effort, the secret place was merely a dungeon in which the person perished; without this effort, indeed, the entire world would be an uninhabitable darkness; and she saw, with a dreadful reluctance, why this effort was so rare. Reluctantly, because she then realized that Richard had bitterly disappointed her by writing a book in which he did not believe. . . . It had not really been written to make money—if only it had been! It had been written because [Richard] was afraid, afraid of things dark, strange, dangerous, difficult, and deep. (114)

It is the revelation of a secret to do with homosexuality (in this case, queer bashing) that centers and generates these thoughts on novel writing. Allegorizing *Another Country*'s own operations, the passage aligns novelistic truth with the "dragg[ing]" of homosexuality "into the light of the world."

50. Baldwin, *Tell Me*, 40.

51. Roach, *It*, 12. The couplet is from *An Essay on Criticism* (1711), lines 299–300. See Alexander Pope, *The Poems of Alexander Pope*, vol. 1, *Pastoral Poetry and an Essay*

on Criticism, ed. Audra Williams and Aubrey Williams (New Haven, CT: Yale University Press, 1961), 273.

52. Roach, *It*, 9, 10.

53. Roach also notes that "there is a kind of freakishness to having It," a freakishness that he goes on to align with gender anomaly: "The uncanny allure of It intensifies when a charismatic performer takes over the typifying marks of gender from the opposite sex, ensuring the prominence of transvestism in the greatest theatrical traditions" (ibid., 11).

54. For discussions of Trilling's homophobia, see Genter, *Late Modernism*, 107; and (discussing his and Diana Trilling's relations with Truman Capote) Solomon, *So Famous*, chap. 2.

55. English, "Another Country," 2; José Esteban Muñoz, *Cruising Utopia: The Then and There of Queer Futurity* (New York: New York University Press, 2009), 1. For a critique of Muñoz's appropriation in this book of the identitarian politics of the liberationist past for his soi-disant truly radical, anti-identitarian utopianism, see Castiglia and Reed, *If Memory Serves*, 5–7.

56. English, "Another Country," 4. English quotes Lee Edelman, *No Future: Queer Theory and the Death Drive* (Durham, NC: Duke University Press, 2004), 53.

57. Paul Welch, with photographs by Bill Eppridge, "Homosexuality in America," *Life*, 26 June 1964, 66–74.

58. Jess Stearns, *The Sixth Man* (London: W. H. Allen, 1962), 15; Helen Gurley Brown, *Sex and the Single Girl* (London: Four Square, 1963), 34–35.

59. For a discussion of these texts and their trope of exposure, see Sherry, *Gay Artists*, 105–9.

60. Stearns, *Sixth Man*, 19.

61. See, e.g., the discussion of the *Life* essay's coverage of cruising in Meeker, *Contacts Desired*, 168–69.

62. The contrast between homosexually identified men and trade is also brought up in a later reference by Eric to the practice of "back-alley cock-sucking" indulged in by the patrons of neighboring taverns in his Manhattan street, one for gays and one for longshoremen: "The longshoremen never go to the gay bar and the gay boys never go to the longshoremen's bar—but they know where to find each other when the bars close." Incidentally, Eric here also reiterates Baldwin's identification of the subculture as deathly, calling the gay bar a "cemetery" (321).

63. The passage anticipates a moment from *The Fire Next Time* in which Baldwin, describing the men he knew in his Harlem childhood, details the psychic barriers to black liberation: "There seemed to be no way whatever to remove this cloud that stood between them and the sun, between them and love and life and power" (298).

64. Rita Mae Brown, "Sappho's Reply," in *The Hand That Cradles the Rock* (1971; repr., Oakland, CA: Diana Press, 1974), 77. Stephan M. Cohen notes that the phrase "an army of lovers cannot fail" was a widely used gay liberation slogan in the early 1970s and derives it from a passage in Plato's *Symposium*, in which Phaedrus states that "if an army should be made up of lovers and their loves . . . they would overcome the world." See Cohen,

The Gay Liberation Youth Movement in New York: "An Army of Lovers Cannot Fail" (New York: Routledge, 2008), 51.

65. Gever, *Entertaining Lesbians,* 114.

66. Julie Enszer, "National Poetry Month: Rita Mae Brown's *Army of Lovers,*" *Ms. Magazine*, 30 April 2012, http://msmagazine.com/blog/2012/04/30/national-poetry-month-rita-mae-brown/.

67. For an astute discussion that considers the "seemingly unrepresentable" nature of lesbianism for Baldwin alongside his "important public intellectual engagements with feminists and lesbians," including Lorraine Hansberry, Nikki Giovanni, Audre Lord, and Margaret Mead, see Brim, *Baldwin and the Queer Imagination*, 155–75; quotes at 156.

68. Susan Sontag, "Psychoanalysis and Norman O. Brown's *Life against Death,*" in *Against Interpretation* (1966; repr., New York: Picador, 2001), 257.

Chapter 3

1. David Fahey and Linda Rich, *Masters of Starlight: Photographers in Hollywood* (Los Angeles: Los Angeles County Museum of Art), 18.

2. Angela McRobbie, "The Modernist Style of Susan Sontag," in *Postmodernism and Popular Culture,* by Angela McRobbie (London: Routledge, 1994), 85.

3. Susan Sontag, "A Note and Some Acknowledgements," in *Against Interpretation* (New York: Picador, 2001), x.

4. Susan Sontag, *Under the Sign of Saturn* (New York: Farrar, Straus and Giroux), 111.

5. Leland Poague, ed., *Conversations with Susan Sontag* (Jackson: University Press of Mississippi), 208.

6. Susan Sontag, *Where the Stress Falls* (London: Vintage, 2003), 260.

7. Sharon Cameron, *Impersonality: Seven Essays* (Chicago: University of Chicago Press, 2007), 7. This paragraph draws on my " 'The Closet of the Third Person': Susan Sontag, Sexual Dissidence, and Celebrity," *Life Writing* 8, no. 4 (2011): 388–89.

8. Laura Mulvey, "Visual Pleasure and Narrative Cinema," in *Visual and Other Pleasures*, by Laura Mulvey (Bloomington: Indiana University Press, 1989), 14–26. For an important discussion of the interrelations of Sontag's photographed image and her sexual identity in her later career, see Lee Wallace, "Sontag's Late Lesbianism," *Celebrity Studies* 6, no. 2 (2014): 206–18.

9. Morin, *The Stars*, 83.

10. Alfred Chester, *The Foot*, in *Head of a Sad Angel: Stories,* 1953–1966, by Alfred Chester, ed. Edward Field (Santa Rosa, CA: Black Sparrow, 1990), 258.

11. Terry Castle describes Sontag as a *lusus naturae* and gives an evocative account of how "the oddity and unexpectedness of her early years" in Tucson and Los Angeles seem not to square with "the singular eminence she achieved." Of course, as is proverbially the case with overnight sensations, Sontag's startling appearance on the cultural stage had an extensive backstory, including a rigorous intellectual apprenticeship at several elite universities (Berkeley, Chicago, Oxford). Terry Castle, "Some Notes on 'Notes on Camp,' "

in *The Scandal of Susan Sontag*, ed. Barbara Ching and Jennifer A. Wagner-Lawlor (New York: Columbia University Press, 2009), 26.

12. Copies of solicited blurbs for the book are held in Farrar, Straus and Giroux, Inc., records, Box 344, New York Public Library.

13. Julian Moynahan, "Makers and Shakers," review of *Against Interpretation*, by Susan Sontag, *Observer*, 12 March 1967, 27.

14. Herbert Marcuse, "The New Sensibility," in *An Essay on Liberation* (Boston: Beacon, 1969), chap. 2, quote at 30.

15. George Cotkin's wide-ranging history of the New Sensibility also makes no mention of Marcuse's use of the term. See Cotkin, *Feast of Excess: A Cultural History of the New Sensibility* (New York: Oxford University Press, 2016).

16. Quoted in Joan Acocella, "The Hunger Artist," *New Yorker*, 6 March 2000, 74.

17. Sontag wrote, "I feel that I have lesbian tendencies (how reluctantly I write this)," and "I am very young, and perhaps the disturbing aspect of my sexual ambitions will be outgrown—*frankly I don't care*." Though Sontag's identification may of course have changed over time, this entry attests to the meaningfulness of lesbian identity for same-sex-attracted women by midcentury that I argued for in the Introduction. See Susan Sontag, *Reborn: Journals and Notebooks, 1947–1963*, ed. David Rieff (New York: Farrar, Straus and Giroux, 2008), 11.

18. Ibid., 218.

19. Ibid., 221.

20. Castle, "Some Notes," provides a good discussion of this dynamic in relation to "Notes on 'Camp.'"

21. Susan Sontag, *As Consciousness Is Harnessed to Flesh: Journals and Notebooks, 1964–1980*, ed. David Rieff (New York: Farrar, Straus and Giroux, 2012), 255.

22. Sontag's cross-identification with gay culture is also evident, for instance, in an early unpublished short story, "Back to School," composed in 1951 when she was eighteen, which concerns a male high school student's experience of cruising and the gay bar scene. The typescript of the story is held in Susan Sontag Papers (Collection 612), Box 164, Folder 4, UCLA Library Special Collections, Charles E. Young Research Library, UCLA. Sontag's experience of same-sex subcultures is perhaps typical of the pre-Stonewall period in that the lesbian scene she described overlapped significantly with the gay male one. See the sixteen-year-old Sontag's descriptions of the gay and lesbian nightlife of San Francisco, to which she was introduced by her first lover, Harriet Sohmers, in Sontag, *Reborn*, 24–28. The young Sontag's preoccupation with queer sexuality was also evident in more public, if cautiously rendered, terms in her University of Chicago undergraduate thesis on Djuna Barnes's *Nightwood*, which "offered a complicated and not entirely unambiguous meditation on what she called sexual 'perversion,'" pointing to the way in which the novel presented heterosexuality as perverse, while also identifying queerness as a reversal of 'normality.'" See Daniel Horowitz, *Consuming Pleasures: Intellectuals and Popular Culture in the Postwar World* (Philadelphia: University of Pennsylvania Press, 2012), 312–13, quote at 312.

23. Craig Seligman, *Sontag and Kael: Opposites Attract Me* (New York: Counterpoint, 2004), 18.

24. Theodore Solaratoff, "Death in Life," *Commentary* 44, no. 5 (1967): 87.

25. Sharon Marcus, "Celebrity 2.0: The Case of Marina Abramović," *Public Culture* 27, no. 1 (2015): 32.

26. Judith Brown, *Glamour in Six Dimensions: Modernism and the Radiance of Form* (Ithaca, NY: Cornell University Press, 2009), 5. Subsequent page references are cited parenthetically in the text.

27. Ibid., 117.

28. Ibid., 98–99.

29. Ibid., 100.

30. Steven Shaviro, *Post-cinematic Affect* (Winchester, UK: Zero, 2009), 9.

31. Ibid., 9–10.

32. Shaviro's discussion here also aligns with Joseph Roach's account of the "public intimacy" generated by the star; see Roach, *It*, 16–17. The "illusion" of audience intimacy with celebrities is discussed in moralizing terms in Richard Schickel, *Intimate Strangers: The Culture of Celebrity in America* (Garden City, NY: Doubleday, 1985). On "stranger intimacy" as a general condition of modernity, see Mark Seltzer, *Serial Killers: Death and Life in America's Wound Culture* (New York: Routledge, 1998).

33. Richard deCordova, *Picture Personalities: The Emergence of the Star System in America* (Urbana: University of Illinois Press, 1990), 98. Subsequent page references are cited parenthetically in the text.

34. Marshall McLuhan, *Understanding Media: The Extensions of Man* (London: Routledge and Kegan Paul, 1964), 318.

35. Leo Braudy, *The Frenzy of Renown* (New York: Oxford University Press, 1986), 279–87. See also Loren Glass, "Zuckerman/Roth: Literary Celebrity between Two Deaths," *PMLA* 129, no. 2 (2014): 225.

36. On Byron, see Tom Mole, *Byron's Romantic Celebrity* (London: Palgrave, 2007); Tuite, *Lord Byron*.

37. On the strictly contemporary status of celebrity, as opposed to fame's association with posterity, see Braudy, "Knowing the Performer." Braudy invokes this value-laden opposition not to endorse it but to suggest the ways in which "the rise of celebrity . . . helps engender some of the more interesting efforts at fame. . . . 'True' fame gets valorized when celebrity, thanks to the rise of the mass media, becomes easier to achieve and more culturally prevalent" (1072). As I note later, Sontag's seemingly unreconstructed faith in immortal literary fame is an example of this kind of valorization, one apparently made all the more pressing for her by her own highly mediatized star image.

38. Van Krieken, *Celebrity Society*, 24. For arguments that stress the relation of celebrity to the historical development of individualism, see also Gever, *Entertaining Lesbians*; and Marshall, *Celebrity and Power*.

39. See, e.g., Pierre Bourdieu, *The Rules of Art: Genesis and Structure of the Literary Field*, trans. Susan Emanuel (Stanford, CA: Stanford University Press, 1996); Michel

Foucault, "What Is an Author?," in *The Foucault Reader*, ed. Paul Rabinow (Harmondsworth, UK: Penguin, 1984), 101–20.

40. Joe Moran, *Star Authors: Literary Celebrity in America* (London: Pluto), 68.

41. Ibid., 19.

42. Richard Bernstein, "Susan Sontag, as Image and Herself," *New York Times*, 26 January 1989, https://www.nytimes.com/1989/01/26/arts/susan-sontag-as-image-and-as-herself.html.

43. This is not to say that her revulsion at mass-media fame was not sincere, or at least largely sincere. For instance, in a 1966 letter to her publisher Roger Straus, discussing an offer to write for *Esquire*, Sontag uses the same term she uses in the 1989 interview: "That is the kind of pop-celebrity fame one should run in the opposite direction from!" In the letter, Sontag indicates how her own widely known writing was putting her in danger of pop celebrity, noting that the latest issue of the "pretty loathsome" *Esquire* has one article titled "Against McLuhan" and one titled "Notes on Stoop." Susan Sontag to Roger Straus, 11 August 1966, Farrar, Straus and Giroux, Inc., records, Box 342A. I take up Sontag's statements on her relations to fame in more detail in the next chapter.

44. Susan Sontag, "The Art of Fiction No. 143," interview by Edward Hirsch, *Paris Review* 137 (1995), https://www.theparisreview.org/interviews/1505/susan-sontag-the-art-of-fiction-no-143-susan-sontag.

45. Susan Sontag, *Styles of Radical Will* (New York: Farrar, Straus and Giroux, 1969), 209.

46. Sontag, *As Consciousness*, 218.

47. Wayne Koestenbaum, "Susan Sontag, Cosmophage," in Ching and Wagner-Lawlor, *Scandal*, 240.

48. Seligman, *Sontag and Kael*, 18.

49. Liam Kennedy, *Susan Sontag: Mind as Passion* (Manchester, UK: Manchester University Press), 9. In noting the difference that Sontag made on the New York intellectual scene, I am wary of overstating the cohesiveness of the older generation. But, as Kennedy notes, for all their sometimes fractious differences, the group that has come to be known as the New York intellectuals evinced "distinct patternings of values and beliefs, and of styles of writing and argument" (8). We also need to be cautious about overstating Sontag's radical break with the liberal tradition. As she herself noted in a 1996 afterword to *Against Interpretation*, she always maintained allegiance to "the canonical treasures of the past" and, despite her aestheticism, was always a "barely closeted moralist." See Sontag, "Afterword: Thirty Years Later," in Sontag, *Against Interpretation*, 310, 309.

50. Kennedy, *Susan Sontag*, 17, 21.

51. For a discussion of the conservative "look" of the New York intellectuals, see James Penner, who contrasts them with the "peacock males" of the counterculture. Penner, *Pinks, Pansies, and Punks: The Rhetoric of Masculinity in American Literary Culture* (Bloomington: Indiana University Press, 2010), 174.

52. Norman Podhoretz, *Making It* (New York: Random House, 1967), 154. Podhoretz was actually of the same generation as Sontag and had his own difficulties with the older New York intellectuals, the chief cause of which was this "tell-all" memoir.

53. Ibid.

54. Ibid., 154–55.

55. Carol Brightman, *Writing Dangerously: Mary McCarthy and Her World* (New York: Clarkson Potter, 1992), 491.

56. "Book News from Farrar, Straus and Company Inc.: Advance Comment on *The Benefactor* by Susan Sontag," Susan Sontag Papers, Box 164, Folder 4.

57. Irving Howe, *Decline of the New* (London: Victor Gollancz, 1971), 258.

58. Penner, *Pinks*, 169. In his chapter 4, Penner provides an incisive discussion of Howe's essay and of other New York intellectual responses to the shifting politics of gender and sexuality during the 1960s. See also his more detailed discussion of the reaction to Sontag, "Gendering Susan Sontag's Criticism in the 1960s: The New York Intellectuals, the Counter Culture, and the *Kulturkampf* over 'the New Sensibility,'" *Women's Studies* 37 (2008): 921–41.

59. Howe, *Decline*, 260.

60. Ibid., 227.

61. Ibid., 260.

62. Sontag, *Against Interpretation*, 14.

63. Morin, *The Stars*, 55.

64. On this aspect of Sontag's writing, see also Mark Greif, "Still Superior," review of *Reborn: Journals and Notebooks, 1947–1963*, by Susan Sontag, ed. David Rieff, *London Review of Books*, 12 February 2009, https://www.lrb.co.uk/v31/n03/mark-greif/still-superior. Greif observes that "an odd, partly disowned, seemingly extraneous but electrifying language of sex serpentines through . . . many of [Sontag's] essays."

65. Susan Sontag, "On Style," in *Against Interpretation*, 32, 31; "virtually independent of the volition of the maker" is from her discussion of Bergman's *Persona*, but the description of the artwork's autonomy applies to Sontag's formalist aesthetic more generally. See Sontag, "Bergman's *Persona*," in *Styles of Radical Will* (New York: Farrar, Straus and Giroux, 1969), 138.

66. The comment is made in an interview with specific reference to *AIDS and Its Metaphors* (New York: Farrar, Straus and Giroux, 1989). See Poague, *Conversations*, 255. On Sontag's essayistic "performativity," see also Marcie Frank, "The Critic as Performance Artist: Susan Sontag's Writing and Gay Cultures," in *Camp Grounds: Style and Homosexuality*, ed. David Bergman (Amherst: University of Massachusetts Press, 1993), 173–84.

67. Susan Sontag, "Resnais's *Muriel*," in *Against Interpretation*, 240.

68. Sontag, "Afterword," 312.

69. Sontag's resistance to being the new McCarthy is something of a leitmotif of her career. A 1963 profile is headlined "A brilliant young author who does not want to be the 'new Mary McCarthy.'" See Donald Stanley, "Susan Sontag," *People: the California Weekly*, 8 December 1963, 14. In the 1966 letter to Roger Straus about the offer to review films for *Esquire*, Sontag writes, "I don't want to be the new Dwight McDonald any more than I want to be the new Mary McCarthy, estimable as these worthy people are." Sontag also

reported that Mary McCarthy once said to her, circa 1969, "Oh, you're the imitation me." See Bernstein, "Susan Sontag."

70. Sontag, "A Note," x (emphasis in original).

71. Sontag, *Against Interpretation*, 5, 6. Subsequent page references are cited parenthetically in the text.

72. In an intriguing twist in her account of the erotics of writing, Sontag elsewhere in *Against Interpretation* identifies Baldwin as a "husbandly" writer in an essay that aphoristically begins, "Great writers are either husbands or lovers." Husbandly writers "supply the solid virtues of a husband: reliability, intelligibility, generosity, decency," while loverlike writers provide "gifts of temperament rather than moral goodness." Sontag cheekily sums up: "As in life so in art both are necessary, husbands and lovers. It's a great pity when one is forced to choose between them." See Sontag, "Camus' Notebooks," in *Against Interpretation*, 52.

73. Phillip Lopate, *Notes on Sontag* (Princeton, NJ: Princeton University Press, 2009), 68.

74. Susan Sontag, *The Benefactor* (New York: Farrar, Straus and Giroux, 1963), 57.

75. Ibid., 58.

76. Oscar Wilde, "The Critic as Artist," in *The Artist as Critic: Critical Writings of Oscar Wilde*, ed. Richard Ellmann (New York: Random House), 389.

77. Loftin, *Masked Voices*, 11.

78. For other discussions of the inappropriateness of the closet metaphor for analysis of the Cold War period, see Michael P. Bibler, "The Cold War Closet," in *The Cambridge Companion to American Gay and Lesbian Literature*, ed. Scott Herring (Cambridge: Cambridge University Press, 2015), 122–38; Sherry, *Gay Artists*, 96–97, 105–9.

79. Loftin, *Masked Voices*, 11.

80. For discussions of the emergence of the closet metaphor during the 1960s, see Henry Abelove, "How Stonewall Obscures the Real History of Gay Liberation," *Chronicle of Higher Education*, 26 June 2015, https://www.chronicle.com/article/How-Stonewall-Obscures-the/231099; Benjamin Kahan, "Ray Johnson's Anti-archive: Blackface, Sadomasochism, and the Racial and Sexual Imagination of Pop Art," *Angelaki* 23, no. 1 (2018): 71; Sherry, *Gay Artists*, 105–9. The mask metaphor as it was deployed in gay subcultural contexts can also, up to a point, be related to the "dramaturgical" conception of social interaction that distinguishes Cold War culture across a wide swathe of sociological, political, and artistic discourses, as discussed by Trask, *Camp Sites*. I agree that there are strong connections between the postwar version of the "homosexual parody" and this culture-wide fascination with the dramaturgical but contend that the germinal conception of a liberationist gay subject militates against an understanding of the mask metaphor as simply an expression of the Cold War pragmatism that Trask describes so well.

81. Susan Sontag, "Bergman's *Persona*," 126. Subsequent page references are cited parenthetically in the text.

82. My argument here is inspired by Eve Sedgwick's discussion of the overlap between the "open secret" of homosexuality and the "empty secret" of male high modernism that "delineates . . . a split between content or thematics on the one hand and structure on the other that is stressed in favor of structure and at the expense of thematics" (*Epistemology*,

165). An examination of the work of such writers as Henry James, Ernest Hemingway, and Wallace Stevens suggests that this operation involves the abjection of the content or figuration of, specifically, "the desired male body" (167). The modernism of these writers is thus a homophobic practice that bears traces of a repressed homoeroticism. I see the late-modernist Sontag's account of Bergman's late-modernist masterpiece operating in a similar fashion, with the female body here the desired body that is not quite jettisoned in the interest of a celebration of form.

83. Sontag, "On Style," 31.

84. Butler, "Imitation," 16.

85. Edmund White, *City Boy: My Life in New York during the* 1960s *and '70s* (New York: Bloomsbury, 2009), 271; Terry Castle, "Desperately Seeking Susan," *London Review of Books*, 17 March 2005, https://www.lrb.co.uk/v27/n06/terry-castle/desperately-seeking-susan.

Chapter 4

1. Susan Sontag Papers, Folder 5; original grammar, ellipsis, and presentation of parentheses. The struck-out words in the final sentence are presumably a reference to Herman Hesse's novel *Demian* (1919). The novel does not actually feature a magic box, which may explain the striking out.

2. Carl Rollyson and Lisa Paddock, *Susan Sontag: The Making of an Icon*, rev. ed. (Jackson: University Press of Mississippi, 2016), 185. Referring to information in a keynote address by Sontag to the 1989 "Memory of Light" symposium, Rollyson and Paddock note that Sontag began writing about Arbus alone, but this writing project expanded into the wide-ranging argument of *On Photography* (New York: Farrar, Straus and Giroux, 1977).

3. In her 1978 *Rolling Stone* interview Sontag stated her opposition to "decade-mongering": "There's something terrible about making the Fifties and Sixties and Seventies into major constructs. They're myths." Yet interestingly this opposition is an elaboration of a defense of the ideals of the 1960s: "The idea is that everything that was hoped for and attempted in the Sixties basically hasn't worked and couldn't work out. But who says it won't work?" Jonathan Cott, *Susan Sontag: The Complete* Rolling Stone *Interview* (New Haven, CT: Yale University Press, 2013), 30. A similar wavering is evident in Sontag's 1996 afterword to *Against Interpretation*, in which she at first evokes the "mythic era known as the Sixties" and her famous book's relation to that era with "reluctance, since I'm not keen on the omnipresent convention of packaging one's life, the life of one's time, in decades." But a couple of pages later Sontag rhapsodizes over what the Sixties represent: "How marvelous it all does seem, in retrospect. How one wishes some of its boldness, its optimism, its disdain for commerce had survived." See Sontag, "Thirty Years Later," 308, 311.

4. Susan Sontag, "Notes on 'Camp,'" 277. Subsequent page references are cited parenthetically in the text.

5. If, as this note suggests, Sontag's thinking on camp helped her approach the topics of Arbus and photography, that foundational work is erased from *On Photography* itself. "Camp" here appears to have an essential but ghostly importance that is in

accord with the sometimes acknowledged, sometimes denied, centrality of the essay to Sontag's work.

6. Castle, "Some Notes," 23.

7. D. A. Miller, "Sontag's Urbanity," in *The Lesbian and Gay Studies Reader*, ed. Henry Abelove, Michèle Aina Barale, and David M. Halperin (New York: Routledge, 1993), 213.

8. Kim Michasiw, "Camp, Masculinity, Masquerade," *differences* 6, no. 2–3 (1994): 171n14; Michasiw here also gives references for work citing Miller as adequate proof of Sontag's homophobia. See also Sasha Torres, who indicates the depth of anti-Sontag feeling in 1990s scholarship when she candidly notes that she "shares Miller's revulsion" of Sontag. Torres, "The Caped Crusader of Camp: Pop, Camp, and the *Batman* Television Series," in *Pop Out: Queer Warhol*, ed. Jennifer Doyle, Jonathan Flatley, and José Esteban Muñoz (Durham, NC: Duke University Press, 1996), 247. Reversing the charge of phobia, Michasiw provides an incisive discussion of how Sontag is constituted as a "phobic object of gay discourse around camp and identity" (164) and of how this enables a gender-conformist stance of militant masculinity on the part of gay writers, concentrating on Miller's essay and (less convincingly) Michael Moon's chapter on Jack Smith's *Flaming Creatures*. See "Flaming Closets," in *A Small Boy and Others: Imitation and Initiation in American Culture from Henry James to Andy Warhol*, by Michael Moon (Durham, NC: Duke University Press, 1998), 67–93. For another account of Sontag's supposed homophobia, see Moe Meyer, "Introduction: Reclaiming the Discourse of Camp," in *The Politics and Poetics of Camp*, ed. Moe Meyer (New York: Routledge, 1994), 1–22. Meyer argues that Sontag's essay initiates "a strategy of un-queer appropriation of queer praxis" (5). An early example of the gay critique of "Notes on 'Camp'" is provided in Esther Newton's pathbreaking ethnographic study of female impersonators, where she reports that one of her informants ("college educated" and therefore "perfectly able to get through" Sontag's essay) was "enraged (justifiably, I felt) that she had almost edited homosexuals out of camp." See Newton, *Mother Camp: Female Impersonators in America*, 2nd ed. (Chicago: University of Chicago Press, 1972), 106n12.

9. Both Marcie Frank and Terry Castle describe Sontag's ambiguously autobiographical relation to camp as "coy." Frank's essay, "Critic," published in 1993 when Sontag was still alive and, for that reason perhaps, more circumspect than Castle's, argues that in "Camp" Sontag "retreats from a full embrace of the autobiographical, offering in its place coy gestures that intensify her [critical] personality" (176). Writing in 2000 and, like Frank and Castle, arguing for the centrality of "Camp" to Sontag's oeuvre, Leland Poague notes that "while numerous sources indicate that she has practiced the androgyny she preaches, Sontag has refused to comment upon the topic of her sexual affiliations." See Poague, "Introduction: The Way She Writes Now: Notes on Sontag," in *Susan Sontag: An Annotated Bibliography*, 1948–1992, comp. Leland Poague and Kathy A. Parsons (New York: Garland, 2000), xxix. Gesturing toward the revisionist account of "Camp," Barbara Ching and Jennifer Wagner Lawlor assert that "nearly all contemporary theorists of camp focus on the essay as an expression of sexual identity," which seems somewhat of an overstatement, given the insistent charges of homophobia leveled at Sontag throughout

the 1990s. See Ching and Wagner-Lawlor, "Introduction: Unextinguished: Susan Sontag's Work in Progress," in Ching and Wagner-Lawlor, *Scandal of Susan Sontag*, 10.

10. Poague, *Conversations*, 70.

11. Daniel Schreiber, *Susan Sontag: A Biography*, trans. David Dollenmayer (Evanston, IL: Northwestern University Press, 2014), 80. The scare quotes in Sontag's title are regularly omitted in commentary. In the interest of an uncluttered reading experience, I have left out the scare quotes in the short version of the title, "Camp," that I use throughout this chapter.

12. Miller, "Sontag's Urbanity," 213.

13. Fabio Cleto, "Introduction" (Section II), in *Camp: Queer Aesthetics and the Performing Subject: A Reader*, ed. Fabio Cleto (Ann Arbor: University of Michigan Press), 88.

14. Van Krieken, *Celebrity Society*, 56.

15. Vivian Gornick, "It's a Queer Hand Stoking the Campfire," *Village Voice*, 7 April 1966, 20.

16. For testimonies to Stein's influence on other film critics, see, e.g., David Noh, "A Man of the Movies: Elliott Stein, 1928–2012," *Gay City News*, 12 November 2012, https://www.gaycitynews.nyc/stories/2012/23/w4228-a-man-of-the-movies-elliott-stein-1928-2012-2012-11-14.html; and Jonathan Rosenbaum, "Elliott Stein (1928–2012)," 9 November 2012, https://www.jonathanrosenbaum.net/2012/11/elliott-stein-1928-2012/.

17. For Stein's supposed influence on *Giovanni's Room*, see Schreiber, *Susan Sontag*, 80.

18. Sontag, *Benefactor*, 54. Subsequent page references are cited parenthetically in the text.

19. Ned Rorem, *Knowing When to Stop: A Memoir* (New York: Simon and Schuster, 1994), 470. Rorem's assertion was subsequently affirmed by Stein himself, who in a 2012 interview said, "I was a great influence on her Notes on Camp thing. She came to see my apartment in Paris and I had decorated my room in, I suppose you could call it, a camp way, with all kinds of objects, sexual, movie star stuff. It was a gay apartment, and she vaguely understood and was sympathetic about it. We talked about it at some length and eventually it became her essay. I can't claim credit for it, but I supplied a lot of the background." Quoted in "Elliott Stein, 1928–2012," *Village Voice*, 14 November 2012, https://www.villagevoice.com/2012/11/14/elliott-stein-1928-2012/.

20. Ira Cohen, "Our Ancestor, Alfred Chester," in Chester, *Head of a Sad Angel*, 364; W. H. Auden, "An Improbable Life," review of *The Letters of Oscar Wilde*, ed. Rupert Hart-Davis, *New Yorker*, 9 March 1963, 155–77.

21. Edward Field, *The Man Who Would Marry Susan Sontag and Other Intimate Portraits of the Bohemian Era* (Madison: University of Wisconsin Press, 2005), 164.

22. Sontag's working notes on the essay are held in Susan Sontag Papers, Box 33, Folder 23.

23. Rollyson and Paddock, *Susan Sontag*, 59–60.

24. Ibid., 111–13. Chester also claimed that he and Sontag once slept together. See Field, *Man*, 168.

25. Rollyson and Paddock, *Susan Sontag*, 112.

26. Susan Sontag to Edward Field, 17 May 1989, Edward Field/Alfred Chester archives, Folder 121, University of Delaware Special Collections.

27. Rollyson and Paddock, *Susan Sontag*, 79.

28. Richard Kluger to Susan Sontag, 30 January 1967, Farrar, Straus and Giroux records, Box 342A.

29. Ibid.

30. Susan Sontag to Richard Kluger, 1 February 1967, Farrar, Straus and Giroux records, Box 342A.

31. Richard Kluger has shared with me his own account of this episode: "I liked and admired Susan, but as I wrote to her, I believed the restraining order she asked Straus to press against S&S unless it revised my already printed jacket copy in order to remove her name was an unreasonable attempt to eradicate her prior public endorsement of Chester's talent—and that I had a greater obligation to present Chester's book to the public in the best possible light rather than to honor what I felt to be Sontag's presumptuous demand. In retrospect, I think I was more irritated by my boss's agreement to do the bidding of fellow publisher Roger Straus in Sontag's behalf than by her wish, perhaps understandable in light of the prevailing homophobic climate of the day, not to be perceived as an affiliate of the gay and lesbian community at a time when her own fortunes as a literary figure were blossoming." Kluger, e-mail to the author, 5 May 2018.

32. Susan Sontag, Letters to the Editor ("Behold Goliath"), *New York Times Book Review*, 31 May 1964, 18.

33. Ibid.

34. Kluger to Sontag, 30 January 1967.

35. Edward Field also trades on Sontag's name recognition by titling his 2005 memoir of the Greenwich Village bohemia of the 1950s and 1960s *The Man Who Would Marry Susan Sontag*. The title indicates Chester's centrality in the memoir, but via an epithet referring to his crazed plan to marry the famous Sontag. Additionally, exploiting the star power of Sontag's image, a photograph of the young Sontag features prominently on the memoir's cover alongside a photograph of Field.

36. Rollyson and Paddock, *Susan Sontag*, 117.

37. Chester, *The Foot*, 258, 259. *The Foot* was originally published in 1970 in issue 9 of *New American Review*.

38. "I want to write, to begin, a romantic mystery about a girl, a young woman. . . . She is perfectly ordinary, I mean, there is nothing as yet at all odd in her character or background. She is probably an American, but she doesn't have to be. There is something romantic and mysterious about her, but as I say it has nothing to do with her intrinsics, for she has only just come into being" (ibid., 258).

39. Herbert Simon, "Designing Organizations for an Information-Rich World," in *Computers, Communication, and the Public Interest*, ed. Martin Greenberger (Baltimore: Johns Hopkins University Press), 40.

40. Quoted in van Krieken, *Celebrity Society*, 56.

41. Ibid., 61. Van Krieken is speaking here specifically about the effect of an academic

"name" reviewing a lesser-known academic's book, but the process obviously applies to all forms of celebrity endorsement.

42. Ibid., 56.

43. On the controversies surrounding these public statements, see, e.g., Schreiber, *Susan Sontag*, 163–65, 226–30.

44. Sontag, "Susan Sontag at Washington University, April 24, 1984," *River Styx* 17 (1985): 9.

45. Van Krieken argues in *Celebrity Society* that "the secret of the nature of celebrity is primarily a matter of the accumulation and distribution of attention" (56).

46. Castle, "Some Notes," 23. Subsequent page references are cited parenthetically in the text.

47. Henry Luhrman, "A Bored Susan Sontag: 'I Think Camp Should Be Retired,'" *Columbia Owl*, 23 March 1966, 8.

48. Sontag, "Susan Sontag at Washington University," 9–10.

49. Luhrman, "Bored," 8.

50. Nora Ephron, "Not Even a Critic Can Choose Her Audience," *New York Post*, 23 September 1967, 29.

51. Lionel Trilling, *Beyond Culture: Essays on Literature and Learning* (London: Secker and Warburg, 1966), xi.

52. Gérard Genette, *Paratexts: Thresholds of Interpretation*, trans. Jane E. Lewin (1987; repr., Cambridge: Cambridge University Press, 1997), 117.

53. Ibid., 135.

54. "Taste: 'Camp,'" *Time*, 11 December 1964, 75.

55. Thomas Meehan, "Not Good Taste, Not Bad Taste—It's 'Camp,'" *New York Times Book Review*, 21 March 1965, 115.

56. John Simon, "Two Camps," *Partisan Review* 32, no. 1 (1965): 156. On Simon's attack, see also Penner, *Pinks*, 173–74.

57. Simon, "Two Camps," 156; Penner, *Pinks*, 173.

58. I borrow this phrase from the subtitle of Michael Sherry's excellent history of the midcentury anxiety about gay influence in the arts, *Gay Artists in Modern American Culture: An Imagined Conspiracy* (Chapel Hill: University of North Carolina Press, 2007).

59. Gornick, "Queer Hand," 1. Subsequent page references are cited parenthetically in the text. Sontag argues that "Camp is a tender feeling" ("Camp," 292).

60. For other discussions of the antigay and anticamp settings of New Left discourse, see Penner, *Pinks*, 220, 240–42; Trask, *Camp Sites*, chap. 3.

61. On the association of (male) homosexuality with tropes of reversal, see, e.g., Edelman, *Homographesis*; Jonathan Goldberg, *Sodometries: Renaissance Texts, Modern Sexualities* (Stanford, CA: Stanford University Press, 1992).

62. On Grove Press, see Glass, *Counterculture Colophon*; on poetic subcultures of the period, see Michael Davidson, *Guys like Us: Citing Masculinity in Cold War Poetics* (Chicago: University of Chicago Press, 2003).

63. Susan Sontag, "Two Camps," *Partisan Review* 32, no. 1 (1965): 157.

64. Ibid., 158.

65. Sherry, *Gay Artists*, 137.

66. Ibid.

67. Mark Finch, "Sex and Address in *Dynasty*," in Cleto, *Camp*, 143.

68. Poague, "Introduction," xxx.

69. Jeffrey Escoffier, "Homosexuality and the Sociological Imagination," in *American Homo: Community and Perversity*, by Jeffrey Escoffier (Berkeley: University of California Press, 1998), 82–83. On the relation of "Camp" to the sociological or "ethnic" conception of gayness, see also Cleto, "Introduction" (Section II).

70. Sherry, *Gay Artists*, 137.

71. Ephron, "Not Even," 29. Ephron states here that she is quoting an earlier interview but does not note the source. Subsequent quotations from Ephron's article record Sontag's comments to Ephron herself.

72. Ibid.

73. Sontag first met Sohmers at Berkeley when she was sixteen. The rekindled affair was the catalyst for Sontag's divorce from Philip Rieff. Sohmers returned to New York in 1959, but she was soon replaced in Sontag's affections by Fornés. See Rollyson and Paddock, *Susan Sontag*, 55–66.

74. Frank, "Critic," 180.

75. Meehan, "Not Good Taste," 113.

76. Susan Sontag, "Jack Smith's *Flaming Creatures*," in *Against Interpretation*, 226. Subsequent page references are cited parenthetically in the text.

77. Juan A. Suárez, *Bike Boys, Drag Queens, and Superstars: Avant-Garde, Mass Culture, and Gay Identities in the 1960s Underground Cinema* (Bloomington: Indiana University Press, 1996), 182. On the film's trials, see also J. Hoberman, *On Jack Smith's* Flaming Creatures *(and Other Secret-Flix of Cinemaroc)* (New York: Granary, 2001), 36–51.

78. Susan Sontag, "A Feast for Open Eyes," *The Nation*, 13 April 1964, 374–76.

79. See Hoberman, *On Jack Smith's* Flaming Creatures, 48.

80. Susan Sontag, "Psychoanalysis and Norman O. Brown's *Life against Death*," in *Against Interpretation*, 257. Subsequent page references are cited parenthetically in the text.

81. Sontag, *Benefactor*, 97.

82. Ibid., 7.

83. Susan Sontag, "The Pornographic Imagination," in *Styles*, 35–73. My account of Sontag's relation to the sexual revolution differs from that of Deborah Nelson, who adduces "Pornographic Imagination" as the main evidence for her argument that Sontag "was a very skeptical fellow traveler, one who embraced the relaxation of sexual hypocrisy while standing well apart from the Reichian optimism about sexuality that guided the sexual revolution." See Nelson, *Tough Enough: Arbus, Arendt, Didion, McCarthy, Sontag, Weil* (Chicago: University of Chicago Press, 2017), 104. I credit Sontag's embrace of "the relaxation of sexual hypocrisy" with more political force than that anodyne phrasing gives it and am interested particularly in its translation into the gay liberation and countercultural movements. Sontag, rather than fundamentally skeptical, I would say,

shifts her position on the sexual revolution depending on the time in which she is writing and the material with which she is engaging. However, it does seem to be the case that Sontag's sexual attitudes became more conservative after the 1960s. On the notorious essay "Fascinating Fascism" (1975), with its moralizing conflation of gay sexuality, gay sadomasochism, and "imputed 'fascism,'" see Frank, "Critic," 178–82, quote at 181.

84. Herbert Marcuse, *An Essay on Liberation* (Boston: Beacon, 1969), 30.

85. Dennis Altman, *Homosexual: Oppression and Liberation* (Sydney: Angus and Robertson, 1972), 141.

86. Susan Sontag, "Some Thoughts on the Right Way (for Us) to Love the Cuban Revolution," *Ramparts*, 16 April 1969, 6.

87. Allen Young, "Out of the Closets, into the Streets," in *Out of the Closets: Voices of Gay Liberation*, ed. Karla Jay and Allen Young (New York: Pyramid, 1972), 29; quoted in Annamarie Jagose, *Queer Theory* (Melbourne: Melbourne University Press, 1996), 42.

88. Altman, *Homosexual*, 139.

89. Jagose, *Queer Theory*, 40–43.

90. Altman's chapter in *Homosexual* on sexual liberation is titled "Liberation: Toward the Polymorphous Whole."

91. Altman, *Homosexual*, 139.

92. Ibid., 94.

93. Eve Kosofsky Sedgwick, *Tendencies* (Durham, NC: Duke University Press, 1993), 8.

94. See Suárez, *Bike Boys*, 183–96. Drawing on Foucault and Butler, Suárez reads *Flaming Creatures*, in its confusion of categories, as working against "literal" gay politics (196), thus implicitly drawing a parallel between Sontag's "polymorphous joy" and queer theory (he does not use the term "queer"). Yet he also understands the film as a "homosexual movie" that is energized by gay sexuality (190).

95. Moon, *Small Boy*, 78.

96. Jack Smith, *Wait for Me at the Bottom of the Pool: The Writings of Jack Smith*, ed. J. Hoberman and Edward Leffingwell (New York: Serpent's Tail, 1997), 107.

Chapter 5

1. Catharine R. Stimpson, "My O My O Myra," in *Gore Vidal: Writer against the Grain*, ed. Jay Parini (London: Andre Deutsch, 1992), 301n7; Dennis Altman, *Gore Vidal's America* (Cambridge: Polity, 2005), 132.

2. Van Krieken, *Celebrity Society*, 56.

3. Gore Vidal, *Sexually Speaking: Collected Sex Writings* (San Francisco: Cleis, 1999), 99.

4. Quoted in Andrew Kopkind, "The Importance of Being Gore," *The Nation*, 5 July 1993, 19.

5. In a 1974 interview, for instance, Vidal said that "I spent most of my life trying to get out of the world of the Auchinclosses and of the American nobles," a claim somewhat at odds with his many loving re-creations of that world in his memoirs and essays. See Anthony Haden-Guest, "The Vidal-Capote Papers: A Tempest in Camelot," *New York*, 11 June 1974, 63.

6. See, e.g., Gore Vidal, *Conversations with Gore Vidal*, ed. Richard Peabody and Lucinda Ebersole (Jackson: University Press of Mississippi, 2005), 104.

7. Sharon Marcus, "Salomé!! Sarah Bernhardt, Oscar Wilde, and the Drama of Celebrity," *PMLA* 126, no. 4 (2011): 1003–4.

8. The classic version of this distinction is given by Daniel Boorstin, *The Image: Or, What Happened to the American Dream* (New York: Atheneum, 1962), 45–76. Also see James Monaco, *Celebrity: The Media as Image Makers* (New York: Dell, 1985); Schickel, *Intimate Strangers*; Braudy, *Frenzy of Renown*; Rojek, *Celebrity*; Fred Inglis, *A Short History of Celebrity* (Princeton, NJ: Princeton University Press, 2010).

9. See Jane Gaines's account of late nineteenth- and early twentieth-century "developments in photographic technology and photo processing that transformed the ordinary person into a celebrity and in turn produced the celebrity as common," in *Contested Culture: The Image, the Voice and the Law* (London: BFI), 184. For critiques of the fame/celebrity distinction, see Joshua Gamson, *Claims to Fame: Celebrity in Contemporary America* (Berkeley: University of California Press, 1994); Su Holmes and Sean Redmond, "Introduction: Understanding Celebrity Culture," in *Framing Celebrity: New Directions in Celebrity Culture*, ed. Su Holmes and Sean Redmond (New York: Routledge, 2006), 1–16. For discussions of the gendered assumptions attached to fame (masculine) and celebrity (feminized), see Gever, *Entertaining Lesbians*, 7–75; Marcus, "Salomé!!," 1010; Weber, *Women and Literary Celebrity*, 18.

10. In this respect, my argument is congruent with those emphasizing the importance of print media forms such as gay and lesbian pulp fiction and physique pictorial magazines for the formation of gay political consciousness in the postwar decades. See Gunn and Harker, *1960s Gay Pulp Fiction*; Thomas Waugh, *Hard to Imagine: Gay Male Eroticism in Photography and Film from Their Beginnings to Stonewall* (New York: Columbia University Press, 1996). See also Loftin, *Masked Voices*, and Meeker, *Contacts Desired*, for discussions of the shaping role on political consciousness of homophile magazines and other subcultural print media. Meeker observes that "coverage of homosexuality" proved to be one way that media such as radio, photojournalism, and paperback books could compete with the newly dominant medium of television during the 1960s, providing "increasingly extended peeks into the arenas of deviance, illegality, and activism" that television executives and censors declared off-limits (112).

11. Eric Schaefer, ed., *Sex Scene: Media and the Sexual Revolution* (Durham, NC: Duke University Press, 2014).

12. Eric Schaefer, "Introduction: Sex Seen: 1968 and Rise of 'Public' Sex," in Schaefer, *Sex Scene*, 3. See also Alan Petigny, "Illegitimacy, Postwar Psychology, and the Reperiodization of the Sexual Revolution," *Journal of Social History* 38, no. 1 (2004): 63–79.

13. Schaefer, "Introduction," 4.

14. Ibid., 3, 4.

15. Ibid., 7.

16. The essays collected in *Sex Scene* are also largely confined to the 1968–73 time frame. See also Robert Hofler, *Sexplosion: From Andy Warhol to* A Clockwork

Orange—*How a Generation of Pop Rebels Broke All the Taboos* (New York: HarperCollins, Itbooks, 2014), which gives a year-by-year account of the production and impact of landmark sexually explicit texts (including *Myra Breckinridge*) over the 1968–73 period. *Deep Throat* actually began its run in 1972, but it reached the height of its notoriety with its obscenity trial the following year.

17. Trask, *Camp Sites*, 177–79.

18. John Weightman, "Myth of the Butch Bitch," review of *Myra Breckinridge*, by Gore Vidal, *Observer*, 15 September 1968. Reprinted in John Weightman, *The Concept of the Avant-Garde* (London: Alcove, 1973), quote at 281.

19. Vidal, *Conversations*, 110.

20. Gore Vidal, *Myra Breckinridge and Myron* (London: Abacus, 1993), 36. Subsequent page references are cited parenthetically in the text.

21. Apparently with Vidal's imprimatur, Bernard F. Dick asserts that Myra's sudden changes in not only gender and sexuality but also personality are intertextual engagements with the shape-shifting characters of classical literature, such as those in Petronius's *Satyricon*. See Dick, *The Apostate Angel: A Critical Study of Gore Vidal* (New York: Random House, 1974), 158–70.

22. Altman, *Gore Vidal's America*, 132.

23. Peter S. Prescott, "Here Comes Gore Vidal with *Charley's Aunt* in Modern Drag," review of *Myra Breckinridge*, by Gore Vidal, *Look*, 16 March 1968, T8, Gore Vidal Papers, 1875–2008 (MS Am 2350), Folder 4188, Houghton Library, Harvard University. The general reviewer perception that *Myra* was "about" homosexuality also indicates the still-common conflation of transsexuality with homosexuality at this time, despite the increasing tendency of medical and sexological researchers to distinguish the two categories. See "The Liberal Moment," in *How Sex Changed: A History of Transsexuality in the United States*, by Joanne Meyerowitz (Cambridge, MA: Harvard University Press, 2002), chap. 6. Meyerowitz places *Myra* in the context of a significant print media focus throughout the 1960s on the figure of the transsexual, evident, on the one hand, in autobiographical books and articles that pleaded for tolerance and, on the other, in tabloid and pulp print media narratives in which the transsexual was eroticized. She notes that Vidal "redrew the eroticized MTF [male-to-female transsexual] as a caricature that allowed him to skewer American sexual mores and to construct, through a single character, scenes of gay male, heterosexual, and lesbian sex" (203). She also records that many transsexuals found the novel "wholly offensive," with one MTF calling it "the worst possible publicity for the transsexual cause," and another writing, "I burn every copy I can get." The most well-known transsexual of the era, Christine Jorgensen, was outraged. She stated in a radio interview that she feared that "fifteen years of progress" would go "down the drain based upon garbage." Jorgensen considered legal action against Vidal, but her lawyers dissuaded her (204).

24. Sontag, *Against Interpretation*, 282, 287. Altman, in *Gore Vidal's America*, wonders whether *Myra* "reveals the influence" of "Notes on 'Camp'" and other Sontag essays (131). Vidal made another, unkind connection of Sontag to the novel, stating on more than one occasion that Myra was partly based on or resembled her. In a 1969 interview,

for instance, he states, "Myra came out of my head like a Minerva who speaks with the same lack of humor as Susan Sontag." "*Gore Vidal il stronca prima d'essere girato il film tratto dal suo romanzo* Myra Breckinridge [Gore Vidal slams the movie based on his novel *Myra Breckinridge* ahead of filming]," *Il Dramma*, 13 October 1969, 73, Gore Vidal Papers, Folder 4174; thanks to Giuliana Ferrari for help with translation.

25. Philip Core, *Camp: The Lie That Tells the Truth* (New York: Delilah, 1984), 185.

26. Trask, *Camp Sites*, 173.

27. The extensive literature on camp has seen much debate over whether or not it is a form of liberatory or resistant politics. For a recent defense of camp's political potential, see David Halperin, *How to Be Gay* (Cambridge, MA: Harvard University Press, Belknap, 2012); Trask, *Camp Sites*, offers a more skeptical view.

28. Trask, *Camp Sites*, 178.

29. Brigid Brophy, "The Tang of Uncertainty," review of *Myra Breckinridge*, by Gore Vidal, *The Listener*, 26 September 1968, 412.

30. Andrew Ross, "Uses of Camp," in Cleto, *Camp*, 310.

31. Stimpson, "My O My O Myra," 195.

32. Margot Hentoff, "Growing Up Androgynous," review of *Myra Breckinridge*, by Gore Vidal, *New York Review of Books*, 9 May 1968, https://www.nybooks.com /articles/1968/05/09/growing-up-androgynous/.

33. See, for instance, the 1991 essay "The Birds and the Bees," in which Vidal states that homosexuals "should be considered benefactors by everyone, while the breeder must be discouraged, though, of course, not persecuted." Vidal, *Sexually Speaking*, 182.

34. Frank, *How to Be an Intellectual*, 140.

35. See Brophy, "Tang of Uncertainty"; Stimpson, "My O My O Myra"; and, most extensively, John Mitzel, "Patriarchy vs. 'Pornography': Some Notes on Myra B.," in *Myra and Gore*, by John Mitzel and Steven Abbott (Dorchester, MA: Manifest Destiny, 1974), 5–44. The phrase "kinky for Myra" is from Brophy, "Tang of Uncertainty," 412.

36. Joyce Haber, "Look Who Says the Novel Is Dead," *Los Angeles Times*, 29 April 1968, 34, Gore Vidal Papers, Folder 4174.

37. The importance of gossip and rumor for celebrity status has been noted by many scholars. See, e.g., Joseph A. Boone and Nancy J. Vickers, "Introduction: Celebrity Rites," *PMLA* 126, no. 4 (2011): 904.

38. Print ad for *Myra Breckinridge*, *New York Times*, 24 May 1968, 25, Gore Vidal Papers, Folder 4185.

39. Gore Vidal, *Point to Point Navigation: A Memoir, 1964 to 2006* (London: Abacus, 2006), 141.

40. Jonathan Beckman, "A Laugh a Year," review of *The Smile Revolution in Eighteenth-Century Paris*, by Colin Jones, *London Review of Books*, 18 June 2015, https://www.lrb .co.uk/v37/n12/jonathan-beckman/a-laugh-a-year.

41. Dick Hallgreen, "City Ignores a Hollywood Symbol," *San Francisco Chronicle*, 16 September 1968, n.p., Gore Vidal Papers, Folder 4192; Boorstin, *The Image*, 57.

42. William Serrin, "Wanna Buy a Statue? Try Myra for Size," *Detroit Free Press*, 24 September 1968, 3, Gore Vidal Papers, Folder 4192.

43. Hallgreen, "City Ignores a Hollywood Symbol."

44. Ross, "Uses of Camp," 320.

45. Raymond Sarlot and Fred E. Basten, *Life at the Marmont: The Inside Story of Hollywood's Legendary Hotel of the Stars—Chateau Marmont* (Harmondsworth, UK: Penguin, 2013), 178–79.

46. Vidal, *Conversations*, 71.

47. Trask, *Camp Sites*, 14.

48. See Davidson, "'Just a Couple of Fags.'"

49. Prescott, "Here Comes Gore Vidal," T8.

50. James MacBride, "What Did Myra Want?," review of *Myra Breckinridge*, by Gore Vidal, *New York Times*, 18 February 1968, https://archive.nytimes.com/www.nytimes.com/books/97/06/22/reviews/hollywood-myra.html?module=inline.

51. Sidney Thomas, "Vidal's 'In' Joke Leaves Reader Out," review of *Myra Breckinridge*, by Gore Vidal, *Atlanta Constitution and Journal*, 3 March 1968, n.p., Gore Vidal Papers, Folder 4174.

52. Fred Kaplan, *Gore Vidal: A Biography* (London: Bloomsbury, 1999), 593.

53. Tuite, *Lord Byron*, 36.

54. Julia Fawcett, "The Overexpressive Celebrity and the Deformed King: Recasting the Spectacle as Subject in Colley Cibber's *Richard III*," *PMLA* 126, no. 4 (2011): 951. Fawcett here draws on Joseph Roach's appropriation in *It* of Pope's couplet "*Something*, whose Truth convinc'd at Sight we find, / That gives us back the Image of our Mind." For Roach's use of the couplet, see Chapter 2.

55. Ibid., 952.

56. Ibid.

57. Ibid. The excessive and spectacular dimensions of Myra, if not her Tiresian life history, were also captured in the gargantuan proportions of her showgirl stand-in. The kind of giant ad the showgirl constituted is, incidentally, known in the trade as a "spectacular": see Sarlot and Basten, *Life at the Marmont*, 178.

58. See D'Emilio, *Sexual Politics*, 134–48; Meeker, *Contacts Desired*, 109–95; Sherry, *Gay Artists*, 105–41.

59. For discussion of these texts, see Meeker, *Contacts Desired*, 109–12, 146.

60. Janet Staiger, *Perverse Spectators: The Practices of Film Reception* (New York: New York University Press, 2000), 135.

61. David McReynolds, "The Gay Underground—a Reply to Mr. Krim," *Village Voice*, 25 March 1959, 4–5; Staiger, *Perverse Spectators*, 135. For another useful genealogy of the term "underground" that concentrates on its 1960s cultural applications rather than its political connotations, see Suárez, *Bike Boys*, 81–86.

62. Review of *Myra Breckinridge*, by Gore Vidal, n.p., *Playboy*, n.d., Gore Vidal Papers, Folder 4174; Paul D. Zimmerman, "Elan Vidal," review of *Myra Breckinridge*, by Gore Vidal, *Newsweek*, 26 February 1968, 88.

63. Hentoff, "Growing Up Androgynous"; Eliot Fremont-Smith, "Like Fay Wray If the Light Is Right," review of *Myra Breckinridge*, by Gore Vidal, *New York Times*, 3 February 1968, https://archive.nytimes.com/www.nytimes.com/books/98/03/01/home/vidal-myra.html.

64. Brophy, "Tang of Uncertainty," 412.

65. Hentoff, "Growing Up Androgynous."

66. Fremont-Smith, "Like Fay Wray."

67. Glass, *Counterculture Colophon*, 129–30.

68. A notable example is his 1992 interview with Larry Kramer, in which Kramer badgers Vidal for his rejection of the "gay" label and asserts, "But Gore, you *are* gay. . . . And I think *you* think of yourself as gay." See Vidal, *Conversations*, 161.

69. A trawl through the extensive holding of press clippings in Vidal's archive demonstrates the shift in the public representation of Vidal's sexuality from preliberation to postliberation moments. In a 1966 interview, when asked about "any plans for sharing his life," Vidal, who had been in a live-in relationship with Howard Austen since 1950, "smiled as only a bachelor can" and described himself as temperamentally unsuited to "domestic bliss"; in a 1968 profile published during *Myra*'s best-selling ascent, the "strikingly handsome bachelor" "refuses to discuss his private life"; but in a 1973 column an answer to a reader's question about Vidal's marital status advises, "The writer never married, but has lived for the last 23 years with Howard Austin [*sic*], a 43-year-old companion secretary." See, respectively, "Americans in Europe: Gore Vidal," *Réalités*, August 1966, 78, Gore Vidal Papers, Folder 4181; Jerry Bauer and Shari Steiner, "Gore Vidal," magazine profile, publication and date not evident but refers to *Myra* as having "just been published in Britain," Gore Vidal Papers, Folder 4187; Robin Adams Sloan, "The Gossip Column," *Daily News*, 23 October 1973, 53, Gore Vidal Papers, Folder 4203.

70. Francesca Stanfill, "Woman Warrior: Sexual Philosopher Camille Paglia Jousts with the Politically Correct," *New York*, 4 March 1991, 29. For a discussion of the parallels between Myra and Paglia, see Woodhouse, *Unlimited Embrace*, 53–54.

71. J. Hoberman, *The Dream Life: Movies, Media, and the Mythology of the Sixties* (New York: New Press, 2003), 278.

72. Ibid., 277.

73. Mitzel, "Patriarchy"; McDonald's testimony is noted in Castiglia and Reed, *If Memory Serves*, 171. Vidal in return dubbed *Straight to Hell* "one of the best radical papers in the country"; see Erin Sheehy, "Straight to Hell: On Boyd McDonald," *n + 1* 25 (2016). https://nplusonemag.com/issue-25/reviews/straight-to-hell/.

Chapter 6

1. *Buckley vs. Vidal: The Historic 1968 ABC News Debates*, intro. Robert Gordon (Memphis: Devault-Graves, 2015), 163. This book provides a transcript of the debates at the Republican and Democratic conventions.

2. William F. Buckley Jr., "On Experiencing Gore Vidal: Can There Be Any Justification

in Calling a Man Queer before Ten Million People on Television?," in *Smiling through the Apocalypse:* Esquire's *History of the Sixties*, ed. Harold T. P. Hayes (New York: McCall, 1969), 943.

3. Kaplan, *Gore Vidal*, 603. Subsequent page references are cited parenthetically in the text.

4. Neil Compton, "Television and Politics," *Commentary* 46, no. 6 (1968): 30.

5. Paul Molloy, "It's the Molloy: Verbal Flying Fists Rival Yippie Clash," *Chicago Sun-Times*, 30 August 1968, 38, Gore Vidal Papers, Folder 2724.

6. Terrence O'Flaherty, "Assignment: TV," *Oxnard Press-Courier*, 25 August 1968, Gore Vidal Papers, Folder 2724.

7. Stephanie Harrington, "Through the Fog," *Village Voice*, 15 August 1968, 12.

8. Quoted in Charles Kaiser, *The Gay Metropolis*, 1940–1996 (New York: Houghton Mifflin, 1997), 148.

9. As well as Sedgwick's work in *Touching Feeling*, discussed in Chapter 1, see, e.g., David M. Halperin and Valerie Traub, eds., *Gay Shame* (Chicago: University of Chicago Press, 2009); Sally Munt, *Queer Attachments: The Cultural Politics of Shame* (Aldershot, UK: Ashgate, 2008); Stockton, *Beautiful Bottom*.

10. Thomas Edwards, "Embarrassed by Jane Austen," *Raritan* 7, no. 1 (1987): 63.

11. Luke Purshouse, "Embarrassment: A Philosophical Analysis," *Philosophy* 76, no. 4 (2001): 520.

12. Rose, *On Not Being Able to Sleep*, 1.

13. Thanks to John Plotz for helping me work out this point.

14. Fredric Jameson, *The Antinomies of Realism* (London: Verso, 2013), 40, 39. In Jameson's historicizing argument, the sliding scale has a specifically musical denotation, as he develops his argument about affective chromaticism in a discussion of Wagner.

15. Heather Love has suggested to me that Goffman's privileging of embarrassment over shame also exemplifies his lack of interest in the idea of the unconscious.

16. My thinking here is indebted to Clara Tuite's argument that scandalous celebrity involves the ritual enactment of various "scenarios of degradation," including public shaming and humiliation, that generate "a cycle of transgression and forgiveness." See Tuite, *Lord Byron*, 10. I want to emphasize, though, the relative affective dialing down of some of these scenarios depending on historical context. Thus, in the era of the open secret, and in the context of the late 1960s in particular, the revelation of homosexuality is potentially more an embarrassment than shameful (as it was paradigmatically in the case of that earlier celebrity, Oscar Wilde).

17. Nick Salvato, "Cringe Criticism: On Embarrassment and Tori Amos," *Critical Inquiry* 39, no. 4 (2013): 682.

18. David Harvey, *The Condition of Postmodernity: An Enquiry into the Origins of Cultural Change* (Oxford: Blackwell, 1982), vii.

19. Judith Butler, *Bodies That Matter: On the Discursive Limits of "Sex"* (New York: Routledge, 1993), 226.

20. Ibid.

21. Sedgwick, *Touching Feeling*, 36.

22. Rowland S. Miller, *Embarrassment: Poise and Peril in Everyday Life* (New York: Guilford, 1996), 22, 27.

23. Erving Goffman, "Embarrassment and Social Organization," *American Journal of Sociology* 62, no. 3 (1956): 269.

24. Ibid., 268.

25. Ibid.

26. It is the social nature of the disruption caused by Buckley's intemperance that licenses my characterization of the affective nimbus of the broadcast as one of embarrassment, even though Buckley's own stated primary affective memory of the event was the "indignation" triggered by Vidal's "pro- or crypto-Nazi" taunt. See Buckley, "On Experiencing," 942.

27. Here I am reversing my view, in an early version of this chapter, that Vidal was also caught up in the embarrassment of the moment and that the smile with which he greeted Buckley's outburst was a version of the awkward, self-conscious grin that the psychological literature on embarrassment identifies as a common physical manifestation of the emotion. Careful study of the footage since that version was published has convinced me otherwise. See my "Embarrassment in 1968: Gore Vidal's Sexuality in the Public Sphere," *Mosaic* 48, no. 1 (2015): 147.

28. Buckley, "On Experiencing," 944.

29. Ibid., 946.

30. *Buckley vs. Vidal*, 164.

31. Gore Vidal, "A Distasteful Encounter with William F. Buckley Jr.," in Hayes, *Smiling through the Apocalypse*, 961. Subsequent page references are cited parenthetically in the text.

32. Buckley, "On Experiencing," 938.

33. *Buckley vs. Vidal*, 26.

34. Ibid., 50, 34.

35. *Buckley vs. Vidal*, 164.

36. Gore Vidal, *United States: Essays 1952–1992* (New York: Random House, 1993), 531.

37. Altman, *Gore Vidal's America*, 149.

38. Ibid., 140. I discuss Baldwin's constructionist account of sexuality in Chapter 2. For Sontag's sense of the cultural variability of sexuality, see, e.g., Cott, *Susan Sontag*, 104–6.

39. Altman, *Gore Vidal's America*, 140.

40. Gore Vidal, "The Twelve Caesars," in *United States*, 525.

41. Vidal, "Author's Note," in *United States*, n.p.

42. Gore Vidal Papers, Folder 616. In *United States*, the essay's first publication is noted as being in the *Nation* in 1959, but this is another inaccuracy, one repeated by several commentators on Vidal.

43. Gore Vidal, "An Afterword," in *The City and the Pillar*, by Gore Vidal, rev. ed. (London: William Heinemann, 1965), 207.

44. Harker, *Middlebrow Queer*, 13.

45. Claude J. Summers, "*The City and the Pillar* as Gay Fiction," in Parini, *Gore Vidal*, 57. Robert J. Corber's reading of the novel as "anti-essentialist" ignores the differences between the original and revised versions and cites only the latter. See Corber, "Gore Vidal and the Erotics of Masculinity," in *Homosexuality in Cold War America: Resistance and the Crisis of Masculinity*, by Robert J. Corber (Durham, NC: Duke University Press, 1997), chap. 5.

46. Summers, "*The City and the Pillar*," 57.

47. Vidal, *The City and the Pillar* (London: John Lehmann, 1949), 121.

48. Gore Vidal, *Palimpsest: A Memoir* (London: Abacus, 1996), 102–3.

49. Ibid., 103.

50. Gore Vidal, *The Judgment of Paris* (London: William Heinemann, 1953), 253.

51. Ibid.

52. Sedgwick, *Epistemology*, 1.

53. Gore Vidal to James Fugaté, [no day date given] August 1954, James Barr Papers, Folder 3, ONE National Gay and Lesbian Archives, USC Libraries, University of Southern California. Fugaté wrote under the name of James Barr; he published *Quatrefoil*, a gay protest novel, in 1950. At the time of his correspondence with Vidal, he was a contributing editor to *ONE*. I am extremely grateful to Craig Loftin for alerting me to the existence of this letter and for providing me with a copy.

54. Vidal, *United States*, 567.

55. On this tension in Vidal's work, see also Altman, *Gore Vidal's America*, 141; and Jörg Behrendt, *Homosexuality in the Work of Gore Vidal* (Berlin: LIT Verlag, 2002), 51–52.

56. Vidal, *United States*, 567.

57. James Fugaté to Tennessee Williams, 10 August 1954, James Barr Papers, Folder 3. Again, I am very grateful to Craig Loftin for providing me with a copy of this letter.

58. Vidal to Fugaté, ibid.

59. James Fugaté to Gore Vidal, 27 August 1954, James Barr Papers, Folder 3.

60. Rose, *On Not Being Able to Sleep*, 203.

61. William F. Buckley Jr., "The Avant Garde," *Firing Line with William Buckley Jr.*, New York, WOR-TV, 7 May 1968. Thanks to members of the audience at a seminar in the English Department at the University of Melbourne for alerting me to this episode of *Firing Line*.

62. *The Homosexuals* and other 1960s exposés named some of the homosexual men that were interviewed, but with their consent.

63. Sedgwick, *Tendencies*, 222.

64. Marcie Frank's discussion of the 1968 broadcast engages incisively with the event of Vidal's outing, but queer theory remains a background concern in her argument, which is focused on Vidal's relation to electronic media. See Frank, *How to Be an Intellectual*, 99–103, quote at 103.

65. Ibid., 103.

66. I discuss this tension in Vidal's self-presentation in my discussion of his feud with Truman Capote, the main target of his effeminophobia, in Davidson, " 'Just a Couple.' "

67. D. A. Miller, *The Novel and the Police* (Berkeley: University of California Press, 1988), 193–94.

68. *Best of Enemies*, dir. Robert Gordon and Morgan Neville, Media Ranch/Tremolo Productions, 2015.

69. Rose, *On Not Being Able to Sleep*, 201.

70. Though I am making this connection specifically in relation to the Buckley-Vidal broadcast in its late-1960s context, as intimated earlier in this chapter, the relation of embarrassment to celebrity today surely constitutes a productive line of inquiry, as indicated, for instance, by the undramatic effect of the public emergence of celebrity sex tapes. Rather than constitute a shame-laden debacle for a celebrity's career, such tapes tend to cause a minor ruffle in the media before being set aside—if they do not actually enhance the fame of the particular celebrity involved.

71. Rose, *On Not Being Able to Sleep*, 203.

72. Quoted in Blake Bailey, *John Cheever: A Life* (London: Picador, 2009), 286.

Afterword

1. Dan Avery, "34 Celebrities Who Came Out in 2017," Newnownext.com, 11 October 2017, http://www.newnownext.com/gay-celebrities-coming-out-2017/10/2017/.

2. Nicole Moormann, "5 Young Celebs Who Won't Be Defined by Strict Notions of Sexuality," takepart.com, 27 August 2015, http://www.takepart.com/article/2015/08/27/five-celebs-sexually-fluid/.

3. Foucault, *History of Sexuality*, 1:159.

4. The forgetting involved has been somewhat different from that recommended by Jean Baudrillard, however, in that I continue to grant efficacy to liberationist desire. See *Forget Foucault*, trans. Phil Beitchman, Nicole Dufresne, Lee Hildreth, and Mark Polizzoti (1977; repr., Cambridge, MA: MIT-Semiotexte, 2007).

5. Foucault, *History of Sexuality*, 1:12.

6. Ibid., 159.

7. For an acute account of the continuities and distinctions between pre- and post-Internet versions of celebrity culture, see Marcus, "Celebrity 2.0."

8. What Sedgwick in *Epistemology* calls the "overarching consistency" (68) of her argument about the closet has been challenged from a variety of angles: on the grounds that it lacks historical nuance, see Chapter 3 in this book, and George Chauncey, *Gay New York: Gender, Urban Culture, and the Making of the Gay Male World,* 1890–1940 (New York: Basic Books, 1994); on the grounds of its inapplicability to contemporary political and cultural developments, see Steven Seidman, *Beyond the Closet: The Transformation of Gay and Lesbian Life* (New York: Routledge, 2002); and on the grounds of its inapplicability to nonwhite contexts, see Martin F. Manalansan IV, "In the Shadows of Stonewall: Examining Gay Transnational Politics and the Diaspora Dilemma," *GLQ* 2, no. 4 (1995): 425–38, and Marlon B. Ross, "Beyond the Closet as Raceless Paradigm," in *Black Queer Studies: A Critical Anthology*, ed. E. Patrick Johnson and Mae G. Henderson (Durham, NC: Duke University Press, 2005), 161–89.

9. I base this list on Peggy Phelan's account of the "trap" of visibility. See Phelan, *Unmarked: The Politics of Performance* (New York: Routledge, 1993), 6.

10. Sedgwick, *Epistemology*, 68.

11. Some argue that social media significantly blurs the distinction between celebrities and ordinary people, as it "enable[s] more people to engage in celebrity practices such as displaying privacy in public," thus "creating opportunities for microcelebrity." However, "practicing celebrity does not in itself confer celebrity status," and "a small number of figures continue to monopolize media coverage." See Marcus, "Celebrity 2.0," 45.

For a subtle analysis of the positive political effects of celebrity outness in relation to social media, see Melissa Hardie, "The Closet Remediated: Inside Lindsay Lohan," *Australian Humanities Review* 48 (2010), http://australianhumanitiesreview.org/2010/05/01/the-closet-remediated-inside-lindsay-lohan/. Hardie argues that in the contemporary moment "closet epistemologies" persist but are also "remediated . . . by the emergence of new social media."

12. Phelan, *Unmarked*, 10.

13. Ibid., 7.

14. Butler, "Imitation," 15–16.

Index

1968, sex becomes publicly discussable, 126–27, 128, 142, 155–56

Abelove, Henry, 7, 184n23
Adorno, Theodor, and Max Horkheimer, 47
affect, 23, 24, 32, 56, 59, 103; and celebrity, 17, 24, 79; chromaticism of, 155; of embarrassment, 18, 152, 155; queer, 75, 85; and self-abasement, 39; of shame, 18, 154
Aldrich, Ann, 11
allure, 73, 78, 79–80; glossed, 80
Altman, Dennis, 121, 122, 125, 127, 129, 164, 212n24
Anger, Kenneth, 99, 120; *Hollywood Babylon*, 131, 149
"anticategorical imperative", 3, 4, 5, 14–19, 164, 169
Arbus, Diane, 99–100
Arendt, Hannah, 75, 110
Arnold, Matthew, 65–66, 108, 110
attention economy, 107–8
Auden, W. H., 104

Baldwin, James, 74, 76, 82; admires blues musicians, 50, 51, 61; ambition of, 23, 35–37, 49–50, 82; and camp, 41, 49, 103, 108, 113; anti-categorization of, 26–30, 37, 41, 44, 49, 56, 57–58; on art as confession, 21, 22, 23–24, 39, 44, 109; and celebrity, 8, 23, 26, 41, 44, 48–52, 55; as conflicted stylist, 47, 68; identifies with Bette Davis, 48–49; fascinated by charisma, 50–51, 60–61; on love, 26, 32, 34, 40, 44, 68–69; as performer, 45, 55; as proto-visible homosexual, 21, 23, 43, 69, 70; as "race man", 28–29, 41, 43, 89; resisted collective gay identity, 4, 12 26, 32, 37, 40, 43, 63, 69, 89, 191n41; sees homosexuality as intractable, 38, 45, 55, 65; seeks human connection, 32, 50–52, 53, 68, 193n2; and shame, 22–23, 35–36, 51, 69; utopian elements in, 62–63, 65, 68
Baldwin, James, Works: *The Amen Corner*, 22; *Another Country*, 23, 31, 33, 35, 43, 44, 45, 46, 51–70, 89, 113; "The Black Boy Looks at the White Boy", 35, 50, 82; *Blues for Mister Charlie*, 87–89; *The Devil Finds Work*, 48; "Everybody's Protest Novel", 26–27; "Freaks and the American Ideal of Manhood", 26, 37; *Giovanni's Room*, 21, 22, 23, 31, 34–35, 46, 53, 55, 61, 63, 64, 68, 103, 113; *Go Tell It on the Mountain*, 21, 22, 39; *Just above My Head*, 32; "The Male Prison", 23, 31, 32, 38–39, 40; *Nobody Knows My Name*, 35, 38; *No Name in the Street*, 22, 23, 36, 46; "The Northern Protestant", 21, 24; *Notes of a Native Son*, 21, 34; *Tell Me How Long the Train's Been Gone*, 8, 43–46, 47, 48, 55, 59

Barth, John, 85
Barthes, Roland, 73
Beat poets, 114
Beckman, Jonathan, 136
Benjamin, Walter, 47, 73
Bergman, Ingmar, 21, 93–95
Bersani, Leo, 15
Black Power, 22, 36, 46, 126, 193n5
Blake, Roger, 11
Boorstin, Daniel, 136
Bowie, David, *Ziggy Stardust*, 129
Bowles, Paul, and Jane Bowles, 105
Braudy, Leo, 44–45, 81
Brim, Matt, 191n41, 198n67
Brooks, Richard, 165
Brophy, Brigid, 130, 145
Brown, Helen Gurley, 65
Brown, Judith, 79
Brown, Norman O., 14, 78, 118, 120, 122
Brown, Rita Mae, 69–70
Buckley, William F. Jr, 4, 143, 151–54, 157–63, 170, 171
Burke, Kenneth, 75
Burns, John Horne, 165
Burroughs, William, *Naked Lunch*, 8
Butler, Judith, 15, 16, 63, 96–97, 158, 178
Byron, George Gordon, 82, 142

camp, 41, 49, 75, 99–100, 110–12, 116; mainstreamed by Sontag, 139; critique of, 112–13, 129; taste 138–39
Canetti, Elias, 73
Capote, Truman, 7, 9, 140
Carby, Hazel V., 190n23
Castle, Terry, 97, 100, 108–10, 111, 112, 198n11, 205n9
celebrity: and affect, 17, 24, 79; ambivalent reception of, 75, 79; and charisma, 44, 47, 49–51, 52, 60–61, 79, 195n27; distance and eroticism in, 79–80; distinguished from fame, 126, 136, 200n37; and embarrassment, 172–73, 219n70; enables liberationist ideas, 176–77; as Faustian bargain, 8; and homosexuality, 3, 4, 45, 126, 170–73, 179, 182n10; identity and, 23, 36, 43; as inauthentic commodification, 47–48, 139; and individual creativity, 6–7, 82, 125–26, 131; inflects everyday life, 132; iterative and standardized, 47, 125–26, 132; literary, 81–83, 179, 184n26; mythic quality of, 74, 132; as performative, 25, 44; public and private in, 3–4, 9, 25, 28, 81, 82, 149, 170, 189n9; and race, 45; risk-taking in, 49, 108, 166; and social media, 176–77, 220n11
celebrity cookbooks, 147–48
celebrity novels, 44
censorship, 7–8, 22, 119, 120, 121, 123, 127, 145, 152
charisma, 61, 195n27; and performance, 61
Charles, Ray, 61
Cheever, John, 1–2, 4, 48, 82, 173; *Journals*, 2
Chester, Alfred, 74, 102, 104–5
Cibber, Colley, 143
Cleaver, Eldridge, 4, 21, 36, 38; *Soul on Ice*, 22
Cleland, John, 8
Cleto, Fabio, 102
closet, metaphor of, 1, 7, 48, 142, 177, 203n82; as alienated victimhood and inauthenticity, 67, 91, 173; as Butlerian site of silent possibility, 96; as enabling liberation rhetoric, 4, 18, 68; and knowingness, 57, 140, 171–72
Cohen, Ira, 104
Compton, Neil, 153
Core, Philip, 130
counterculture, 13, 76, 85, 102, 114, 117, 118, 120, 126
cross-dressing, 59–60, 129

Daughters of Bilitis, 11, 186n42
Davis, Miles, 61

deCordova, Richard, 80, 87, 88
D'Emilio, John, 11
Drake, St. Clair, and Horace Clayton, 190n22
Dyer, Geoff, 2

Eckman, Fern, 28–29, 53
Edelman, Lee, 15, 29, 62, 63
Edwards, Thomas, 154
effeminacy, 2, 139–40, 168, 182n7, 218n66
Eliot, T. S., 47
embarrassment: associated with homosexuality, 152–54, 170–71; and celebrity, 219n70; distinguished from shame, 18, 154–56, 216n16; essentially relational and public, 155, 157–59, 172; revelatory effect of, 171–72
English, Daylanne, 54, 62
Ephron, Nora, 117
Escoffier, Jeffrey, 116

Fawcett, Julia, 143–44
feminism, 14; second-wave, 126, 128
Field, Douglas, 46
Field, Edward, 104, 105
Finch, Mark, 116
Fornés, María Irene, 104
Forster, E. M., 50
fort/da game, 74, 93
Foucault, Michel: argues sexuality is a form of power/knowledge, 14–15, 176; queer theory's uses of, 14, 112, 164; sees sexuality as central to modern subjectivity, 6–7, 14, 176
Franck, Georg, 107–8
Frank, Marcie, 118, 133, 134, 171, 205n9
Fremont-Smith, Eliot, 145
Freudianism, 117, 121, 122
Fugaté, James ("James Barr"), 167, 168, 169, 218n53

Gass, William, 110
gay liberation movement, 122, 125, 149
Genet, Jean, 90, 114; *Un chant d'amour*, 119, 120
Genette, Gérard, 111–12
Gever, Martha, 182n10
Gide, André, 38–40
Ginsberg, Allen, 9, 10, 170
Glass, Loren, 6, 23, 41, 81, 145, 179, 189n9
Goffman, Erving, 155, 158–59
Gornick, Vivian, 113–14, 139
Graves, Robert, 164
Grove Press, 145–46

Hair, 129
Hardie, Melissa, 220n11
Harman, Graham, 79–80
Harrington, Stephanie, 153
Harvey, David, 156
Hayes, Harold, 152–53, 157, 159–60
Hentoff, Margot, 132–33, 145
Hess, Harry, 71–72, 75
Hoberman, J., 147
Hoffman, Martin, 116
Hollywood, 139, 147, 179; in *Myra Breckinridge*, 128, 130–33, 136
homosexual/heterosexual binary, 2, 19, 164
homosexuality: and authenticity, 117, 122, 175; and celebrity, 45, 126, 170–73; confused with transsexuality, 212n23; considered private, 151–52; as driver of ambition, 49; etiologies of, 165–66; pathologized, 53, 62, 116, 195n39; and population control, 133; as mode of performance, 58–60, 61, 64; public discussion of, 143–44; sociological discourse of, 116; as weapon, 49, 77
homosexuals, prison, 23
Howard, Richard, 105
Howe, Irving, 85, 111
identity: and authenticity, 80, 87, 90, 91, 175; Baldwin on, 26, 27–34, 37, 64, 68, 70; categorized, 122, 164; and celebrity, 43, 50, 142–43;

and gay liberation, 61–62, 67; generates artistic ambition, 37, 49, 50, 77; media representation of, 156, 178; performed, 2, 4, 9, 23, 39, 55, 59–60, 89–90; polymorphously disappearing, 122; racial and ethnic, 41, 167; has sexuality as chief component, 88, 175; and shame, 25, 32–33; as weapon, 49, 77; Vidal's unstable position on, 125–26, 130, 164–66, 168–69
Isherwood, Christopher, 116, 140, 169

Jackson, Charles, 165
Jagger, Mick, 129
Jagose, Annamarie, 122
James, Henry, 46, 51
Jameson, Fredric, 155
Johns, Jasper, 7
Jones, LeRoi, 87
Joyce, James, 47
Joyce, Justin and Dwight McBride, 28, 41

Kant, Immanuel, 3
Kaplan, Fred, 152, 154, 157, 159, 170
Karlson, Eric, 11
Kazin, Alfred, 84
Keats, John, 95–96
Kennedy, Liam, 84
Kinsey, Alfred, 164, 165, 166–67
Kissack, Terence, 187n45
Kluger, Richard, 105–6, 207n31
Knopf (publisher), 34
Krim, Seymour, 12, 144

Lacy, Steve, 175, 177
Lawrence, D. H., *Lady Chatterley's Lover*, 8, 120
Legg, Dorr, 169
Leys, Ruth, 24
lesbianism, 70, 77–78, 93–95, 182n10, 198n67
liberation, sexual, 11, 12, 14, 16, 62, 63, 65, 69, 75, 114, 126, 173; through androgyny, 121; celebrity's contribution to, 176–77, 178; engenders queer theory, 96, 156; glossed, 10, 211n10; metaphors of, 91–93, 177; outcomes of, 10, 15, 176–77; and open discourse, 143, 146, 156, 179, 182n7; politics of, 23, 26, 163, 147, 177; Sontag and, 100–2, 117–18, 123; Vidal's relationship with, 146, 163
Loftin, Craig, 91, 182n7
Lopate, Phillip, 89

MacBride, James, 140, 144
MacInnes, Colin, 30–31, 33
Mailer, Norman, 35, 46, 82, 161, 169
Marcus, Sharon, 6, 126, 131, 132
Marcuse, Herbert, 14, 76, 120, 121, 122, 145
Marshall, David, 5
mask, metaphor of, 28, 87–95, 179; as adaptative negotiation, 91; as knowing performativity, 90
Masters, R. E. L., 10–11, 12
Mattachine Society, 11, 186n42
McCarthy, Mary, 84–85, 87
McDonald, Boyd, 147
McLuhan, Marshall, 81, 82, 129, 133
McRobbie, Angela, 73, 74
Meehan, Thomas, 112, 114, 117
Meeker, Martin, 12, 211n10
Mekas, Jonas, 119
Meyerowitz, Joanne, 212n23
Michasiw, Kim, 205n8
Miller, D. A., 101, 104, 111, 171, 172
Miller, Henry, *Tropic of Capricorn*, 8
Mills, C. Wright, 116
Mitzel, John, 147
modernism, 85, 120, 183n19
Montez, Maria, 147
Moon, Michael, 129
Morales, Natalie, 175
Moran, Jim, 136–39
Moran, Joe, 9, 82
Morin, Edgar, 47, 49, 73, 86
Morrissey, Paul, 130

Mulvey, Laura, 74
Muñoz, José Esteban, 62–63
Myra Breckinridge (Vidal), 8, 123; and gay liberation, 125, 127, 128; as meta-camp, 130–31, 140; plot summary of, 128–29; protagonist as celebrity, 133–34, 142, 146; provides cover for Vidal's sexuality, 128, 142–43, 146, 155, 163; publicity campaign for, 134–39, 140; as satire, 128, 129, 130; as *succès de scandale*, 126, 145
Myra Breckinridge Cookbook, The, 147–49

Nelson, Deborah, 209n83
Nelson, Emmanuel, 46, 194n13
New Journalism, 184n22
Newman, Paul, 151, 160
New Sensibility, 76, 81, 84, 85; conflated with sexual license, 86
New York intellectuals, 84–86, 108, 111, 115, 201n49

Odets, Clifford, 88
Ohi, Kevin, 57
open secret, 4, 18, 140, 171-72, 177

Paglia, Camille, 146
Palahniuk, Chuck, 179
Partisan Review, 75, 84, 87, 108, 110, 111, 113, 163
Partridge, Eric, 113
Penner, James, 85, 113
Petigny, Alan, 127
Phelan, Peggy, 178
Poague, Leland, 116, 205n9
Podhoretz, Norman, 84–85
postmodernism, 75, 85
Prescott, Peter, 140
Purshouse, Luke, 154

queer theory, 2, 101, 181n6; critiques sexual categorization, 3, 6, 14, 156, 157; critiques visibility, 3, 15, 157, 177–78; descended from liberationist discourse, 96; and embarrassment, 171–72; influenced by Foucault, 14, 112, 164; on knowingness, 171; relativism of, 67; on sexual identity, 3–5, 15–17; utopian strand in, 10, 62, 63

"race man", 28–29, 41, 43; glossed, 28, 190nn22, 23
Rahv, Philip, 85
Reay, Barry, 2, 67, 68, 182n7
Rechy, John, 10, 114
Reich, Wilhelm, 13, 14, 77
Resnais, Alain, 86
rights-based reform, 12, 187
Roach, Joseph, 44–45, 52, 61, 109
Rocky Horror Picture Show, The, 129
Rollyson, Carl, and Lisa Paddock, 76
Rorem, Ned, 103–4, 107
Rose, Jacqueline, 24, 154, 170, 172
Ross, Andrew, 131, 139
Ross, Marlon, 41, 45, 192n66
Roszak, Theodore, 13
Roth, Philip, 46, 48, 82

Said, Edward, 7, 35, 36
Salvato, Nick, 155
Sarlot, Raymond, and Fred Basten, 139
Sarne, Michael, 147
Schaefer, Eric, 127
Sedgwick, Eve Kosofsky, 14–15, 122, 167, 171, 203n82; on the closet, 177, 219n8; on shame, 24–26, 37, 38, 158
Seinfeld, 1–2
Selby, Hubert, 113
Seligman, Craig, 78, 83
sexual categorization, 2, 15–16; critiqued by queer theory, 3, 6, 14, 101, 156, 157; Baldwin on, 26–30, 37, 41, 44, 49, 56, 57–58
sexual revolution, 13, 126, 146, 147; and the media, 3, 10–11, 126, 127, 149; Vidal on, 123, 128
sexuality: and subjectivity, 6–7, 14, 176;

and aesthetics, 119–21; as liberation, 120–21
Seyrig, Delphine, 86
Shakespeare, William, 50
shame: audience role in, 154; connected to fame 22, 23, 25, 36, 153, 154; distinguished from embarrassment, 154–56, 216n16; energizes queer agency, 25, 37, 38; glossed, 24; and identity, 25, 32–33; intersubjectivity of, 24; produces relationality, 40; as theatrical, 24, 25, 39
Shaviro, Steven, 79–80
Sherry, Michael, 114, 115, 117
Simon, Herbert, 107
Simon, John, 113, 114–15, 117
Smith, Jack, 131, 144; *Flaming Creatures*, 118, 123, 129
Sohmers, Harriet, 104, 117, 199n22
Solaratoff, Theodore, 78
Solomon, Jeff, 7, 17, 186n32
Sontag, Susan: ambivalent reception of, 75–78, 84–86; association with gay men, 106, 123; attitude to psychology, 89, 97, 121; on camp; 100–2, 110–11, 116, 130, 139, 205n9; and celebrity, 8, 82–83, 102, 107, 110; compares homosexuals and Jews, 115, 117; conflates sexuality and aesthetic joy, 119–21, 203n72; contradictory allure of, 73, 75, 77–78, 85, 86; disparages "decade-mongering", 204n3; lesbianism, 101, 109, 117, 123, 199n17; and the mask, 87–94; on mass media, 9, 110; and New York intellectuals, 84–86, 110–11; on the politics of sexuality, 121; resisted lesbian identity, 4, 12, 76; seen as appropriative, 101, 102, 104, 105, 123, 205n8; sees race as political, 89; star effect of, 73–83, 86–87, 95, 111; style of, 73, 86, 90; sees homosexuality as personal weapon, 77; sympathetic to homosexuals, 112, 117
Sontag, Susan, Works: *Against Interpretation*, 73, 75, 76, 84, 86, 89, 112, 118–20; *The Benefactor*, 75, 85, 90, 103, 120–21; "Notes on 'Camp'", 75, 90, 99–104, 108–11, 204n5; *On Photography*, 99; *Styles of Radical Will*, 75, 93, 95
Staiger, Janet, 144, 145
stardom. *See* celebrity
Stearns, Jess, 11, 65, 116
Stein, Elliot, 99, 100, 102, 120; contribution to Sontag's "Notes on 'Camp'", 103–4, 117
Stein, Gertrude, 7
Stimpson, Catharine, 127, 132
Strauss, Helen, 22, 35
Stonewall Inn riots, as temporal marker, 1, 5, 7, 9, 10, 106, 117, 133, 143, 146, 147
Suárez, Juan A., 210n94
Suetonius, 164
Summers, Claude, 165, 166
surrealism, 120

temporality, queer, 62–63
Thek, Paul, 112
Thomas, Sidney, 140–42
Time magazine, 75, 112
Tomkins, Silvan, 24
trade, 67, 197n62
Trask, Michael, 130
Trilling, Lionel, 43–44, 47, 54, 55, 62, 84, 108, 110, 111, 112, 115
Tuite, Clara, 142, 216n16
Tukhamen, Mikko, 191n41
Turner, Graeme, 3
Tyler, Parker, 131

underground, 129, 144–46
utopianism, 10, 15, 17, 178; Baldwin on, 63, 65, 68; in queer theory, 10, 15, 96–97, 118, 164; Sontag on, 95–96, 97, 118; as universal pansexuality, 118, 122, 145, 175

van Krieken, Robert, 5, 107–8
Vidal, Gore, 27, 74, 76, 82; inconsistently anti-categorical, 125–26, 164, 165–69; dispute with William Buckley, 151–54, 157–63, 170–71, 217n27; and celebrity, 8, 123, 172–73; ideas informed by classics, 164; critiques celebrity culture, 128; dislikes camp effeminacy, 139–40, 168, 218n66; on psychoanalysis, 133; resists gay identity, 4, 12, 32, 125, 130, 139, 163, 167, 215n69; sees homosexuality as natural, 139, 164–65, 170, 173; on Alfred Kinsey, 166–67; on television, 133; on universal bisexuality, 125, 133, 164, 165, 168
Vidal, Gore, Works: *The City and the Pillar*, 27, 163, 165–66, 167; *The Judgment of Paris*, 166–67; *Myron*, 146–47; *Point to Point Navigation*, 136. *See also Myra Breckinridge*
visibility, 3, 5, 78, 80, 177; politics of, 178; precursor of liberation, 4, 156; proto-, 4, 15–16, 21, 23, 35, 40, 43, 69, 116, 156
vomiting: as metaphor for artistic compulsion, 21, 22, 23–24, 39; and shame, 25, 33

Warhol, Andy, 7, 129, 144
Waters, John, 130
Weightman, John, 128
White, Edmund, 97
Wiegman, Robyn, 181n6
Wilde, Oscar, 90, 91, 93, 104, 112
Williams, Tennessee, 9, 88, 89, 169
Womack, H. Lynn, 8
Woodhouse, Reed, 55–56, 59
Worthy, Ken, 11–12
Wright, Richard, 26

Post45

Joseph Jonghyun Jeon, *Vicious Circuits: Korea's IMF Cinema and the End of the American Century*

Lytle Shaw, *Narrowcast: Poetry and Audio Research*

Stephen Schryer, *Maximum Feasible Participation: American Literature and the War on Poverty*

Margaret Ronda, *Remainders: American Poetry at Nature's End*

Jasper Bernes, *The Work of Art in the Age of Deindustrialization*

Annie McClanahan, *Dead Pledges: Debt, Crisis, and Twenty-First-Century Culture*

Amy Hungerford, *Making Literature Now*

J. D. Connor, *The Studios after the Studios: Neoclassical Hollywood (1970–2010)*

Michael Trask, *Camp Sites: Sex, Politics, and Academic Style in Postwar America*

Loren Glass, *Counterculture Colophon: Grove Press, the* Evergreen Review*, and the Incorporation of the Avant-Garde*

Michael Szalay, *Hip Figures: A Literary History of the Democratic Party*

Jared Gardner, *Projections: Comics and the History of Twenty-First-Century Storytelling*

Jerome Christensen, *America's Corporate Art: The Studio Authorship of Hollywood Motion Pictures*